ARISTOTLE AND AUGUSTINE ON FREEDOM

Aristotle and Augustine on Freedom

Two Theories of Freedom, Voluntary Action and Akrasia

T. D. J. Chappell

Lecturer in Philosophy
University of East Anglia

St. Martin's Press

© T. D. J. Chappell 1995

First published in Great Britain 1995 by
MACMILLAN PRESS LTD
Houndmills, Basingstoke, Hampshire RG21 2XS
and London
Companies and representatives
throughout the world

A catalogue record for this book is available
from the British Library.

10   9   8   7   6   5   4   3   2   1
04 03 02 01 00 99 98 97 96 95

ISBN 0–333–62537–4

Printed in Great Britain by
Ipswich Book Co Ltd
Ipswich, Suffolk

First published in the United States of America 1995 by
Scholarly and Reference Division,
ST. MARTIN'S PRESS, INC.,
175 Fifth Avenue,
New York, N.Y. 10010

ISBN 0–312–12467–8

Library of Congress Cataloging-in-Publication Data
Chappell, T. D. J. (Timothy D. J.)
Aristotle and Augustine on freedom : two theories of freedom,
voluntary action, and akrasia / T.D.J. Chappell.
p.   cm.
Includes bibliographical references and index.
ISBN 0–312–12467–8
1. Free will and determinism.   2. Aristotle—Views on free will.
3. Augustine, Saint, Bishop of Hippo—Views on free will.
B105.L45C45 1995
123'5'0922—dc20   94–38184
                                                          CIP

In memoriam

Gillian Patriciae Chappell

30.4.1937–
13.12.1989

Quia fecisti nos ad Te
et inquietum est cor nostrum
donec requiescat in Te

By liberty, then, we can only mean a power of acting or not acting, according to the determinations of the will; that is, if we choose to remain at rest, we may; if we choose to move, we also may. Now this hypothetical liberty is universally allowed to belong to everyone who is not a prisoner and in chains. Here, then, is no subject of dispute.

David Hume: *An Enquiry concerning Human Understanding* (1775), VIII.1

It does not seem to be self contradictory to suppose that [the acceptance of determinism could lead to the decay or repudiation of participant reactive attitudes]... But I am strongly inclined to think that it is, for us as we are, practically inconceivable. The human commitment to participation in ordinary inter-personal relationships is too thoroughgoing and too deeply rooted for us to take seriously the thought that a general theoretical conviction might so change our world that, in it, there were no longer any such things as interpersonal relationships as we normally understand them.

Peter Strawson: 'Freedom and Resentment', *Proceedings of the British Academy*, 1962

Contents

Preface

Aristotle and Augustine probably seems like an incongruous pairing to many readers. As I hope this book will show, it is not as odd a conjunction as it may look at first sight. To instance one straw in the wind (though it is no more than that): for all his professions of Platonism, we know that St Augustine read Aristotle's actual words, but we do not know that he ever read Plato's actual words. He tells us in the *Confessions* that he read the *Categories* at school; but the nearest we get to evidence that he had read Plato is the famously unspecific phrase *in platonicis libellis*, also in the *Confessions*. (However, of course, Augustine did not find the *Categories* an inspiring read; and it is perhaps also worth pointing out that Augustine, in the *City of God*, remarks casually that Plato's and Aristotle's philosophies were virtually identical in content!)

More seriously, what I hope to show is that Aristotle and Augustine develop theories of freedom and the voluntary which are in many ways strikingly analogous. Both are more concerned to describe freedom than to prove its existence. Both describe freedom of action by describing voluntary action. Both conclude that abandoning belief in freedom means abandoning belief in voluntary action too – which very few are willing to do. Again, it is striking that both their descriptions of voluntary action show that voluntary actions must be (i) uncompelled; (ii) not ignorant; and (iii) done in pursuit of perceived attainable goods.

But don't agents sometimes act voluntarily in pursuit of perceived attainable evils? Aristotle says not: any such actions would be inexplicable as voluntary actions. Augustine, agreeing that such actions are inexplicable, still insists that they can occur. This – as I argue – is the true place, in Augustine's theory of freedom, of his famous 'theory of will'. It is also the real point of contrast between Aristotle and Augustine.

This book had its origins in an Edinburgh University doctoral thesis supervised by James Mackey and David Wright, to both of whom I am grateful for the benefit of their wisdom, scholarship and advice.

xi

I have also learnt much from a number of others who have listened patiently to my heterodoxies, and done their best to straighten them out: David Bostock, David Charles, Willie Charlton, Roger Crisp, Brian Davies, John Divers, Steven Everson, Philippa Foot, Peter Geach, Justin Gosling, Dave Horner, Mike Inwood, Fergus Kerr, Christopher Kirwan, John Lucas, Christopher Martin, Stephen Priest, David Pugmire, Hayden Ramsay, Dory Scaltsas, Richard Sorabji, Richard Swinburne, Charles Taliaferro, Lubor Velecky. If I have sometimes resisted their good sense, that is hardly their fault.

In another way, I am indebted to the Whitefield Institute, Oxford, for their generous support, both financial and moral, during my postgraduate research; to Wolfson and Merton Colleges, Oxford, for electing me to a Junior Research Fellowship and a Lectureship in philosophy respectively, the tenure of which posts has facilitated the metamorphosis of thesis into book; and to the University of East Anglia, for repeatedly believing my claim that the book really was about to come out. I am also grateful to my daughter Miriam, for being herself, and to my parents for their love, support and encouragement during my studies; I am sad that my mother did not live to see them bear fruit.

But my biggest debt of all is to my wife Claudia, without whom this project could never have been begun, let alone finished.

T. D. J. CHAPPELL
Wolfson College, Oxford
Merton College, Oxford

Part I
Aristotle

1

The Limits of the Voluntary

> While it has been the tradition to present [freedom] as the positive term requiring elucidation, there is little doubt that to say we acted 'freely'... is to say only that we acted not *un*-freely.... Like 'real', 'free' is only used to rule out the suggestion of some or all of its recognised antitheses.... Aristotle has often been chidden for overlooking 'the real problem': in my own case, it was when I began to see the injustice of this charge that I first became interested in excuses.
>
> J. L. Austin, 'A Plea for Excuses', *Proceedings of the Aristotelian Society*, 57 (1956–7), pp. 1–30

1.1. 'POSITIVE' AND 'NEGATIVE' THEORIES OF FREEDOM

Austin's famous remark, in my epigraph, is notable for at least two reasons. First, Austin takes it that 'freedom' is not something arcane and mysterious, but as near and familiar to us as voluntary action. If this is right then an adequate theory of the nature of voluntariness may well be sufficient for an adequate theory of the nature of freedom to act.

This suggests a simple strategy for the inquirer into freedom to act. The strategy would be to develop a theory of freedom to act by just developing a theory of what it is to act voluntarily. This is the strategy that will be followed here. If it seems to the reader to be just too banal to end up discussing the philosophically rather down-to-earth topic of voluntary action, when the reader hoped for a high-soaring treatment of something called 'metaphysical freedom', then the reader should ask himself: *How else* is one to go about explicating the nature of free action, but by explicating the nature of voluntary action? What else could possibly be involved in discussing freedom; and how would it be relevant?

Of course, this statement of strategy needs an immediate caveat. The caveat is that an adequate theory of the nature of freedom to act is not a proof of the existence of freedom to act. Austin risks obscuring this point when he says that 'In examining all the ways in which it will not do to say simply "X did A", we may hope to dispose of the problem of freedom' (loc. cit.). But I will admit it at the very beginning: if I aim to show that there is free will, I aim to do so principally by means of showing, like Strawson in 'Freedom and Resentment', how many other beliefs we would have to abandon along with a belief in free will, if we were to abandon that belief. In particular, as already suggested, we would have to stop believing in the existence of any genuinely voluntary action.

The second notable thing about Austin's remark is its suggestion that free action is not a 'positive term requiring elucidation', but (in effect) a paradigm case. When we talk about action *sans phrase* (says Austin), we *mean* free action. Austin explicitly equates 'all the ways in which each action may not be free' with 'all the ways in which it will not do to say simply "X did A"' (Austin, loc. cit.). For him, qualifications are only added when the action is in some way or other less than fully free. Therefore we arrive at our definition of free action, according to Austin, by a kind of subtraction. If you imagine a case of human action, then take away from it all the possible factors that could militate against its being an ordinary case of human action, what you are left with is typical action. And (he argues) typical action, as normally understood, just is free action. I shall call any theory of this Austinian sort a *negative theory of free action*. Austin rightly points out that the claim that Aristotle himself has a negative theory of free action is readily supportable from the ethical writings:

> Whatever someone does which it is up to him not to do, and which he does without ignorance and through his own agency (*di' hauton*) – everything of this sort is necessarily voluntary, and this is what the voluntary *is*. (EE 1225b7–10)

> Since the involuntary is what is done under compulsion and through ignorance, it would seem that the voluntary is what is done which has its origin in the agent himself, when the agent is aware of the particular circumstances of his action. (NE 1111a22–24)

My first task is to give an account of this negative theory, which is to say an account of the cases which for Aristotle constitute what I call 'the less than fully voluntary'.

Before that, a comment on the very idea of a *purely* negative theory of free action, such as Austin proposes. I agree with Austin that, if we want to understand what 'freedom to act' means, the cases where it is impeded are revealing. But how simple a matter is it to 'say simply "X did A"'? Does that fact of X's doing A, once arrived at, really require no further explanation? Iris Murdoch noted that 'Oxford philosophy' (by which I think she meant chiefly Austin himself) 'has developed no serious theory of motivation' (Murdoch 1970, p. 53). Is there really nothing of interest or importance to be said which might contribute towards the development of a positive theory of free action? If it turns out that there is anything non-trivial and plausible to say towards such a positive account, then it follows that a negative theory alone is incomplete.

And indeed (as I will argue), besides his undoubted interest in what free action isn't, Aristotle also has plenty to say about what free action is. Aristotle does have a well-developed negative theory about what kinds of opposing factors count as impairments or suspensions of normal freedom to act. But he has an even better-developed positive theory about what typical action consists in, what it is for an agent to have a normal freedom to act. It is unfortunate that Aristotle's positive doctrine is frequently overlooked (as here, I suspect, by Austin), or else treated as if it had no bearing on the issue of freedom.

In this book I present both negative and positive aspects of Aristotle's theory of voluntary action as free action. It will turn out that the negative and positive conditions of free action which we can supply from Aristotle are corollaries of each other.

But – against Austin – it is Aristotle's positive theory which is prior and more fundamental. For to define and enumerate the kinds of obstacles that there are to free action is to list the varieties of ill-formed free action that there are. But this can only prompt the prior question: 'What is the normal "form" of free action?' And Aristotle does believe – unlike, perhaps, Sartre (v. Sartre 1949) – that we can answer this, can define freedom of action by giving it a certain structure. His positive theory describes that structure.

But I start with the negative theory. What, for Aristotle, must not be the case regarding an agent, if he is to do a free or voluntary action? One passage normally considered vital has been cited already:

Since the involuntary is what is done under compulsion and through ignorance.... (NE 1111a22)

On the basis of these words, it is standardly assumed that Aristotle believes there to be two, and only two, negative conditions of free or voluntary action:

(i)   Voluntary action must not be compelled.
(ii) Voluntary action must not be done in ignorance.

Does NE 1111a22 give us all the conditions of involuntariness that there are? In Section 1.4 I shall argue that the logic of Aristotle's own position requires a third condition, which, however, needs further and more explicit development than Aristotle gives it. This third negative condition, the sense of which will be explained in 1.4, is this:

(iii) Voluntary action must not be irrational behaviour.

Two methodological observations are in order before I begin exegesis of the evidence for these conditions:

A. I use 'behaviour' to include all human performances, movements and physical manifestations, without prejudice to the question whether such performances count either as action or as free action.
B. As Austin notes, most of Aristotle's account of the negative conditions of the voluntary is concerned with exculpation from responsibility for bad deeds, with blame rather than with praise. As I have said, this does not necessarily mean that Aristotle is only, or even mainly, concerned with excuses. Whatever he says about exculpation from blame I believe applies, *mutatis mutandis*, to exclusion from praise.

1.2.   COMPULSION, DURESS, PERSUASION AND FREE ACTION

It is an obvious intuition that I cannot act freely or voluntarily if I am under compulsion:

We talk of whatever is compelled (*to biaion*) as being involuntary, indeed of whatever is involuntary as being compelled.' [EE 1224b11–12; the latter clause evidently goes too far.]

What comes about by force (*to biai*) is thought to be involuntary. (NE 1109b35)

The distinctions which Aristotle goes on to draw concerning compulsion and its relation to the voluntary are all qualifications or dilutions of the meaning of *bia*. What, then, is the basic theme on which the variations are to be played: what is to count as a case of straightforward compulsion?

2a. Straightforward Compulsion: External Compulsion

Aristotle opens his discussions of voluntariness and compulsion in the EE with a plausible generalisation: What something is compelled to do is whatever is unnatural (*para physin*, EE 1224a20) for it to do. Correspondingly, what something does freely or spontaneously is whatever is natural (*kata ten physei kai ten kath' hauta hormen*, EE 1224a18) for it to do. This opposition *para physin / kata physin* can be given fairly precise sense. The movement or process (*kinesis*) which is natural to X, is whatever *kinesis* originates within X. The *kinesis* which is unnatural to X, is whatever *kinesis* originates outside X:

A thing is compelled to undergo a process if that process has its origin (*arkhe*) outside the thing in question, and is present in it in such a way that nothing is contributed by the thing which acts (or rather is acted on). (NE 1110a1–3)

When some external factor moves or stops a thing contrary to its own impetus, we call it compulsion; when it does not, we say there is no compulsion. (EE 1224b7–9)

Three examples of this kind of compulsion. (*First example*) Aristotle reports that the movement of a stone thrown upwards, or of a flame made to burn 'upside down', were called 'forced' movements by Greeks of his time:

We say that a stone borne upwards, and a flame borne down, are moved by force and necessity. (EE 1224a17)

This kind of movement is contrasted by Aristotle with the opposite movements (downwards for a stone, upwards for a flame), the movements 'according to the natural and characteristic impetus of the thing' (EE 1224a18). These (he reports) were not called forced movements (a19) – though admittedly they were not called *voluntary* movements either: 'the opposite is nameless' (a20). These movements are 'natural' for these things because they are the movements which, according to Aristotle's physics, these things will display if left to their own devices, the movements which originate within these things 'when the origin of the movement is within the thing and is not brought about by compulsion' (EE 1224b15).

This general point is applicable to human beings, whose 'natural' movement *qua* human beings is voluntary action, as we shall see further in Ch. 2. Thus Aristotle tells us that an 'origin (*arkhe*) outside the agent' means an origin which is 'a necessity which moves or halts the object contrary to its impetus' (EE 1224b13). A case of this would occur if (*second example*) 'someone were to take someone else's hand, when he was opposing both his wish and his choice, and use it to strike a third person' (EE 1224b13–15; cp. NE 1135a27).

Where I cannot prevent my limbs being utilised for another's purposes, I am straightforwardly compelled to perform whatever movements that other wishes. The impetus to action (*horme*) does not arise within me. Hence I am not responsible for whatever is so done, because in such a case I do not act voluntarily.

(*Third example*) In the NE there is the more famous example of the captain in his ship: 'as, for example, if a wind or men who had overpowered me should carry me away somewhere' (NE 1110a3). The captain is not responsible for the movements of his ship unless they are the results of his own impetuses (*hormai*): that is, unless they are under his control, which they are not if typhoons or brigands commandeer his sails. He too is straightforwardly compelled, and therefore exonerated.

2b.   External Non-Compulsion

The plausible generalisation is, then, that I am responsible for all my behaviour which originates within me, but for none of it which originates outside me. However, this generalisation is only a starting-point for Aristotle. He thinks that, before it is accepted (if it can be), this statement should be tested against obvious objections, some more compelling than others. This procedure will allow us both to elaborate the original rule of thumb, and to note any exceptions to it.

The first objection to the rule of thumb is this. If compulsions arise only without and free actions only within, why not say that I am compelled (e.g.) by what is pleasant (perhaps in the case of an unrestrained or wicked action), or by what is noble (perhaps in the case of a virtuous action)?

Aristotle's response is as follows. Of course it is true that 'what is pleasant' and 'what is noble' are (descriptions of) things – states of affairs conceived by me as desirable goals – outside me. But one cannot legitimately move from the rule of thumb to the claim that *any* outside influence on my behaviour, since it is outside me, must be a compulsion. To do so would destroy the very idea of a contrast between the voluntary and the involuntary which Aristotle is trying to establish:

> If someone said that what is pleasant, or what is fine, acts as a compulsion because *it* is an external necessity, on this view every action would be compelled. For everything that everybody does is done for the sake of these things. (NE 1110b9–11)

It may be true that when, say, I seduce my neighbour's wife, I act on an external influence, namely her beauty. But does this look like a case of compulsion (which is supposed to be unpleasant, b12)? Since I am clearly not physically pained by the experience, but the opposite (b12–13), doesn't the plea of compulsion just look like a rather flimsy pretext (b14–15)?

More importantly, we should distinguish (although Aristotle does not, explicitly) between something's being an *influence* on an agent's behaviour, and its being the *origin* (*arkhe*) of that behaviour. The seduction case is not assimilable to the case in which the sea-captain finds himself, because the origin of the sea-captain's movement is the winds (or the pirates). If the captain can do anything at all, he may hope, at best, to influence his ship's movements, but (as the case is described) he cannot be the origin of those movements. In the seduction case, as I have described it, it is the other way round. The origin of my behaviour (Aristotle would say) is not the lady's beauty, but my desire to seduce her. Her beauty is an influence on, perhaps even a necessary condition for, my behaviour; but it is not the origin of that behaviour. Hence my behaviour's origin is not, in truth, outside me, and so cases like this provide no counter-example to Aristotle's rule of thumb.

2c. Internal Compulsion

So the rule of thumb survives the first objection, if it is modified to say that 'Voluntary action is behaviour that finds its origin, and not just some of the influences on its occurrence, within the agent; compelled behaviour is behaviour that finds its origin, and not just some of the influences on its occurrence, outside the agent.' But what if the objector now goes on the other tack? He has attempted to argue that no behaviour truly originates within the agent, and hence that no behaviour is voluntary. He may now attempt to argue a second objection: that even behaviour which does truly originate within the agent is not necessarily voluntary.

This is a problem which Aristotle notes at EE 1224a23 ff., drawing a contrast between things like stones and things like human beings. Things like stones either undergo 'natural' movement (according to the impetus which is the originating principle (*arkhe*) within them) or 'unnatural' movement (according to some other principle, outside them). For things like human beings, however, this simple contrast is not available: 'In inanimate things, the principle originating movements is a simple one, but in animate beings (*ta empsykha*) there are a number of such principles' (EE 1224a28). The simple contrast between origin outside and origin within is not available for animate beings, because at least some animate beings do not have one and only one kind of originating principle within them: they have two, reason (*logos*) and appetition (*orexis*) (1224a26). This is the case, at any rate, with humans ('in humans both [reason and appetition] are present': a28).

(Aristotle seems unsure whether or not to say the same of other animals, drawing first a distinction between the 'animate' as having more than one principle in them and the 'inanimate' as having only one, and then a second distinction between humans as having more than one principle in them and the rest, both animals and inanimate objects, as having only one.)

Can an agent's behaviour genuinely have its origin within that agent, and yet be not voluntary action but compelled behaviour? Aristotle's answer to this in the NE is markedly different from that in the EE. In the NE, his position is evidently that any impetus which originates in me is entirely my responsibility. It is a sufficient criterion of voluntariness that the agent should be the *arkhe* of his action, that the action should originate in him. Accordingly, the only true compulsion is external compulsion, that which is applied to me against my wishes by other agents or outside forces. On this criterion of compulsion, the question of whether I can help obeying the pull of my own desires towards certain objects is strictly irrelevant: 'It is no good to say that what we do in passion or desire is involuntary' (1111a24–25) precisely because, whatever we do in these states, *we* do.

However, if we accept the EE's point about there being more than one kind of principle of origination of movement in humans (as the Aristotle of the NE undoubtedly did: NE 1102a29 ff.), a more tolerant approach is suggested, which indeed, in the EE, Aristotle adopts; most explicitly at EE 1225a25–33. Here Aristotle virtually contradicts the teaching of NE 1111a24–25. He compares those who act under the influence of desire (*epithymia*) with those who are possessed by spirits (*enthousiontas*):

> We do not say that it is up to [the possessed] to say what they say or do what they do... *but neither do we say this of those who act under the influence of desire...'* (EE 1225a30-31)

In the case of desire-led action, too, it now appears, it can sometimes be true that we can lack control, either over some of our thoughts and emotions (1225a32), or over the actions resulting from our thoughts and reasonings (1225a33). In what cases, then, can this loss of control of one's beliefs, wants or behaviour be said to occur? For unless we can give a clear answer to that question, this excuse of being overpowered by desire will be available to every scoundrel for every indulgence. Aristotle remarks that the crucial question ('what everything leads up to', 1225a26) is that of 'what a nature is able to bear' (a27). But what a person's nature can and cannot bear is not up to him (a28). Hence (in Philolaus' words), 'some arguments are too strong for us' (a34).

So it seems that, in the EE at least, Aristotle does allow for a breach of his rule of thumb: there can, on this account, be internal compulsions. (The only place in the NE where Aristotle definitely entertains the idea that internal compulsion can diminish voluntariness is NE 1148a18–22.) Action on such a compulsion will contrast both with action on an external compulsion (where the origin of the action, as we have seen, is not within the agent); and also with action on either an internally or externally derived urge which, however, does not count as a compulsion (where there will be a conscious assent, on the agent's part, to acting in this way, so that although the urge was strong he could have resisted it).

The criterion of an internal compulsion, then, is given by the answer to the question 'Is this urge too strong for this nature to resist?' (EE 1225a27). This, of course, is a question to which (even given the same strength of urge) the answer will vary from one nature to another. Hence the assignment of responsibility and exculpation, in cases where a plea of internal compulsion is entered, will be a subtle matter. But this subtilising of the account need not mean that *carte blanche* has been given to every scoundrel for every indulgence. It might, rather, seem an advantage of the EE account over the NE account that this kind of being overpowered is here allowed as an excuse.

(It is curious, incidentally, that Kenny (1979), one of the most distinguished recent commentaries on the EE, makes no mention of this important point of difference between the EE and the NE. Especially if its allowance of internal compulsion is considered to be an advantage of the EE's account over the NE's, one might have thought that Kenny would want to stress this point.)

Thus the rule of thumb needs to be modified a second time, to read: 'Voluntary action is behaviour that finds its origin, and not just some of the influences on its occurrence, within the agent and to which the agent consents without being overpowered; compelled behaviour is either (i) behaviour that finds its origin, and not just some of the influences on its occurrence, altogether outside the agent; or else (ii) behaviour that finds its origin within the agent's psyche, but to which the agent does not consent because he is overpowered by something in his psyche which nevertheless can be distinguished from *him*.'

2d. External Duress

This, I think, completes Aristotle's remarks on compulsion strictly so called. But he does have something to say about what I will call 'duress', which seems a close relation of compulsion:

> Actions can be said to be done under compulsion and by necessity in another sense: namely when people do something which they take to be painful and base, but which if they do not do, they will suffer blows or chains or death. (EE 1225a3–6)

Compulsion is physical necessity; duress is practical necessity. Action under duress is exemplified by action under a threat, like the tyrant's threat to one's family if one does not comply with his wishes (NE 1110a6–7), or the threat perceived from the storm by the sailor who jettisons the cargo (NE 1110a8–9). Aristotle says that there is some doubt about whether action under duress is voluntary or involuntary (NE 1110a7–8), and indeed his own remarks seem to illustrate this uncertainty.

In the NE, Aristotle begins with puzzles and moves towards a simpler account. He begins by calling actions under duress *mixed* (*miktai*, NE 1110a11), half-voluntary and half-involuntary. His reason for calling actions under duress involuntary is, apparently, to do with considerations about second-order choice. It is clear that no one would *choose to choose* between having their relatives slaughtered and cooperating in a tyrant's atrocities: no one would voluntarily enter a situation where these were the only options on offer for voluntary choice. Neither option is the kind of thing that one would ever choose to do, for its own sake and considered in its own right. Hence action under duress is (he says), in a way, both voluntary and involuntary:

> Such things are indeed voluntary – though considered in their own right (*haplos*) they are perhaps involuntary... .(NE 1110a18–20)

They can be seen as involuntary because 'no one would choose any of these for its own sake (*kath' hauto*)'. On the other hand, they can also be seen as voluntary, for two reasons. (i) Because they are chosen (*hairetai*, a13) at the time they are done, even if not at any other time. But it is the chosenness or otherwise of an action at the time it is done which counts for its (in)voluntariness (a14). And (ii) because the rule of thumb applies to them: the origin of an action under duress is within the agent. Hence such actions are mixed, although 'they are generally more like voluntary actions' (NE 1110a12).

In the EE, by contrast, Aristotle begins with a simpler account and introduces more and more difficulties for it. (This contrast, incidentally, seems rather good evidence for dating at least this part of the EE earlier than the corresponding part of the NE. If an early essay on a subject starts well then runs into perplexities, it is natural when returning to the topic to start by re-examining those perplexities.) At first he seems to be in much less doubt than in the NE about the status of actions under duress. He does not start by calling them 'mixed' or raising considerations about second-order choice.

He simply says that all actions under duress must be voluntary, because in every case of duress it is true that 'it is open to the agent not to act, but rather to undergo the [threatened] suffering' (EE 1225a7–8). However, unfortunately, he then goes on to complicate this picture, in three ways.

(i)   If (he says) it was up to the agent (*eph' hautoi*, a10) to avoid or not avoid the situation of choice under duress, then the agent is responsible for being in that situation, and so his choice under duress, however painful, is voluntary (EE 1225a9–12). If, however (a12–14), he had no chance of avoiding that situation, then one may say that his action is under compulsion of a sort (*biai pos*, a13), though not full-blown (*haplos*) compulsion. (Compare NE 1110a18.)

(ii) Furthermore, the agent's action under duress is now said to be less than fully voluntary because he does not choose the action which he does for its own sake, but for some further purpose, e.g. saving his family's lives: 'He does not deliberately choose (*proairetai*) that very thing which he does; he deliberately chooses that for the sake of which he does it' (EE 1225a14; cp. NE 1110a19–20).

(iii) Finally, Aristotle simply contradicts EE 1225a7–8:

Therefore an agent acts under compulsion and necessity, or at least not naturally, when he does something bad either for the sake of something good, or for the sake of deliverance from a greater evil. *And so involuntarily,* for such things are not up to him. (EE 1225a18–20)

Here Aristotle's remarks under (i) and (ii) seem, by his own lights, to be misguided. To say that I am *involuntarily* put in a situation in which I have to make a certain *voluntary* choice is, obviously, not to say that that voluntary choice is not voluntary; to say that something is not chosen for its own sake, but as a means to something else, is obviously not to say that it is not voluntarily chosen as a means. Both these remarks seem more relevant to questions about second-order choice than first-order choice. Surely, then, it is the simpler remarks, at the beginning of the EE account and the end of the NE account, which are more correct. Actions done under duress are done voluntarily and not, strictly speaking, under any sort of compulsion, as application of the doubly modified rule of thumb clearly shows. The origin of an action done under duress is within, not outside, the agent, who consents to what he does and is not overpowered by any urge like physical desire. So actions under duress are neither involuntary nor 'mixed', but simply voluntary. As for considerations about second-order choice: Aristotle's own observation (NE 1110a13) that it is the chosenness of the action at the time at which it is done seems to render these irrelevant. The question whether one would choose to be confronted with such choices is a question about the nature, not of voluntariness, but of human well-being (*eudaimonia*).

It follows that action under duress is more sharply distinct than Aristotle recognises from action under compulsion, for one is a species of voluntary, the other of involuntary, action. That this distinction is not sharp for Aristotle is evident from the fact that he does not, in the NE or EE, even have separate terms for 'compulsion' and 'duress'. In EE 2.8, Aristotle does regularly use two words for 'compulsion and duress', *bia kai ananke* (whereas, in NE 3.1, the talk is almost all of *bia*, apart from *anankasanta* at 1110a28). But even when Aristotle uses both words, he uses both for both phenomena. So EE 1225a2 (where he switches from talking about compulsion to talking about duress): 'Actions can be said to be done under compulsion and by necessity (*bia kai anankasthentes*) in another sense...' (cp. EE 1224a11–12). (In the *Magna Moralia*, however, it is interesting to note that this distinction *is* drawn by the author (who is not necessarily Aristotle): v. MM 1188a37–b28.)

2e. Internal Duress

I quoted EE 1225a25–33 above in discussing internal compulsion. The keen-eyed reader will have seen that the immediately preceding passage, a23–25, is not about internal compulsion at all, but internal duress:

> It seems more plausible to say that someone acts under compulsion and involuntarily (*biai kai akon*) if they act so as to avoid violent pain than if they act so as to avoid slight pain. And, in general, it seems more plausible to say that someone acts under compulsion and involuntarily if they act so as to avoid pain than if they act so as to enjoy pleasure. (EE 1225a23–25)

It seems clear from this passage that (in the EE at least) Aristotle would admit, under the heading of duress, not only the possibility of acting so as avoid torture by another, but also the possibility of acting so as to avoid torture by (e.g.) one's own unsatisfied longings. EE 1225a25–28, then, would give Aristotle's rationalisation of this 'common opinion' (*doxa*): there can be such internal duress, and hence it can be admissible to act so as to avoid a worse alternative which one's own constitution presents. This will only be true in some cases, of course. Only some internal urges will genuinely leave one with no practical alternative to acting on them. Other urges may make it practically very difficult to do otherwise than act on them; yet giving into them will not be in any sense a practical necessity. Therefore such giving in, where it is a bad thing, will be a proper subject neither of pity nor even of condonation (v. NE 1110a24). (If, incidentally, a25–28 is really about internal duress, then it might be said that a25–28 cannot be relevant in the context of internal compulsion in which I quoted it above. However, given Aristotle's lack of an adequate distinction between compulsion and duress in general, and his toing and froing between the two topics at EE 1225a3–33 in particular, there is no good reason why a25–28 cannot be relevant to both cases.)

2f.   Duress and Persuasion

Duress, then, is not very like compulsion. It is much more like something else to which Aristotle also alludes very briefly in the same context, persuasion:

> What is compelled and necessary appears to be opposite to the voluntary and to persuasion in practical matters, as do compulsion and necessity. (EE 1224a13–16)

It might at first sight be thought from this remark that Aristotle has the following spectrum of cases in mind:

compulsion/ necessity (i.e. duress?) // persuasion/ the voluntary.

There would be a spectrum from entirely voluntary action (at one extreme), through voluntary action under persuasion and under duress, to entirely compelled 'action' (at the other extreme). But clearly Aristotle is not thinking of such a spectrum. First, as we have already seen, he makes no distinction in sense between *bia* and *ananke*. Given this, it seems probable that no important distinction is made at EE 1224a13–16 between persuasion and the voluntary either. This also is a distinction which Aristotle should have made. Action at another's instigation through persuasion is, it seems clear, quite often distinct as to its degree of voluntariness or spontaneity from action which an agent simply instigates himself. To see this consider its culpability. That 'I was persuaded to do as I did' can perfectly well be a partially exonerating factor of a kind.

A second reason why the above spectrum will not work as a tool of analysis is that there is no easy gradation between compulsion and duress; for the pair compulsion and duress are not elements of the same spectrum at all. The same, however, is not true of the triplet duress, persuasion and the voluntary. Notoriously, being persuaded can take many forms, some of which are very like choosing to act purely on one's own initiative, while others are so compelling and unfair as to be close to duress. On the one side, emotional blackmail does not seem very different from any other sort of blackmail. On the other, there is evidently a close similarity between acting on another's presentation to me of reasons for action, and acting on my own presentation to myself of reasons for action. So then persuasion shades into duress on the one side, and into spontaneous voluntary action on the other. However – *pace* Aristotle – there is no such slide from compulsion to duress. In the range from duress, via persuasion, to uninfluenced original action, it remains true that the origin of the agent's behaviour is within the agent himself – however strong the influences which are brought to bear on that behaviour. In the case of compulsion, however, the origin of the agent's behaviour is (by definition) outside the agent; the agent is, at best, only an influence upon that behaviour and not its origin. (And this is true, in a way, even if the compulsion is 'internal'.)

Then if duress is so different from compulsion, should Aristotle have discussed it at all in these contexts? The answer to that is, I believe, Yes. But this is not because action under duress is a species of action under compulsion; nor yet because action under duress is a species of the involuntary. As I hope I have shown, action under duress is neither of these. It is because action under duress is a species of action having limited responsibility. What the existence of the class 'actions done under duress' illustrates, rightly understood, is the idea that an action can be fully voluntary, yet not fully responsible. This is a remarkable and perhaps counter-intuitive idea, and it may be discomfort with this idea which causes Aristotle to try to fit duress under the heading of compulsion. Under that heading, however, it gets more and more anomalous the more one looks at it.

If it is true in general that action under duress is voluntary, and yet its doer bears only limited responsibility, does it follow that all duress exonerates? Apparently not: in both NE and EE Aristotle notes that, just as there can be degrees of forceful influence on my behaviour which yet do not amount to compulsion because they are not irresistible, so there can be degrees of duress which are not sufficient to justify the action performed under that duress. So at EE 1225a14–16, Aristotle remarks that it would be absurd for a person to say that he had killed someone under duress because, had he not done so, he would have lost a game of blind man's buff: 'there needs to be something worse and more painful than that which he will endure if he does not act' (a17). And again at NE 1110a27–29, 'It seems absurd of Euripides' Alcmaeon to talk of the factors which "force" him to kill his mother.' In general, 'It is the mark of a small spirit to endure what is shameful for the sake of nothing noble or proportionate' (NE 1110a23). If one is to go through some painful or despicable course to some desired end, the end must be worth the pain or shame of the course. In cases where it is worth it, there can even be praise for the person who takes the necessary course (NE 1110a20). But some courses are *so* shameful that *nothing at all* could make them worth taking (NE 1110a26–27) – Alcmaeon's action in Euripides being a case in point. All of this evidence tends to support the claim that action under duress is indeed voluntary action.

1.3.   THE VARIETIES OF IGNORANCE

Having completed my consideration of Aristotle on compulsion and duress, I turn to Aristotle's discussion of ignorance and the voluntary. Here too his method is to begin with a very plausible general rule, and then note a list of exceptions to it or refinements of it.

The plausible generalisation here is: 'What is done in ignorance cannot be voluntary': 'All action in ignorance is not voluntary action' (NE 1110b18). But this bald observation is patient of much refinement and qualification, for it is set (as the last quotation is set) in the midst of an impressive variety of both broad and subtle distinctions.

What emerges from the drawing of these distinctions is that knowledge and ignorance are not set in binary opposition for Aristotle. There is a wide range of degrees of knowledge/ ignorance, set between extremes which Aristotle (to an extent) defines for us. Hence, insofar as they depend upon knowledge/ ignorance, neither are voluntariness/ involuntariness in binary opposition.

The first distinction which, strictly speaking, we should make about ignorance is one which Aristotle does not make. Aristotle uses the word *agnoia* for 'ignorance'; but, as Kenny rightly notes, 'It is clear that *agnoia* includes not just lack of knowledge, but also positively mistaken belief' (Kenny 1979, p. 48). That is, *agnoia* covers both <believing that not-*p* when *p* is true> and <not believing that *p* when *p* is true>. It is *agnoia* if (say) I switch off the lights on the mistaken belief that there is no one else in the room. It is also *agnoia* if I simply switch off the lights without considering whether there is anyone else there.

This noted, the first distinction which Aristotle makes excludes a large class of cases of ignorance, as being of a kind which is not relevant to the (in)voluntariness of any behaviour. This is Aristotle's distinction between what I shall call principle ignorance and particular ignorance.

3a. Principle and Particular Ignorance

This distinction is most clearly drawn at NE 1110b27 ff. Aristotle admits the Platonist view that it is proper to speak cognitively of moral beliefs. We can indeed say that good people *know* what is right. Likewise we can say that bad people do not know what is right. But *this* ignorance does not excuse their badness. 'Every scoundrel is ignorant of what he ought to do (*dei prattein*) and what he should avoid'; but in the case of a scoundrel it would be wrong to draw the normally permissible inference from the scoundrel's being ignorant to some degree to his being involuntary to the same degree, and so likewise not culpable to that same degree. For 'ignorance in the *proairesis*...is not the cause of involuntariness, but of wickedness' (b31–2). And Aristotle immediately makes it clear that by 'ignorance in the *proairesis*' he means precisely ignorance of principle as opposed to ignorance of particulars (NE 1110b34–1111a1). (As has often been noted, this is a confusing use of the phrase, for Aristotle stresses elsewhere that *proairesis*, deliberate choice, is always choice of means and not of ends. So we might have expected 'ignorance in the *proairesis*' to mean ignorance about means. But on the contrary, it means ignorance of an end. Since, as we shall see in Ch. 3, voluntary action which involves *proairesis* is the paradigm case of Aristotelian voluntary action, perhaps we may salvage the position by suggesting that Aristotle's point is that 'ignorance in the *proairesis*' is the kind of ignorance which is still there even when there is no ignorance of the sort that impedes voluntariness around.)

I can always be blamed for my ignorance of right principle; I always ought to have had this sort of knowledge. Why should we take this line? If Aristotle's requirement seems unreasonable, consider these two exchanges, representing respectively the two forms of ignorance noted above, <believing that not-*p* when *p* is true> and <not believing that *p* when *p* is true>:

(1)   A.   You shot my father!
      B.   But I don't believe that killing is wrong.
(2)   A.   You stole my watch!
      B.   Oh, sorry – I forgot that stealing is wrong.

Are either of B's responses conceivable as *excuses*? We can understand B excusing himself with 'But I didn't mean to', or 'I didn't know it was your watch', or 'But I was forced to' (etc.); but how could 1B and 2B ever count as excuses, rather than as frank admission of guilt or of lunacy respectively?

There is one analogy for knowledge of moral principle which Aristotle clearly has in mind at NE 1142a27 ff., and also at 1147a21, a27; though, as we shall see in Section 2.1, this analogy is heavily qualified by Aristotle, e.g. at NE 1140b23–24. This is the analogy between knowledge of moral principle and mathematical knowledge. No one calls me hopeless at mathematics if I do not happen to know what Goldbach's conjecture is; but they do call me hopeless at mathematics if I am incapable of learning what Goldbach's conjecture is. I may lack all sorts of factual mathematical knowledge, yet still be a genius at applying the principles of mathematics. But if I have lots of factual knowledge about maths, but no understanding of mathematical principle, then there is something radically wrong with me as a mathematician. Likewise, in ethical matters, to lack particular knowledge may affect my voluntariness, but will not affect my virtue. Whereas to lack principle knowledge will not affect my voluntariness, but will affect my virtue – for I will, *ipso facto*, be wicked. (Hence all the remaining distinctions which Aristotle makes apply only to particular and not to principle ignorance.)

Principle ignorance, then – or 'ignorance of the universal' as Aristotle also calls it, *he katholou agnoia* – is mistaken or absent belief about what is good. What about particular ignorance (*he kath' hekasta agnoia*)? At NE 1111a2–19 Aristotle distinguishes six respects of particular ignorance:

(a) ignorance of the agent (*tis*),
(b) ignorance of the act (*ti*),
(c) ignorance of the scope of the act (*peri ti e en tini prattei*),
(d) ignorance of the means for the act (*tini*),
(e) ignorance of the purposive tendency of the act (*heneka tinos*),
(f) ignorance of the manner of the act (*pos*).

I think it would be implausible to suggest that this was meant as an exhaustive and definitive list (despite NE 1111a3). It might be doubted whether any list of respects in which one might possibly experience particular ignorance could be either. (Compare EE 1225b1–8, where Aristotle distinguishes out only (c), (d), and (e) of the above list.) Aristotle's purpose is simply to give examples of the kind of accidental unawareness of specific circumstances which counts as particular ignorance.

For consider the objection to this account, that we could redescribe most cases of particular ignorance as exemplifying any one (or all) of Aristotle's respects of ignorance. Thus fencing with a sharp foil under the mistaken impression that it has a button on the end fits most obviously into Aristotle's respect (d). But we can also call it (a) ignorance that I am an agent with a sharp foil, (b) ignorance that my act is fencing with a sharp foil, (c) ignorance that the victim of my thrust is being stabbed, not touched, (d) ignorance that my act will result in death, not exercise, and (e) ignorance that I am fencing too hard.

Hence it seems that action in particular ignorance is more to do with mistakes of one type – about the extension of predicates – than with six types of ignorance. But this is not a very important objection. Aristotle's main point is not (implausibly) that there are rigidly separable kinds of problems about the extensional knowledge relevant to any behaviour, but simply that there may at one time be a great variety of different problems (of whatever kind) about that extensional knowledge. What matters, for particular ignorance, is not the number of different respects in which the agent can truly be described as ignorant, but the number of different relevant true propositions of which that agent is ignorant.

3b. Active Ignorance and Passive Knowledge

The next distinction drawn by Aristotle is apparent at EE 1225b11–12:

> Since we speak of understanding and knowledge in two senses, one referring to the *possession*, the other to the *use* of what we know...

Aristotle argues here (a point of some importance, as we shall see in Ch. 4, for Aristotle's discussion of akrasia) that when some item of knowledge is only potential and not actual, it is all right to say that the agent acts in ignorance of it. This is surely true. Relevant knowledge which is not accessible to me at the time of action – even if it is then 'there in my head' in some potential form – is not properly speaking knowledge which I have. The agent who 'has' merely passive knowledge of a relevant particular is, then, exculpated – unless, says Aristotle, the agent could have actualised it (EE 1225b16–17). Which brings us to another distinction, between actions done on and in ignorance.

3c. Action on and in Ignorance

Aristotle's distinction between acting *in* ignorance (*to di' agnoian prattein*) and acting *on* ignorance (*to agnoon prattein*) is drawn at NE 1110b25–30: 'When someone is drunk or in a rage, it seems that he does not act *in* ignorance; ...yet not knowingly either, but *on* ignorance.' The point of distinction here is this. An ordinarily ignorant agent acts *in* ignorance. When he acts, he is unaware of some fact or other which is relevant to his action. Since he (of course) does not know that he is or was going to be ignorant, *a fortiori* he never chose to be ignorant, and so deserves 'pity and understanding' (NE 1111a2). A drunkard or a man in a fury, by contrast, acts *on* ignorance. Not only does he act under influences which are liable to blind him to relevant facts; normally, he also knows, when so acting, that he is acting under influences which are liable to blind him to relevant facts; or at any rate he knew that it was going to be so when he began to allow himself to become drunk or enraged.

Hence, at least to a degree, the person who acts on ignorance has chosen his state of ignorance. He has allowed himself to get in a state where there is a real danger that his actions will be importantly compromised by ignorance. And such voluntary ignorance or risking of ignorance is, according to Aristotle, culpable (because – note well – it is voluntary):

> Likewise the person who lacks [knowledge] would be blamed, if through lack of care or pleasure or pain he lacked knowledge that it was easy, or even necessary, for him to have. (EE 1225b14–17; cp. NE 1114a2–3)

3d. Repentance and Disowning

The fourth and last of Aristotle's distinctions about under what circumstances an action in ignorance may be excused, applies only to actions done in ignorance, and in particular ignorance. It is this:

> An action said to be 'done in ignorance' in this sort of sense must also be painful to the agent, and must result in regret (*metameleia*). (NE 1111a21)

If an action done in ignorance is not followed by pain and regret, then it may be not voluntary (*oukh hekousion*), but it is not involuntary (*akousion*) (1110b18–25). I suspect that Aristotle's main point here is not, despite appearances, to single out some emotion(s) (pain or repentance or regret) the very occurrence of which is diagnostic of involuntariness-through-ignorance of this sort. It is rather to mark a logical distinction resting on a counterfactual. If A does *x* in ignorance of *p*, then

A does *x* *involuntarily* if A would not have done *x* if A had known *p*;

but A does *x* *not-voluntarily* if A would still have done *x* even if A had known *p*.

For practical purposes, therefore, the question is: will A disown the deed *x*? If A will disown *x*, then A did *x* fully involuntarily, and so, *ceteris paribus*, is exculpated. But if A refuses to disown *x*, then A did the deed not involuntarily, nor yet voluntarily, but non-voluntarily. In this case A is not only not exculpated; he is actually incriminated to a degree. For the fact that A will not disown the deed suggests something about A's character. It suggests that A is, in general, the kind of person to do this sort of thing voluntarily, even though A's doing of *x* was not (on this occasion) demonstrably not a voluntary action. Hence, where A shows no regret for having done *x* in ignorance, A is not as fully culpable for *x* as if A had actually meant to do *x*. But neither is A as fully exculpated from *x* as A would be if A's doing of *x* had been involuntary rather than non-voluntary.

Aristotle's emphasis on the development of character shows here. If a deed *x* is blameworthy, then for me to be the kind of person who would have done *x* is itself for me to be a proper subject of a degree of blame – whether or not I actually am the person who does *x*. In the case where I am that person, I am not only to be blamed for applauding the deed: I am also to be blamed for doing it. The point then is that Aristotle marks the distinction in degree of voluntariness between the involuntary and the non-voluntary precisely because he wants to mark a corresponding distinction in degree of responsibility.

To conclude, Aristotle's decision procedure for determining whether an agent who acts in some kind of ignorance and does something bad is or is not a voluntary agent, and so is or is not to be exculpated, can be summarised in this flow chart:

A. Is the ignorance of principle(s) or of particular(s)?
A1. Of principle(s): agent acts voluntarily and hence culpably.
A2. Of particular(s): proceed to B.

B. Is the apparent 'particular ignorance' in fact active ignorance which the agent could have helped? Or is it a case of passive knowledge? Or neither?
B1. Active ignorance: agent acts voluntarily and hence culpably.
B2. Passive knowledge: proceed to D.
B3. Neither: proceed to C.

C. Is the action action in particular ignorance or on particular ignorance?
C1. On: agent acts voluntarily and hence culpably.
C2. In: proceed to D.

D. Does the agent show regret?
D1. No: agent acts semi-voluntarily and hence semi-culpably.
D2. Yes: agent is exculpated.

This concludes my exegesis of Aristotle's treatment of the relation of free action to (i) compulsion and (ii) ignorance. By now certain broad themes are emerging. One is that, although the desire to ascribe praise and blame is not (on my view of Aristotle) the only possible motivation for an inquiry into what factors make for (in)voluntariness, it is evident that, for him, voluntariness and responsibility stand in direct proportion. Another is that there can be degrees to ignorance, compulsion and duress, and hence also to (in)voluntariness and responsibility.

1.4. IRRATIONALITY

I come to the third negative condition of voluntary action which, I said, the logic of Aristotle's position requires. Saying that 'the logic of Aristotle's position requires' this third negative condition means, of course, that I am going to argue for it myself, because Aristotle does not, at least not directly. But that there is here a hole which Aristotle should have filled is not too difficult to show.

Compare his negative conditions of voluntary action with his positive account. In this (exegesis of which is yet to come, in Chs 2–3), Aristotle will tell us explicitly that voluntary action is

(i)   action which originates within the agent in a particular way (a condition corresponding to the negative condition about compulsion);

(ii)   action on certain sorts of knowledge and information (a condition corresponding to the negative condition about ignorance);
       and we should add that Aristotle is committed also to holding that it is

(iii) action which is rational behaviour.

The negative condition to which this third part of the positive account corresponds is the condition that voluntary action must not be irrational behaviour, a phrase the sense of which I now hope to make clearer. The argument for positing this third negative condition spills over unavoidably into the forthcoming positive account; but here it is, prolepses and all.

To put it briefly: Belief *plus* want or pro-attitude does not equal voluntary action; but belief *in combination with* want or pro-attitude does. On Aristotle's own theory, there is in the constitution of a voluntary action more than just the absence of ignorance (which implies, positively, the presence of true belief(s) relevant to the manifested behaviour) and the absence of compulsion (which implies, positively, the presence of unhindered pro-attitude(s) relevant to the manifested behaviour). It is neither sufficient nor necessary for the occurrence of a voluntary action that the agent's true belief(s) and unhindered pro-attitude(s) *should be* relevant to the performance of the manifested behaviour. What is sufficient and necessary for a voluntary action is that those belief(s) and pro-attitude(s) *should be seen by the agent herself to be* relevant to the performance of the manifested behaviour.

Consider a person A who exhibits some behaviour B. Let us suppose (i) that there is nothing in the situation to impede B. Let us also say (ii) that, in every important respect relevant to B, A is not ignorant. Does it follow, from the stipulation of these two conditions alone, that B is a voluntary action? If it does follow, then my negative conditions (i) and (ii) are both necessary and sufficient for voluntary action. But if it does not follow, then (i) and (ii) may be necessary, but they are not necessary and sufficient for voluntary action.

My argument for negative condition (iii) is that it does *not* follow. For if A, in the situation described, is to do B as a voluntary action, this condition is not necessary and sufficient:

(C1) that A should do B *while* feeling relevant pro-attitude(s) action upon which is not impeded, and while holding some relevant belief(s) not subject to any kind of ignorance.

What is necessary and sufficient for A's performance of B as a voluntary action is this:

(C2) that A should do B *because of the combination of* some unimpeded pro-attitude(s) which A feels, and some relevant belief(s), not subject to any kind of ignorance, which A holds.

The crucial difference between (C1) and (C2) is in the words 'because of the combination of'. To say that A does B because of the combination of desire D and belief P is to say something quite different from, and not implicit in, saying that A does B while feeling desire D and while holding belief P. All my negative conditions of voluntary action (i) and (ii) entitle us to say is the latter and not the former.

This is why, on their own, (i) and (ii) cannot be the necessary and sufficient conditions of voluntary action. For the satisfaction of (i) and (ii) by some piece of behaviour is no guarantee that that piece of behaviour can plausibly be seen as a voluntary action rather than as just a piece of (random) behaviour. I might want some toast, and believe rightly that this thing here is toast, and go ahead to eat the toast without being compelled to do so. Yet, in this case as described, it could still be true that I did not eat the toast *because* I wanted toast and believed this thing to be toast. There might be no explanatory connection at all between my beliefs and desires and my toast-eating behaviour. That behaviour might be purely coincidental to those beliefs and desires.

Of course (it may be replied), someone whose toast-eating behaviour exhibited no such explanatory connection would be counted, by most people, as an idiot or lunatic, even if not an ignorant or compelled lunatic. But that is precisely the point: that negative conditions (i) and (ii), taken on their own, give us no means whatever of distinguishing the chance, random movements of a lunatic (or certain sorts of machine) from the voluntary actions of a rational agent. To make that distinction, we need to postulate a third negative condition of voluntary action: that it should not be irrational behaviour.

Note that behaviour which is irrational, in this sense, is not simply a sub-class of behaviour which is compelled – although that seems to be Aristotle's implication when he writes of the possessed that, even though their behaviour is actually intelligent ('they do the things that characteristically go with understanding', EE 1225a29), 'still we do not say that it is up to them to say what they say or do what they do'. Likewise, Aristotle describes incontinent people as being like actors (NE 1147a23), and as being like the sleepwalker or the madman or the drunkard (NE 1147a14). Now he says (rightly, I think) that the behaviour of people in such states is not fully voluntary; but he seems to be implying (wrongly, I suggest) that such behaviour is not fully voluntary because it is compelled. In the case at least of the sleepwalker and the madman, it would have been at least as plausible for him to say rather that such behaviour is not fully voluntary because it is irrational. In such cases, that is, the explanatory connections which we would look for, in a voluntary action, between wants and beliefs and the manifested behaviour are simply absent.

For irrational behaviour differs from compelled behaviour (as that is described in Aristotle's own account) for the following reasons. Compelled behaviour, we have seen, may (a) originate outside the agent. But irrational behaviour can perfectly well originate within the agent, and still be irrational; hence irrational behaviour is not externally compelled. Otherwise it may (b) originate within the agent, against the overpowered agent's consent. But that formula implies that something like a normal process of combining wants and beliefs towards an action goes on in the agent, but is frustrated by an overriding force – otherwise there would be no consent for the compelled behaviour to be against. If no such process occurs, as (by definition) it does not in irrational behaviour, then there is no such consent for the resulting behaviour to override; hence irrational behaviour is not internally compelled either.

Nor is irrational behaviour a sub-class of action in ignorance. That might seem to be Aristotle's implication when he describes the person who fears nothing as a 'madman' (*mainomenos*, NE 1115b27). Fearlessness might be thought to count as a case of ignorance-like irrationality in the context of Socrates' famous argument (*Laches* 194c–d) that courage was a species of knowledge. Again, Aristotle also calls the person who is ignorant of every aspect of his own action a *mainomenos* (NE 1111a7).

Now no doubt crazy courage, and such radical ignorance as Aristotle means, are cases which do deserve the name 'madness' (*mania*). But that does not mean that ignorance of either of these sorts is equivalent to what I mean by 'irrationality'. In a case of irrational behaviour in my sense, the problem is not what it is in a case of ignorance (as that is described in Aristotle's own account). It is not that the agent has no beliefs, nor that the agent has wrong beliefs. The problem is that the agent's beliefs fail to connect in any conceivably appropriate way with the agent's behaviour.

It is because irrational behaviour will not fit under either of Aristotle's own headings of ignorance or of compulsion that I say he needs to postulate a third negative condition of voluntary action. Does Aristotle himself ever recognise the need for that third negative condition?

I cheerfully admit that the answer to that seems to be: hardly at all. It is well known that Aristotle has a theory of practical reason (to which I shall be coming shortly) in which a certain form of voluntary action, action on what is called *proairesis* by Aristotle, plays a starring role. Action on *proairesis* is, evidently, voluntary action which is rational; but it is also sharply distinguished by Aristotle from the voluntary in general (*to hekousion*). Moreover, at first sight it looks as if the point of distinction between the voluntary and action on *proairesis* is exactly that action on *proairesis* is necessarily rational, while voluntary action is not. (So, e.g. NE 1112a13–17.)

But my claim is not only about action on *proairesis*; it is about any voluntary action. The claim I have just argued for is that, contrary to the apparent sense of passages like NE 1112a13–17, not only *proairesis* but voluntary action too is necessarily rational in the sense defined above. (What, then, is the right way to distinguish between voluntary action and action on *proairesis*? I will answer that question in Section 3.2) For the explicit making of this claim there is little or no evidence in Aristotle's ethical writings. The best evidence is to be found in the MM, but this is of dubious authorship. At MM 1188b25–28, the author does indeed give three conditions of voluntariness, not two:

> The involuntary is what happens under necessity, and under force; and thirdly it is what comes about in the absence of understanding (*dianoia*).

But clearly the three conditions of a voluntary action given here are not my three. They are the conditions that the action should involve (a) no compulsion, (b) no duress, and (c) the presence of 'understanding': meaning what? *Dianoia* might easily be the Greek for 'rationality' (in a loose sense); but it becomes clear, when we read MM 1188b29–35, that what the author means by requiring the presence of *dianoia* in a voluntary agent is very little different from what Aristotle means by requiring that a voluntary agent should not be ignorant.

The only places in the writings generally accepted as genuinely Aristotle's to which one might, tenuously, point for direct evidence of my third condition would be these two:

> We should define 'what is to be deliberated about' as what the man of sense (*ho noun ekhon*) would deliberate about – not the fool or the madman. (112a20)

> [The beasts] do not have *proairesis* or the ability to reason; they stand outside nature, as madmen do among humans. (NE 1149b35)

The first passage might be adduced to support the claim that it is only the *mainomenos*, meaning the irrational agent in my sense of 'irrational', who does not reason in his voluntary action. But this will not do. (i) The passage says rather that the *mainomenos* does reason, but, like the fool, not about the right things; clearly then this kind of madman cannot be the 'irrational agent' of my terminology. (ii) The passage is taken from the beginning of Aristotle's discussion of deliberation, which is for him an ingredient or precondition of *proairesis* (NE 1112a15).

The second passage might be taken to mean that what the animals have in common with the *mainomenos* (again, meaning the irrational agent in my sense of 'irrational') is that neither acts voluntarily because neither reasons: the animals because they act on instinct or the like, the madman because he is mad. But this will not do either. (i) The passage, explicitly, is talking about exceptions from *proairesis*, not from voluntary action. (ii) Aristotle says at NE 1111b8–10 that 'animals, like children, do share in the voluntary, but not in action on *proairesis*'.

So neither of these passages can be used to give direct support to the claim, which I nonetheless have argued for, that Aristotle is or should be committed to the doctrine that all voluntary action is rational (in my sense of that word). However, this absence of direct support, such as would be given by the discovery of an Aristotelian term meaning 'rational' in my sense, is no problem. As Ch. 3 will show, my claim is not short of other forms of grounding.

Let me conclude this chapter by noting that, in explanation of my third negative condition of the voluntary, I can now essay a tentative definition of rational and irrational behaviour. The definition is this: An agent's rational behaviour is such of that agent's behaviour as is susceptible to explanation by reference to the combination of that agent's wants and beliefs, where that combination has a causal influence over the behaviour because it is seen by the agent as providing a reason for the action.

Irrational behaviour, then, is just behaviour which cannot be explained in the above way: human movement or doing for which there is no contrast between two ways of describing it, as behaviour, with its efficient causes (on the one side), and as action, with the reasons for which it is done (on the other). And if behaviour which satisfies the other two conditions of voluntary action is, nonetheless, irrational behaviour, there seems, as we have seen, to be no good reason to describe it as voluntary behaviour rather than (say) random, accidental, instinctive, or automatic behaviour. This doctrine of the necessary rationality of voluntary action is one for which I would claim the support of Donald Davidson. In his words:

> Central to the relation between a reason and the action it explains is the idea that the agent performed the action because he had the reason... . When we ask why someone acted as he did, we want to be provided with an interpretation. His behaviour seems strange, alien, outré, pointless, out of character; perhaps we cannot even recognise an action in it. When we learn his reason, we have an interpretation, a new description of what he did, which fits it into a familiar picture [which]... includes some of the agent's beliefs and attitudes... .To learn that the agent conceived his action as a lie, a repayment of a debt, an insult, the fulfilment of an avuncular obligation, or a knight's gambit is to grasp the point of the action in its setting of rules, practices, expectations, and conventions.... And there is no denying that... when we explain an action, by giving the reason, we do redescribe the action.
>
> Donald Davidson, 'Actions, Reasons and Causes', in Davidson (1980), pp. 9–10

2
Freedom, Ability and Knowledge

It seems clear, at the outset, that Aristotle analysed voluntary action in terms of efficient causality *and* knowledge.... . These two elements are central to Aristotle's account: neither causation nor knowledge alone is sufficient to analyse the concept; both causal and teleological considerations may play a role in it without inconsistency. Most recent work [e.g. Anscombe (1957), von Wright (1971), Stoutland (1970, 1976)] has sought to analyse voluntary action in terms either of causation *or* of knowledge and teleology (but not both). Aristotle's theory (if it proves defensible) may avoid those difficulties which undermine contemporary accounts which take one of these features alone as the analysans; for it would yield a (partially) causal account of intentional action and the basis for a (partially) causal analysis of freedom to act.

David Charles, *Aristotle's Theory of Action*, p. 59

In my account of the three negative conditions of voluntary action to which Aristotle is committed in Ch. 1, I remarked that each of these conditions has a corollary which is a part of Aristotle's positive account of voluntary action. In Ch. 2, I begin my exegesis of that positive account by examining the positive corollaries of the negative conditions about (i) compulsion and (ii) ignorance. For treatment of the corollary of condition (iii), about irrationality, v. Ch. 3.

2.1.   FUNCTION, PROCESS AND ABILITY TO DO OTHERWISE

If any human behaviour, to count as voluntary action, must be uncompelled, what does Aristotle think will count as such uncompelled behaviour? We have already glanced at his brief answer to this at EE 1224a16–20. The opposite of compelled behaviour, for any item, is whatever behaviour is natural for that item. Thus an uncompelled stone falls towards the centre of the earth because there is nothing in the situation to prevent it doing this, which is what it is natural for stones to do; and a flame, under normal conditions, rises away from the centre of the earth for the same sort of reason. Now as for flames and stones, so for humans: the way to understand what Aristotle thinks counts as uncompelled human behaviour is to ask: What does he think counts as natural human behaviour – behaviour characteristic of humans as such?

The brief answer to the question is that Aristotle counts as natural human behaviour all voluntary action. And (the point that matters here) he counts as voluntary action any behaviour which – besides satisfying the other conditions – is action done on any appetition (*orexis*). There are, in his view, three sorts of appetitive principle, i.e. three sorts of appetition which (can) act as efficient causes of action: desire, especially physical desire (*epithymia*); 'spirit' (*thymos*); and 'rational wish' (*boulesis*). Other things being equal, any action done with any of these as its 'principle', arising within the agent, will be a voluntary one.

(But here note Aristotle's contrast between what humans do voluntarily and what they do naturally (*physei* or *automatoi*). The existence of this contrast does not contradict my thesis that voluntary action is natural for humans. For when Aristotle says that humans do something 'naturally' in the sense of 'naturally' which he *opposes* to 'voluntarily', the point is always that the humans do that in virtue of something in them which is less than the most fully developed or truly human part of them. For humans at their acme, there is no conflict between the two: their acting voluntarily is just the focal case of their acting naturally.)

To answer the question more fully and informatively, we may consider Aristotle's theory of human nature. This theory leads Aristotle to a detailed answer to our question. It also offers us an understanding of the place of humanity within the cosmos, and underlies much of what Aristotle has to say, both about political or social man (the subject of the ethical discourses: NE 1094b7–10, 1097b8–11), and also about women, children, barbarians, animals, plants, and other genera even further removed in type from the Aristotelian ideal. It is only in the context of that wider view that the specific answer is given. We turn therefore to the wider view.

1a. Function

The starting-point for understanding Aristotle's theory of human nature is the concept of the function (*ergon*) which he took over from Socrates and Plato (*Republic* 352e–353a). Aristotle's doctrine of function is given at NE 1097b22–1098a20. Here Aristotle is seeking a more precise answer than 'Happiness' to the question 'What is the human good?' He suggests that 'such an answer may quickly be found, if we consider the *function* of humanity' (NE 1097b25). The idea is that, if we look at what humanity characteristically and by nature does or is or pursues, then this will give us a clearer view of what is good for humanity:

> It seems that what is 'good' and 'well' for the flute-player, and for the statue-maker, and for every sort of craftsman (indeed, for whatever things have any function and any sort of activity), is implicit in their functions. Likewise, presumably, with humanity – unless humanity has no function. (NE 1097b26–28)

It is an obvious feature of human life that it includes many different particular kinds of skills (*tekhnai*) in which a person might display excellence (*arete*). Now we can provide a simple and non-circular analysis of the meaning of 'excellence' for each of these particular skills. For excellence at (e.g.) harp-playing is indeed, in Aristotle's phrase, 'implicit in the function'. The knowledge of what counts as excellence in harp-playing is directly deducible from the knowledge of what counts as *harp-playing*: 'We say that the function of an X and a good X is the same in kind' (NE 1098a8–9). So to define what performing a function is, just is to define what performing that function *well* is. Aristotle wants to suggest that human living itself is, in some way, a functional activity (*energeia*) of this sort. Defining what this activity is will enable us to deduce what doing this activity well is. And this will be the human good.

Aristotle's claim that humans, *qua* humans, must have a function connects clearly enough with a much more general claim of Aristotle's, that the whole of nature displays purpose: 'In the functions of nature (*physis*) what happens is not random but *for the sake of* something' (dPA 645a24–5; cp. dGA 744a16). Aristotle also believes that the whole of nature displays economy of design. At Pol 1252b1–5, he gives us the 'Delphic knife' principle, that every distinct species made by nature has a single function:

Nature makes nothing in a niggardly way, as the Delphic knife is made by metallists [to serve several purposes at once]; but one thing for one purpose, because in this way each of the organs of nature is best perfected, serving not many ends but a single one. (Pol 1252b1–5)

Having concluded that humans *qua* humans have a function, Aristotle turns to the question of what that function is. In line with his general theory of classification by genus and species, Aristotle tells us (NE 1097b35) that what is sought when one looks for something's function is what is characteristic of that thing or unique to it (*to idion*). Thus the human function cannot be given by the mere fact that humans are alive, nor can it be 'the life of nourishing and the life of growth' (1098a1). For these we have in common even with plants. Nor, for similar reasons, can the human function be 'some kind of life of sensation' (NE 1098a2–3); for this also is shared, 'with horses and cows and every kind of animal'. Hence it follows, or at least Aristotle thinks it follows, that 'what is left is some practical activity of the part that has reason' (NE 1098a4; cp. dA 413a21–b11). What humans have which they share with no other creature is the ability to partake in a life of rational action.

Note then that, in the NE and the *Politics* at least, the way to find the function of *x* is to look for the one thing which that *x* characteristically does or is that differentiates *x* from everything else. But clearly there are problems with this.

For one thing, there is a logical problem. In the NE, Aristotle apparently works on the assumption that, if *x*, *y* and *z* all do *F*, then doing *F* cannot be the function of any of them. A notorious problem follows, from this account and an examination of NE X.8, about what the function of the gods could be. For apparently contemplation, *theoria*, is the divine function. But humans are capable of contemplation as well as of 'the practical activity of the part that has reason', and sometimes it seems that contemplation is what is meant to be the human function. But if that is right then nothing is left over to be the distinctive function of the gods.

But the problem is wider than that. The same problem could be raised about any creature at all, other than (presumably) the human being. If 'function' means 'what *x* characteristically and uniquely does or is', then for Aristotle plants have no function, because he holds that everything they do or are (viz., whatever is entailed by 'the life of nourishing and the life of growth') is also done by or involved in the nature of other, more sophisticated creatures. But the same will be true of, say, horses. For while they are different from plants in as much as they not only have 'the life of nourishing and the life of growth', but also 'some sort of life of sensation', they do not (according to Aristotle) have anything like 'a [life] of action of the part that has reason'. On this understanding of function, it turns out that in fact only humans have a function; it is not just the gods who are excluded. (At any rate if we start with humans, and 'differentiate away' from them; perhaps if we started from, say, manatees, and 'differentiated away' from them, it would turn out that on this account only manatees had a function.) Either result hardly accords with Aristotle's doctrine of the purposefulness of all nature, mentioned above.

How are we to tidy this up? One way of producing a solution of a kind, which will not square with every piece of evidence but will make sense of a fair number of them, is to attend more closely to the role played in Aristotle's thinking by the concept of a hierarchy of nature.

1b.   The Hierarchy of Nature

Aristotle never explicitly argues for this concept, except perhaps at dA 413a21–b11; he seems to feel entitled to take it for granted. But it is clear enough that the idea of a hierarchy of nature is at work in such a passage as NE 1145a15–33. Here Aristotle suggests that 'there are three forms in respect of character which are to be avoided, wickedness, akrasia and beastliness' (a17). What is 'beastliness', and what is its opposite? Aristotle replies that its opposite 'might be most suitably called *virtue above our natures* – a heroic and divine sort of thing' (a19–20). Beastliness, for him, is 'below' humanity, and godlikeness is 'above' it; he even quotes the common opinion that 'humans become gods through over-abundance of excellence' (NE 1145a23). The opposite is also true: one can become bestial through over-abundance of badness (a23–25). Further, barbarians (and, Pol 1252b8–9 tells us, slaves too) are more likely to be bestial than Greeks (a31–32). Finally, maimed or diseased or brain-damaged persons are less than fully human, and sometimes so much so as to be bestial (a32–33). (By this Aristotle need only mean that to be so crippled is to be unable to perform the human function properly, or at all; not necessarily that to be in such a state is to be a fit object of contempt.)

All this is clear evidence that Aristotle believed in a hierarchy of nature, wherein some kinds are 'higher' (and therefore superior) and others 'lower' (and therefore inferior). We can add to this evidence that of various other passages, to fill out the picture of an Aristotelian doctrine of a hierarchy of nature.

(i) Aristotle's god or gods is/ are, of course, far superior to everything else in Aristotle's universe: NE 1141b1–2, 1154b22–32.

(ii) Internal to the individual human person, there are, for Aristotle just as much as for Plato, inferior and superior parts:

The soul rules over the body with an absolute governance… it is natural and fitting for the body to be ruled by the soul. (Pol 1254b5–7, 8; cp. Plato, *Republic* 443d–e; NE 1102a26–1103a1, 1113a5–9; VV 1249a31 ff.)

(iii) Likewise there are inferior and superior parts within the human race:
  (a) God-like, ordinary and bestial humans ranked as above.
  (b) Men/ husbands superior to women/ wives: Pol 1254b13–15.
  (c) Masters superior to slaves: Pol 1254b13–15.
  (d) Greeks superior to barbarians: Pol 1252b8, quoting Euripides' *Iphigeneia in Aulis* 1400; Pol 1255a28–32.
  (e1) Fathers superior to children: Pol 1259b2–5, NE 1134b8–12.
  (e2) Children, like animals, not full moral agents: NE 1111b8–10; cp. NE 1153a27–31.

(iv) Again, there are inferior and superior parts in nature generally:
  (a) Tame animals superior to wild ones: Pol 1254b10–13 (because, perhaps, they are closer to being ruled by reason; cp. NE 1102b29 ff).
  (b) Animals, like children, not (full?) moral agents: NE 1111b8–10.

For the next rungs on the ladder, we may refer to NE 1097b34–1098a4, or to dA 413a21–b11. It seems that the 'hierarchy of nature' is ordered as follows:

  (c) Animals capable of all of these: thought (*nous*), sensation (*aisthesis*), change in the sense of alteration of place (*kinesis kai stasis he kata topon*), and change in the sense of nourishment and growth (*kinesis kata trophen*) (dA 413a23–25); e.g. (?) humans;

(d)   animals capable of all of these except one: e.g. horses (NE 1098a3) are incapable of exercising *nous*;

(e)   animals capable of all of these except two: e.g. an ant is, apparently, incapable of exercising *nous* or experiencing *aisthesis*;

(f)   animals capable of all except three: e.g. a barnacle is incapable of exercising *nous*, *aisthesis* or *stasis kata topon*;

(g)   animals (or rather, by now, living things) capable of all of these except four: e.g. a plant has only the 'life of nourishment and growth' (NE 1098a2; cp. dA 413a26–b10);

(h)   the inanimate (superiority of the study of the soul: dA 402a1 ff.).

1c.   Hierarchy and Function

How does this doctrine of the 'hierarchy of nature' help us clarify the doctrine of function? The answer is that it suggests that we should redefine 'function of *x*'. Any *x*'s function is not simply 'what *x* characteristically and uniquely does or is'. It is, more exactly, 'what the species *x* characteristically and uniquely does or is *that differentiates* x *from species below* x *in the hierarchy of nature*'.

This redefinition of the concept of function, which (like the concept of function found in the biological writings) presupposes the concept of a species, enables us to overcome the logical difficulty noticed above. On this definition, it will not be true that nothing except humanity has a function. If – as seems possible – the creatures found in nature can be more or less precisely ranked for their complexity, then each creature in the 'hierarchy of nature' will have a function which defines its place in that hierarchy. X, which does A and B but not C, will fit into the hierarchy between Y, which does A but not B or C, and Z, which does A, B and C. Here we cannot say that Z does not have A as a function, simply because Z does A, but X does A too. Nor will it be true of X that it does not have B as a function, simply because X does A and B, but X does A and B too. The characteristic we are looking for when we look for a creature's function, on this account, is not simply what differentiates that creature from any other creature; it is what differentiates that creature from all lower creatures.

There are obvious problems here. (i) There may indeed be some activities A, B and C for which it is true that, say, humans perform A, B and C, but elephants only A and B (perhaps: running, eating, making hydrogen bombs). But so what? First, we could just as easily cite some activities P, Q and R for which it is true that elephants perform P, Q and R, but humans only P and Q (perhaps: running, eating, uprooting trees with the trunk). And second, as the hydrogen-bomb example suggests, the differentiating activity of the species which is capable of one more activity than any below it might be an *abhorrent* activity, one which (it might be said) ought to *demote* that species in the hierarchy of nature, not promote it.

More specifically (ii), this redefinition still contradicts the 'Delphic knife' principle (Pol 1252b1–5). For apparently there is still one class of things without any function at the bottom of the hierarchy, viz., whatever is left behind when all the things with functions have been distinguished from it and put above it in the hierarchy. Lastly (iii), does this procedure really tell us that the function of humanity is what Aristotle says it is?

I will pass over (i). On (ii), there is little problem about there being no function for whatever is left at the bottom of the hierarchy. For this need not be a species, or even a natural kind, of any sort; therefore it need not have a function. What is left behind by the definition and specification of all species and their corresponding functions is simply the *un*defined, or the 'unlimited'; which of course does not have a function any more than 'matter as such' has any form.

Aristotle's problem in answering (iii) is not only that it is unclear that what he wants to call the human function has been arrived at strictly by the method for differentiating between species' functions which he claims to be using. More worryingly, he does not even have a single answer to the question:

(a) 'What remains is some practical activity of the part that has reason...' (NE 1098a3–4).
(b) 'Man is a social animal by nature' (NE 1097b11, Pol 1253a3).
(c) 'Contemplation would then be the human's complete happiness' (NE 1177b24–25).
(d) 'The human function ... is the activity of the soul *and* practical actions rationally done...' (NE 1098a14).

It is commonly said that Aristotle has two accounts of the good for humans, one intellectual (or exclusively intellectual) and the other practical (or inclusive of practical and intellectual elements). On the face of it, the above four quotations present not two but four different verdicts on the nature of the good life. (a) is clearly the practical good, (c) the intellectual good; however, in addition to these, (b) suggests a political good – not necessarily the same as a practical good, as Aristotle himself admits even while trying to run them together (NE 1141b23) – and (d) suggests a composite, intellectual-cum-practical good, which cannot properly be identified with either of its components as represented in (a) and (c).

Can we make sense of this jumble? Many commentators think not (e.g. Clark (1978) arranges the evidence in the same sort of way as I have, but jibs at the conclusions I will now draw from that arrangement). Suppose first that some kind of connection can indeed, as Aristotle suggests at NE 1141b23, be made between (b) and (a) – of what kind, I will not discuss here. Suppose, second, that we make sense of the relations between (a), (c) and (d) by introducing a concept which stands alongside that of the function: the concept of the meta-function.

What I mean by my meta-function/function contrast is that any creature in the Aristotelian hierarchy of nature has, not one, but two final goods (*tele*). Aristotle does not just talk of excellence *within* an expertise, function, or species. He also talks of the excellence *of* an expertise, function or species. That is the whole point of the hierarchy of nature: it allows us to say both that some creatures, and their activities, rank higher than others, and that some creatures (at least at the human level) achieve the final good (*telos*) of their own rank more nearly than others.

Correspondingly, the function of any creature or practitioner of an expertise is to achieve excellence within its own rank in the hierarchy of nature. The meta-function of that creature or practitioner is to rise to a higher rank in the hierarchy of nature.

There is good evidence for something like this view in Aristotle:

(i)   There is the point noted above, that 'humans become gods through over-abundance of excellence' (NE 1145a23).

(ii) This interpretation makes sense of the puzzling words of NE 1098a16–18: 'The human good appears to be an activity of the soul according to its excellence; but if it has several sorts of excellence, according to the best and most final (*teleiotate*) sort'.

(iii) There is NE 1141a21–22: 'It would be incongruous if someone thought that political excellence or practical wisdom were the best excellence, unless man is the best thing in the universe'.

(iv) Most conclusively, there is NE 1177b27 ff.:

But this kind of life [the life of contemplation] is too much for human capacity. For a man who lives it will not live it in virtue of his humanity, but in virtue of something divine in him. The activity of this part will differ from the activity of the composite human (*tou synthetou*) by as much as this part differs from that composite... insofar as one can, one should join the immortals (*athanatizein*). (NE 1177b27–35)

Granted the coherence of the very idea of a hierarchy of nature, we may then say that each species in it, at least in the higher reaches of the hierarchy, has both a function and a meta-function. What excellence is for each species is given (NE 1098a8–9 again) by the definition of that species' function; for each species there is an objective (*telos*) of excellence in realising the function of that species. But there is also a meta-function (and a meta-objective) for each species, which is *to ascend the hierarchy of nature*: to rise beyond the performing of its own function to the performing of the function of the next species up.

The application of this line of thought to the case of human, divine and animal functions is clear. The human function, on this view, is not the contemplative life, but a practical life of the best possible kind (NE 1095a16). The divine function is simply the contemplative life (v. NE 1154b26 and Mph 1072b14 ff.). The gods are (it appears) the next and possibly only species, or kind, above humanity in the hierarchy of nature. So the contemplative life, while it is not the human function, is the human meta-function.

Likewise, we might suggest, the point of Aristotle's remark that tame animals are superior to wild ones (Pol 1254b10–13) is exactly that tame animals, by their participation in human life, come closer than wild ones to transcending their own function. Aristotle's view is, of course, that animals never actually achieve this transcendence. But there is a case where something very like this kind of transcendence does, in Aristotle's view, occur: namely, in a child's development into adulthood (NE 1103b14–25).

My contrast between function and meta-function has one further upshot, which brings us back to a more direct attention to the subject of voluntary action. On this view, Aristotle's theory entails that the human species (at least) is capable of making choices about how and whether to fulfil its function, or its meta-function, or both. (I suspect that choosing to fulfil *neither* is not an option.) Therefore Aristotle is already assuming that humanity is a kind of creature which exhibits voluntary choice. We can now add that, for Aristotle, the realising of the human function itself is typically found in voluntary action. For one of Aristotle's several ways of characterising the human function is in terms of the characteristic human process or movement (*kinesis*). Aristotle says this is uncompelled, contingent, voluntary movement which is up to the agent. Examining this claim will enable us to apply what has been established about the human function to answering the question with which I began this chapter, the question of how to characterise the kind of movement or process of which humans are typically the moving principle (*arkhe*).

1d.   Process, Principle, Contingency and Ability to Do Otherwise

At NE 1110a15–18, while arguing that what is done under duress is done voluntarily (cp. Section 1.2d), Aristotle makes these rather cryptic remarks:

> The agent acts voluntarily. For in such cases the principle (*arkhe*) of the moving of the parts of the body is in the agent himself. And when the principle of action is within the agent, it is up to the agent to act or not to act. (NE 1110a15–18)

Does Aristotle tell us anything new in these words? Certainly the old 'principle inside/ principle outside' contrast is being applied here as a criterion of the voluntary in a way which is familiar from Section 1.2a. What are new are (i) the gloss on this procedure which follows ('when the principle of action is within the agent, it is up to the agent to act or not to act'); and (ii) the more extended formula 'the principle *of the moving of the parts of the body* is in the agent himself', in place of the NE's usual 'the principle is in the agent himself'.

Both these amplifications help clarify Aristotle's meaning. (i) links the enigmatic phrases 'the principle is in me' (*arkhe en autoi*) and 'it is up to me' (*ep' autoi*). It tells us that Aristotle believes that it is a condition of voluntary action that I should be able to do otherwise: that when I do *x*, I must have been able to do not-*x* if my doing *x* is to count as voluntary action. And (ii) focuses our attention on Aristotle's use of two terms which are to be vital in his further elaboration of this claim, namely 'principle' and 'process'.

To take these in turn.

(i) Ability to do otherwise as a condition of voluntary action appears very clearly in both the NE and the EE. Aristotle would not agree with those moderns who contrast cases of actual compulsion with cases where my action is (they say) causally determined, yet not, in any normal sense, compelled. In such a case, it is often said, I am not forced to act as I do – 'it is me acting' – and yet I could not do otherwise. Aristotle's contrast between the allurements of pleasure and the coercion of force (NE 1110b9 ff.) is not meant to be aligned with this modern contrast. Aristotle's contrast makes the exactly opposite point: that pleasures are not, normally, causally determining factors, as successful applications of force are; and that only a scoundrel would attempt to equate the two on each and every occasion. The passages of the EE (discussed in Section 1.2b) in which Aristotle argues that pleasures can sometimes compel, give further evidence that he believed that pleasures do not normally compel.

On Aristotle's view, if *for any reason* I could not have done otherwise than I do, I do not act voluntarily. Conversely, if determinism is true, then all action is compelled. So, at NE 1113b7–10, Aristotle makes ability to do otherwise a condition of moral responsibility because it is a condition of voluntary action:

> Excellence (*arete*) is up to us also, and likewise badness (*kakia*). For in those matters where it is up to us to do something, it is also up to us not to do that thing; wherever we can say No, we can say Yes too. Thus when it is up to us to do what is admirable (*kalon*), it is also up to us to do what is shameful. (NE 1113b7–10)

Compare EE 1225b8: 'What an agent does, without ignorance and by his own power, *which it is up to him not to do*, is necessarily voluntary action.'

(ii) The view that voluntary action is necessarily contingent is spelled out by what Aristotle has to tell us about the meanings of the terms 'principle' and 'process'. Here the exiguous argument of NE 1110a15–18 can be filled out by reference to EE 1222b15–1223a20 (cp. MM 1187a30–b30).

What is humanity the principle of? What kind of causal sequences do human beings, as such, originate or tend to originate? According to EE 1222b17–18, one thing that human beings are principles of is other human beings; for to be a principle of some natural kind *x* involves the ability to produce other principles of that kind. But humans are 'principles' for Aristotle in another sense, which is more important for our uses. This is the sense in which Aristotle takes, as his example of a process of which humans are the principle, *voluntary action*:

> A human is the principle of a certain sort of process; for action (*praxis*) is a process (EE 1222b28–30).

> Indeed man alone, among the animals, is the principle of certain actions (*praxeon tinon*); for we do not say that any of the other animals *acts* (*prattein*) (EE 1222b19–21).

(In spite of this latter remark, Aristotle himself sanctions the use of *praxis / prattein* for animal behaviour at NE 1111a26–27, where he says that what is done through passion (*thumos*) or desire (*epithumia*) should not be called 'involuntary', because the undesirable consequence would be that 'then none of the other animals would act voluntarily'. (This consequence would follow because, presumably, animals always act either on *epithumia* or on *thumos*, and never on reason (*logos* or *nous*): so if only action on reason can be called voluntary, animals' actions cannot be called voluntary.) We have three names for two kinds of action, apparently: 'the voluntary' (*to hekousion*), 'action' (*praxis*), and action on *proairesis*. Aristotle is quite clear that 'the voluntary' does not equal 'action on *proairesis*' (NE 1111b7–8), but less clear about whether 'the voluntary' equals 'action' or 'action on *proairesis*'.)

Here, in any case, two questions arise. First, what does it mean for humanity to be the principle of 'certain sorts of *praxis*' which are examples of processes? Second, even if we cannot properly speak of animal *praxis*, is there anything in their case corresponding to this kind of being a principle?

An obvious answer to the first question, given the last two quotations, is also suggested by NE 1110a15, as above: 'In such cases the principle of the moving of the parts of the body is in the agent himself.' For a human to be the principle of 'certain sorts of *praxis*' is, at least, for him to be (or contain) 'the principle of the moving of the parts of the body'. The human is principle of some particular actions if and only if the movement(s) of, or change(s) in, his body which that action involves, are causally originated by himself, that is to say by his own desires or other natural appetitions.

(For the different types of appetition (*orexis*), and the evidence that Aristotle does not think of any sort of appetition, even the highest (*boulesis*, rational wish: cp. Section 3.1) as one which exercises the highest part of the soul, v. NE 1102b13–1103a10. On the other hand, it is *not* the case, as one way of taking the hierarchy of nature doctrine might suggest, that only the 'highest' appetitive principle in humans, 'rational wish', can give rise to voluntary (or 'truly' voluntary) action. Action is no less voluntary for having as its principle such a force as proud spirit (typical of the *thymos*) or strong emotion (typical of the *epithymia*); as evidence of which, recall that Aristotle thinks there are right ways to be affected by such forces. V., e.g., NE 1119a31 ff.)

This answer in turn suggests an answer to the second question, about animals. There is a correspondent to human *praxis* in animals, even if their behaviour cannot be called *praxis*. To put it non-committally, an animal is, in the proper sense, a principle of some particular process if and only if that process is causally originated by itself – that is to say by its own natural appetitions.

Aristotle, then, sets the animals and their functions, their typical processes and the originating appetitions which cause those processes, below humanity. And, as already seen, he sets the divine and its typical activity above humanity:

> Such principles as these, from which movements arise, are principles in the truest sense. The name is especially fitting for those principles from which the same processes invariably follow. (No doubt God rules over a principle of this sort.) (EE 1222b21–23)

The divine characteristically originates necessary, non-contingent processes; Aristotle has in mind both contemplation and the perfect circular motion of the 'fixed stars' (Mph 1072a7–b31). Animals characteristically originate processes which are unworthy of the name of *praxis*, or at any rate of the name of *proairesis*; elsewhere Aristotle tells us that animals 'move without defined (self-conscious) purpose' (dA 434a4) . What kind of processes will humans characteristically originate when they originate *praxis*, given that (as we have seen) Aristotle takes seriously the thought that humanity is set between animals and gods in the hierarchy of nature?

Aristotle's answer is that *praxis* is a kind of process which, unlike animal movements, is not (in some sense) sub-purposive; and which, unlike the divine process, *does* 'admit of coming to be otherwise' (EE 1223a2). It is a sort of doing what you want to do which is not available to animals; but what you will want to do, if you are human, is not fixed by necessity in the way that divine processes are. Aristotle's argument for this conclusion is entertainingly opaque.

The argument evidently turns on a geometrical analogy. We have what we call principles in geometry, although this name is only given analogously, and is not strictly appropriate to such principles (1222b23–25). If these principles are changed, so, necessarily, is every consequence that follows from them (b25–27, b33–37). This is the point of analogy with genuine principles which justifies the geometrical principles' being called principles too. The points of disanalogy with genuine natural principles are (i) that mathematical principles do not move anything (b23–25), and (ii) that mathematical principles do not 'admit of coming to be otherwise' (1223a1).

What we may learn from the geometrical analogy is that principles of any given kind (more or less contingent and prone to obstruction) necessarily give rise to processes of the same kind (NE 1222b41–1223a3, following Kenny (1979)'s interpretation of *enteuthen* at 1223a2). By contrast with the mathematical principles, it follows that the genuine principles (i) do produce actual processes, and (ii) produce processes which do 'admit of coming to be otherwise'. Now Aristotle expects us to find it obvious that humans are contingent principles. Given that, it follows (i) that humans are genuine principles, and (ii) that humans characteristically produce processes which do 'admit of coming to be otherwise' – namely the voluntary actions which result from the principles of appetition contained in the human. Since Aristotle has also said (EE 1222b29–30) that *praxis* is the process characteristic of humans, it follows, further, that *praxis* is a process which 'admits of coming to be otherwise'.

Human action seen as *praxis* is, then, a process which can be placed in the middle of a range of processes of different degrees of contingency, between the products of chance and the animals' movements on the one hand, and the divine activity on the other. As a process originated by one or other of those contingent principles of appetition found within humans, *praxis* is what naturally comes about when humans are not compelled or otherwise impeded from doing what they want to do and are free to abstain from doing. And this is why we may say that Aristotle sees action resulting from those three principles of appetition as being the positive correlative of the negative condition on voluntary action about compulsion.

2.2 ARISTOTLE'S EPISTEMOLOGY

The negative requirement that a voluntary action should be uncompelled has for Aristotle the positive corollary that it should satisfy the details of the above description. In brief, and barring such exceptions to this rule as internal compulsion (Section 1.2c): to be voluntary in the sense of not being compelled, an action must be done in circumstances where the principle of the action is one of the three kinds of appetition which arise 'within me'. Aristotle believes that when this condition is satisfied, it will also be true that the principle of the action is contingent, i.e. such that I could have done otherwise.

What description(s), in turn, must be satisfied as a corollary of the negative requirement that a voluntary action should not be done in ignorance? The answer is that, to be voluntary in the sense of not being done in ignorance, an action must be performed on relevant knowledge. What, then, is Aristotle's account of knowledge? And what is his account of relevance?

We saw in my discussion of ignorance (Section 1.3a) that Aristotle makes a crucial distinction between ignorance of moral principles (which does not exculpate or affect the voluntariness of the action) and ignorance of particulars (which normally does). One reason why this is so is that, for Aristotle, knowledge of moral principles (e.g. 'stealing is wrong': Section 1.3a) is just as much a matter of appetition as of knowledge. My knowing that stealing is wrong does not merely entail that I have a belief of the form 'I ought not to steal'; it also entails that there is some sense in which it is natural to my character to want (or otherwise be motivated) not to steal. This is why Aristotle can both speak of the possession of moral principles as knowledge, and also insist that ignorance of such principles is not excusable in the way that ignorance of particulars usually is.

Aristotle's account of knowledge of particulars – and the relationship of that knowledge, in humans, to knowledge of scientific universals – can be very fully explored by considering his discussions of the philosophy of perception at AP° 2.19 and in the dA and the *Parva Naturalia*. The upshot of these discussions is a full, interesting and complex theory of knowledge; but I shall not attempt to engage with this vast topic here. Instead, I shall say more about another important (but more manageably sized) question, namely Aristotle's account of knowledge of moral principles.

2a.   Aristotle on Knowing a Moral Principle

From the fact that ignorance of moral principles does not exculpate, we might infer that ignorance of moral principles, unlike ignorance of particulars, does not impede the voluntariness of an action. Recalling the distinction between <not believing that p when p is true> and <believing that not-p when p is true> (Section 1.3), we may say that this is true in the case where I am ignorant of moral principle in the sense that I hold to a false moral principle, but not in the case where I hold to no moral principle. (In the latter case, I might even be responsible for the fact that I cannot act voluntarily in a given situation.) However, even if false beliefs about moral principle are not so much an impediment to voluntary action as to virtue, it is important for a study of voluntary action to consider what any moral or practical principles – true or false – are like, and how they are acquired. (On the words 'moral' and 'practical', v. Cooper (1975), p. 1. But I am not marking any important distinction by my uses of 'moral' and 'practical'.)

One thing that is clear is that the practical (or appetitive) and the cognitive status of knowledge of moral principles are both given the same weight by Aristotle. In taking this position Aristotle is consciously opposing two sets of predecessors. On the one hand, Socrates held that all the virtues were simply items of rational knowledge (*logoi*), and thought that their being understood was sufficient to guarantee their being acted upon. Against him and his ilk, Aristotle repeatedly insists on the practical nature of moral knowledge and moral inquiry (v., e.g., NE 1103b23), and aims to show that the virtues are more fundamentally qualities of character than forms of knowledge (NE 1106b36 ff.). On the other hand, sophists contemporary to Socrates, notably Protagoras, typically held that virtue merely meant having the kind of character which rational argument *might* show to be defensible – but whether rational argument actually did so, was a question of purely theoretical interest. Against such sophists Aristotle contends that the virtues are not merely those qualities of character which correspond to right reason, but those qualities of character which actually belong together and cooperate with right reason (NE 1144b26–30):

> Virtue is not just a disposition corresponding to right reason (*kata ton orthon logon*); it is rather a disposition [working] together with right reason (*meta tou orthou logou*). Socrates thought that the virtues were items of rational knowledge (*logoi*) (for he held that

all virtues were species of knowledge (*epistemas*)). But we say that the virtues are together with rational knowledge (*meta logou*).

This raises important and difficult questions about the precise relation of appetition and cognition in the case of *orthos logos* – knowledge of moral principles. What if my appetition is to steal and my cognition is that I ought not to steal? Aristotle's answer becomes clearer if we compare Aristotelian moral principles with other sorts of Aristotelian first principle.

2b. Desire and Moral Principles

Aristotelian moral principles are in important ways analogous to other kinds of argumentative first principle. But Aristotle's argumentative principles, in general, are not utterly indisputable prime starting-points for all argument. Rather, they are points at which one kind of argumentative method is exchanged for another, namely 'induction' (*epagoge*) for 'deduction' (*syllogismos*):

> Let us not forget that there is a distinction between arguments *from* (*apo*) first principles, and arguments *to* (*epi*) first principles. (NE 1094a31–32)

> Induction concerns the first principle and the universal, but deduction proceeds from the universals. For there are first principles, from which deduction begins, and concerning which there is no deduction – there is rather induction. (NE 1139b28–31)

Thus Aristotelian first principles are themselves results of a prior rational process. There can, paradoxical as it may sound, be argument to first principles (i.e. inductive argument, *epagoge*), as well as argument from those first principles (i.e. deductive argument, *syllogismos* or *logos*). (But note that both *syllogismos* and *logos*, besides meaning 'deduction' as opposed to 'induction', can also mean 'argument' in general: so NE 1094a32, and APr 68b30. This, no doubt, is one root of the mistaken view that Aristotelian induction is not a proper form of argument. It also helps explain the notorious problem about *proairesis* (v. Section 3.1), that sometimes (e.g. 1112b13) it has to do only with means, and at other times seems to be of ends too (e.g. 1139a33). Strictly, *proairesis* is practical reasoning from first principles, but the word is ambiguous in just the same way as *logos* and *syllogismos*, so that sometimes it is more loosely used by Aristotle to suggest practical reasoning *to* first principles: v., e.g., NE 1144a20).

In what, then, does argument to first principles consist? One of Aristotle's answers is that induction in his sense can take the form of induction in something rather like the modern sense of the phrase, i.e. a generalising from some instances of a regularity to the claim that all instances will display this regularity (APr 68b15–29). Another is that induction can take the form of definition, *horismos*: 'Definition is a "thesis" or a "laying something down"', according to APo 72a21. There is also NE 1142a26: 'Intuition (*nous*) is about definition, about which there is no deductive argument (*logos*).'

Now practical reasoning too may consist both of inductive and deductive parts. Argument to moral or practical first principles is of an analogous kind to any other argument to first principles. It starts from what is uncertain to the reasoner and proceeds to what is more certain, just as deduction proceeds in the opposite direction. An example would be when a number of non-cogent considerations – conditional practical imperatives, as we might call them – taken together, yield a more cogent overall view; this overall view then becomes the 'first principle' of deduction – what we may call an unconditional practical imperative. Thus: 'I have a reason to do *x*, and a reason to do *y*; but my reason to do *y* outweighs my reason to do *x*; so I have more reason to do *y*' is inductive reasoning; and a deductive reasoning, about how to achieve *y*, may then follow on from 'I have reason to do *y*', taking this as its first principle of action, or practical imperative. (Cp. Section 4.1, on the distinction between conditional and unconditional practical imperatives.)

Hence the answer to the earlier question, about cognitive/appetitive clashes, is given: one important form which argument to moral first principles will frequently take is precisely that form of argument where various candidate principles of action are in play against each other, some of which have to do with appetition and others with a belief about what is right. In a rightly-habituated Aristotelian agent, desires and moral principles do not (any longer) clash at all: in fact, in the scope of the actions which follow from them, they become *identical*. But it is obvious already that this need not be so in an agent who is not (or not entirely) rightly habituated. (Cp. my discussion of 'syllogism conflict' akrasia in Section 4.2.)

So far, then, I have shown that knowledge of moral principles is for Aristotle both a cognitive and a practical matter, and that it involves the right ordering both of beliefs and also of dispositions – and hence of appetitions too. Three questions arise here. First, what of the view of those who think that Aristotle does not believe in the existence of moral principles, as opposed to particular moral truths, at all? Second, what entitles us to speak of knowledge rather than merely belief, or perhaps just commendation, in moral matters – what grounds the objectivity of judgements about moral principles? And third, how are moral principles applied?

The answer to the first question is, I think, just that it is mistaken to claim that Aristotle does not believe in the existence of moral principles. Contrary to a recent consensus, one source of which is McDowell (1978), Aristotle surely does believe that there are moral principles in the strong sense of indefeasible material moral rules. ('Material' rules or absolutes in the sense that such rules prescribe that we not do certain sorts of action which can be *non-evaluatively* picked out, e.g. 'Do not lie'. The opposite of a material absolute is a formal absolute, i.e one that gives a particular shape to a moral theory without picking out anything in a non-evaluative way: e.g. 'Never act so as not to maximise consequences' or 'Act only in a universalisable manner'. For the distinction cp. Finnis (1991).) For examples of such rules v. NE 1107a9–26 (against *schadenfreude*, shamelessness, envy, adultery, theft, murder) and NE 1110a28 (matricide): 'But there are, perhaps, some things that one *cannot* be forced to do, but rather one should die, even if this means suffering most terribly' (1110a27). It is true, as I have already acknowledged, that there is more to knowing a moral principle of such a sort than merely being able to state it: 'such a principle must become part of one's nature' (*dei gar symphuenai*, NE 1147a23). But that does not show that such rules *cannot* be stated.

Aristotle's answer to the second question, about the objectivity of knowledge of moral principles, is given by his notion of the ideal moral agent. This is the *phronimos* or practically wise man, the man of virtue, who is himself the standard of what is right in ethics:

In all such matters it seems that what *is* the case, is what *appears* to be the case to the good man… the measure of each thing is virtue, and the man of virtue considered as such. The [real] pleasures then will be those that he finds pleasant; what is [truly] enjoyable will be what he enjoys. (NE 1176b17–19; cp. NE 1113a32–34)

> Concerning all these things [sc. the fine, the advantageous, the pleasant] the good man is the one who is likely to get it right (*katorthotikos*) and the bad man is the one who is likely to go wrong (*hamartetikos*). (NE 1104b32)

> Perfection and what is best is evident to the good man if it is evident to anyone. (NE 1144a32)

Aristotle's answer to the question 'Which moral principles are objectively true and right?' is: 'Those the man of virtue believes to be objectively true and right'. Here it will be pointed out that this answer just prompts the further question 'Who is the man of virtue?'. This is true, but it need not lead to a collapse into triviality; for the answer to this further question need not be merely 'Whoever agrees with me about which moral principles are true and right'. In fact Aristotle would welcome this further question. For it in turn directs our attention to a third question, which he thinks absolutely crucial and fundamental to ethics, namely 'What kind of people do we admire, or want to be like?' Some intimations of how he thinks this question should be answered may be gathered from the (quite definitely substantive and non-trivial) portraits of the man of virtue which he himself offers us in such passages as NE 2.6 ff. We may disagree with the details of this portrait, perhaps with the whole picture; but, once we recognise its existence, we can hardly go along with the standard general accusation that Aristotle is unhelpfully vague and formalistic in his ethics. On the contrary, he often seems much too specific for his judgements to be to our tastes. Consider, for example, NE 1125a12–16: 'It seems to befit the great-spirited person to move slowly, and to talk in a deep voice, with a deliberate diction...'.

What of Aristotle's answer to the question 'Which applications of right moral principles are right?'? *How* does one know how to apply moral principles in particular cases?

There are two points to Aristotle's reply to this question, the first of which leads us on to the second, and the second of which brings us, in a sense, full circle. The first point is that some actions are such clear cases of the application of a given principle that, if we fail to recognise them as such, we thereby demonstrate our own badness. For example, plain and straightforward cases of murder or adultery or envy surely ought, on Aristotle's view, to be *by definition* actions which quite unproblematically deserve condemnation and avoidance; and given the existence of such cases we can extend the judgements we make in them to other similar cases.

But – the second point – I say 'by definition' because, of course, it is only because such cases are straightforward that to condemn the relevant actions is unproblematic. What is difficult is to deal with the cases which are not so straightforward. To put it another way, what is difficult is to decide which cases are to be assimilated to which. (Compare a modern example: is abortion *more like* standard cases of murder? or standard cases of contraception?) Now what methodology does Aristotle's account of practical wisdom offer us for the difficult cases? How in such cases are we to know which way to take the particulars with which we are presented?

The answer to this is that Aristotle does not offer us any methodology, because he believes there is none (v. NE 1142a24 ff.: 'here too there will be an end to reasoning'). I have argued that there can, in his view, be moral rules. But those moral rules cannot contain within themselves a set of instructions about how they are to be taken in every circumstance. For even if they did, a similar problem would arise for those instructions: do they contain within themselves instructions about how they are to be taken? All that we can have, in hard cases, is a *sense* for which cases resemble which; Aristotle's name for this sense is 'the [moral] eye' (NE 1143b14; 1144a30).

Aristotle's recognition that justifications run out does not mean that he is lost in featureless subjectivism. For there is a standard for judging different applications of our moral sense. And this standard (to complete the circle) is *the man of virtue*. Just as Aristotle's answer to the question 'Which moral principles are objectively true and right?' was 'Those the man of virtue believes to be objectively true and right', so also his answer to the question 'Which applications of moral principles are objectively right?' is 'Those the man of virtue believes to be objectively right'. Once again, this answer may prove less unhelpful than it initially seems: for Aristotle's picture of what the man of virtue is like includes some detail about how the man of virtue, on his understanding, behaves in particular situations. As before, we are free to disagree with Aristotle's understanding of how, say, Alcmaeon (1110a28) or the great-souled man (1124b18) should act in their particular circumstances; but we are not free to complain that he not only offers us no 'science of behaviour' but also says nothing about how particular people should behave in particular situations.

But here we are beginning to move on from discussing knowledge, whether of particulars or (as for the most part here) of principles, to discussing the rightness or wrongness of applications of moral or practical principles in particular situations. And the question of how *rightly* to apply principles is only approachable once we have an answer to the simpler question: 'What is it to apply a practical principle in a particular situation at all?' For an answer to that question, we need to consider Aristotle's third positive condition of voluntary action, the condition of rationality. This is the topic of Chapter 3.

3

Practical Reasoning

But the question, which things should be chosen in preference to which others, is not easy to give an answer to; for there are many differences in particular circumstances.

Aristotle, NE 1110b7

In Chapter 2 I discussed some aspects of the positive accounts of unhindered appetition and of knowledge which Aristotle offers us as corollaries to his negative requirements of voluntary action, that it should be behaviour which is neither compelled nor done in ignorance. In Chapter 1 I argued that there is a third negative requirement of voluntary action to which any half-decent theory of the voluntary is committed, about 'irrationality'. Since Aristotle's theory of the voluntary is a good deal more than half-decent, he too is committed to this third negative requirement – whether or not he recognises his commitment. It should follow that he is also committed to the positive corollary of this requirement. So it is clearly time to examine Aristotle's positive account of the rationality of action.

It may be clear why I have left this third positive account till last. The rationality of an action consists in the combining in that action of an unhindered appetition with relevant knowledge. So plainly we cannot discuss Aristotle's account of the rationality of action without first considering his accounts of appetition and hindrance, and of knowledge and relevance – which is what, albeit in outline and incompletely, I have done in Chapter 2.

Aristotle's positive account of rationality is an account of *how* relevant knowledge and unhindered appetition combine to be the reason for, and hence the cause of, a voluntary action. Examining what he has to say about this leads me to consider, first *proairesis* (as I shall call it, without prejudicial translation of the word: 3.1–3.2), then 'deliberation' (*bouleusis*) (3.3), and third, Aristotle's doctrine of the 'practical syllogism' (3.4).

55

3.1.   *PROAIRESIS*

What is *proairesis*? Aristotle discusses it in detail in two passages of
the NE, III.2 and 1139a21–b13. I will concentrate here on III.2, as this
actually purports to give us a definition of *proairesis*. Aristotle works
his way towards this definition inductively (in his sense), by giving
us a list of things which *proairesis* is not. Broadly speaking he aims to
establish, on the one hand, that *proairesis* is not (simply) an appetition; and, on the other, that it is not (simply) an opinion or belief,
either (NE 1111b11–13). Aristotle holds that a correct understanding
of *proairesis* entails seeing it as being in crucial ways both different
from and similar to both appetition and belief. (*Pace* Charles 1984,
p. 58, that is surely the upshot of the VI.2 discussion, which concludes: 'We may then say that *proairesis* is appetitive intelligence – or
intelligent appetition' (NE 1139b5).)

For Aristotle as for the Plato of the *Republic*, there are (as we have
seen already: Section 2.1) three kinds of *orexis* or appetition, corresponding to the three parts of the soul: (physical) desire, *epithymia*,
'spirit', *thymos*, and (cognitive) wish, *boulesis*. No one of these sorts
of appetition is identifiable with *proairesis*, though the third might
have seemed the most plausible candidate to Aristotle's contempo-
raries.

'Desire' is disqualified from being identifiable with *proairesis* for
these reasons:

(a) '*Proairesis* is not shared with irrational creatures, but desire (and
     spirit) are' (NE 1111b13).
(b) 'The victim of akrasia acts on desire, but not on *proairesis*;
     whereas the self-disciplined person acts on *proairesis*, but not on
     desire' (NE 1111b14–15).
(c) 'Desire can contradict *proairesis*, but desire cannot contradict
     desire' (b16).
(d) 'Desire is concerned with the pleasant and the painful, *proairesis*
     with neither' (b17).

'Spirit' is disqualified too (b19), although Aristotle gives us little
explicit argument for this claim apart from (a) above. Possibly
(a)–(d) are all meant to apply to spirit too, *mutatis mutandis*.

Aristotle gives two reasons why '[rational] wish' (*boulesis*) cannot
be equated with *proairesis*, 'though the two seem very close in
nature' (1111b20–34):

(e) There can be wish for things which are either impossible *tout court*, or impossible for me; there cannot be *proairesis* of either (b21–26; cp. 1139b7–13).

(f) Wish is of the end, *proairesis* of the means (b27–29).

Given the success of these six arguments, which I will not here dispute, and given Aristotle's classification of appetitions into three sorts (ditto), it follows that *proairesis* is no kind of appetition. The mere presence of an appetition, of whatever kind, is no guarantee of the presence of a *proairesis*.

Aristotle then argues that *proairesis* is not simply a sort of cognitive state or belief (*doxa*) either. He begins this discussion by saying that 'Belief can evidently be about anything', which is not true of *proairesis* (1111b31). It seems that *doxa* here means 'belief' in its widest sense: not that sense in which 'belief' is opposed to knowledge, as at NE 1139b17 and 1145b32 ff., but a sense which includes both knowledge and (mere) belief. (This is also suggested by 1140b27.) That wide sense certainly seems to be the one employed at 1112a11, where Aristotle allows that belief may precede and accompany proairesis – having just remarked (a7) that proairesis involves certain knowledge, not hazy belief. (For more on 1112a7–8, see below.)

The suggestion, then, is that the mere presence of a belief, of whatever kind, is no guarantee of the presence of a *proairesis* either. Why not?

(g) (cf. (e)) Belief can concern any matter at all, not just those things that are up to us (NE 1111b33; cp. 1139a36 ff.).

(h) Belief is qualified as either true or false; *proairesis* as right or wrong (NE 1111b34–35; cp. 1139a21–22).

(g) and (h) are offered to show that the genera *proairesis* and belief are not identical. Aristotle then goes on to argue that *proairesis* is no species of belief, either:

But *proairesis* is not [the same as] some particular belief, either. For our beliefs about good or evil do not determine the sort of people we are; but our *proairesis* of good or evil does (NE 1112a1–3).

(Notice that this is one of the passages where Aristotle uses 'proairesis' in the broad sense in which it can mean choice of an end as well of means to an end. Notice also what the passage implies about akrasia. For the most obvious example of those who believe something to be good, even though they do not choose (*proairousi*) it, is provided by those who suffer from akrasia; and Aristotle has just said (NE 1111b14) that the akratic 'acts from desire, but *not* from *proairesis*'. We are presumably to infer that the akratic, or at any rate this sort of akratic, does not choose (in the sense of choice which involves *proairesis*) what he believes to be good, and indeed does not (in that sense) choose anything else either. Since it is 'our *proairesis* of good or evil' that determines what sort of people we are, this in turn must imply that we can make no judgement about what sort of person the akratic is; except of course that he is an akratic.)

NE 1112a1–3 introduces six more specific arguments (i–n) for the claim that *proairesis* is not identical to some species of belief:

(i) *Proairesis* makes our characters good or bad – not belief (a1–3, as above; cp. 1139a33–34).

(j) (cf. (g)) *Proairesis* is practical, belief theoretical (a3–5).

(k) (cf. (h)) Belief is qualified as either true or false, *proairesis* as either right or wrong (a6–7).

(l) What we believe (*doxazomen*) to be right, we do not know for sure (*ou panu ismen*) to be right. But action on *proairesis* is action on knowledge of what is right, not on (mere) belief (a7–8).

(m) I can have good 'abstract' moral beliefs without being a good person (a9–10; cp. (i) and 1147a22).

(n) That [moral] belief is a necessary condition of *proairesis* does not show that it is *proairesis* (a11–13; cp. 1139a33).

(a–n) are, as I say, presented by Aristotle as negative arguments. But plainly they also give us a good idea of the cards in Aristotle's own hand. Given a clarification of (f) and the exclusion of (l), the combination of these arguments with Aristotle's positive remarks gives us a fair account of his doctrine of *proairesis*.

(l) should be excluded from consideration if, as I have argued, the whole point of NE III.2 is to show that *proairesis* involves the combination of unhindered appetition and relevant knowledge. If that is right, then in this context *doxa* ought to mean 'belief' in its widest sense, not that sense in which 'belief' is opposed to knowledge. Of course it is true that non-defective action on *proairesis* is action on knowledge, not on (mere) belief. Action on belief which is not also knowledge is action in ignorance, and hence not voluntary action, and hence (*a fortiori*) not action on *proairesis* either. But this is a point against belief-as-opposed-to-knowledge, not against belief in the wide sense which includes knowledge. To repeat, if Aristotle's aim is to show that *proairesis* must mean the combination of unhindered appetition and relevant knowledge, because either alone is insufficient for *proairesis*, then attacking the idea that *proairesis* could be equivalent to belief in the narrow sense, as (l) does, is somewhat beside the point.

The clarification of (f) is this. NE 1111b27 does say that *proairesis*, which we have seen described elsewhere as 'rational appetition', is 'of the means to the objective', not of the objective. But it is as well to note at once that this need not mean that the setting-up of an objective (*telos*) is an altogether non-rational process. Aristotle's pronouncement that there is no argument (*logos*) about definitions (NE 1142a26) does not mean that the setting-up of a definition (*horos*) is an altogether non-rational process. It means rather that, if the setting-up of a definition is a rational process (as, we are told elsewhere, it is – see next paragraph), that rational process is not, strictly, *logos* (which here means deductive reasoning). Likewise, Aristotle's pronouncement here that there is no *proairesis* of objectives does not mean that the setting-up of an objective is an altogether non-rational process. It means rather that, if the setting-up of an objective is a rational process (as, we are told elsewhere, it is), that rational process is not, strictly, proairesis.

As we saw in Ch. 2, there are both broad and narrow senses of both *logos/syllogismos* ('reasoning') and of *proairesis*. This leads to parallel ambiguities concerning practical and theoretical reasoning. Aristotle sometimes calls induction a kind of reasoning (*syllogismos*, APr 68b30) (the broad sense), and sometimes opposes induction to reasoning (*syllogismos* in the narrow sense: APr 68b13). Notoriously, he also describes *proairesis* as being (i) of means only and not of ends (1111b27), (ii) of ends (1110b32, 1144a20–23), and (iii) of both means and ends (1145a4–6). This is because, like 'reasoning', '*proairesis*' has a narrow sense, in which it cannot include the rational processes involved in the setting-up of an objective; but also a broad sense, in which it can.

Given these qualifications about (l) and (f), we may proceed to outline what positive information Aristotle gives us about *proairesis* by way of his negative points about it. (a) *Proairesis* is something distinctive to mature humans, unlike voluntary action (1111b8–9). (b) It is limited not simply to mature humans, but more specifically to self-disciplined, mature humans, such as those who generally act not suddenly (NE 1110b10) but 'from a settled disposition of character' (NE 1104a35). (c and d) *Proairesis* is concerned with non-abstract (m), character-forming (i) beliefs (*inter alia*, n) about what is right (k) in practical affairs (h, j). It can overrule any desire in a way that no desire can (c). The scope of someone's *proairesis* is 'those things that he thinks to be up to him to bring about' (NE 1111b26). Thus there is no *proairesis* about (e) impossibilities, (g) matters which are not 'up to us', or (j) 'theoretical questions', i.e. those covered by science.

These remarks establish that *proairesis* is not simply either a belief nor an appetition. Since this is argued to pave the way for the conclusion that *proairesis* involves the *combination* of belief and appetition, it is followed, in the NE, by this definition of *proairesis* (NE 1112a13–17):

What then is the essence (*ti*) and quality (*poion ti*) of *proairesis*, since it is none of the aforementioned [sc. desire, spirit, or wish]? It seems to be voluntary in nature – but not everything voluntary is done on *proairesis*. Then may we say that action on *proairesis* is [voluntary action] that has been deliberated about in advance (*to probebouleumenon*)? Indeed, for *proairesis* is accompanied by reasoning and understanding (*meta logou kai dianoias*). Indeed the very name '*proairesis*' seems to imply that what is chosen by *proairesis* is chosen (*haireton*) before (*pro*) other things.

I have tentatively translated *to probebouleumenon* as 'voluntary action that has been deliberated about in advance'; I might also have put 'voluntary action that has been settled on in preference to other possibilities'. For there is a question here whether the Greek *pro* means 'before in time', or 'before in preference' as it does at EE 1225b8 (cp. MM 1189a13). Joachim (1955) (pp. 100–101), Gauthier-Jolif (1970) (p. 198), and, it appears, Kenny (1979) would argue that *pro* here is temporal; certainly there is further evidence for the temporal view at least of the NE passage at e.g. NE 1113a2–12 (a passage cited by Joachim (1955), p. 100). A Rylean or Wittgensteinian commentator might want to argue, as might Ross (1925) and Burnet (1900), that, on the contrary, *pro* is not temporal but (as we might say) preferential. Hardie (1968, p. 164) takes something from both sides: he thinks that *pro* in *probebouleumenon* is temporal, but *pro* in *pro heteron* is preferential; for this view he has the support of EE 1226b8. Again, it may be that Aristotle is deliberately playing on the fact that *pro* in *proairesis* and related phrases can be either temporal or preferential. On the whole it is perhaps best to suggest that *proairesis* should be understood, at least in the passage we are considering, as referring primarily to a choice made *before* action or any mediate part thereof, and accompanied by reasoning which is simultaneous with the choosing (*meta logou kai dianoias*: NB that *meta* + genitive cannot mean 'after').

This brings us to ask: Accompanied by what kind of reasoning does *proairesis* occur? The answer to that will begin to be made clear in my discussion of deliberation (*bouleusis*) in Section 3.3. The same conclusion also puts us in a position to offer an answer to the question to which I now turn: what is the difference between 'action on *proairesis*' and (mere) 'voluntary action'?

3.2. THE DIFFERENCE BETWEEN ACTION ON *PROAIRESIS* AND VOLUNTARY ACTION

I said in Ch.1 that voluntary action must, for Aristotle, mean action which is (i) uncompelled, (ii) not done in ignorance, and (iii) rational. But this may seem to make pressing for my account the question of how (merely) voluntary action is different from action on *proairesis*. For one fairly standard view of Aristotle has it, roughly speaking, that it is precisely in their being rational that actions upon *proairesis* differ from merely voluntary actions. A (merely) voluntary action, on this view, is any action which is (i) uncompelled and (ii) not done in ignorance. Action on *proairesis*, by contrast, is any action which is (i) uncompelled, (ii) not done in ignorance, and (iii) rational.

Then does my claim that any voluntary action is, for Aristotle, rational, confuse voluntary action and action on *proairesis*? No. To see this, consider the following conflict of texts. (*Text A*) The definition of 'action on *proairesis*' is 'voluntary action upon deliberation' (NE 1112a15–17). (*Text B*) Deliberation means practical reasoning (NE 1112b13–29). (*Text C*) Children and animals are incapable of action on *proairesis*, though they are capable of voluntary action (NE 1111b9). From these three premises it follows that children and animals are incapable of practical reasoning. Yet (*Text D*) in the dMA, Aristotle gives us a quite general indication that 'creatures' – *ta zoia*, a broad and inclusive word used without any indication that it is not meant to be taken broadly and inclusively – act on practical reason:

'I must drink,' says desire, and 'this is drinkable' says perception or imagination or intuition; at once he drinks. This is how animals are impelled into movement and action... (dMA 701a32–35).

Of course, some of Aristotle's examples of practical reasoning in the dMA clearly are about specifically human deliberation: v., e.g., 701a13: 'Every *man* must walk'. But there is nothing in 701a32 ff. which indicates that humans alone are under discussion. On the contrary, the reference is explicitly to *ta zoia* in general. Moreover, earlier in the dMA account, Aristotle says explicitly that the behaviour of *all* animals displays something like that explicability in terms of purposes which, in Ch.1, I explained was what I mean by the rationality of voluntary action:

> All creatures (*panta ta zoia*) move and are moved for the sake of something: since the terminus of all their processes of change is what they are *for*. And we see that what moves the creature is [such things as] understanding, imagination, *proairesis*, wish, and desire... (dMA 700b15–18).

(NE 1118a17–23 makes a similar point, even while Aristotle is belittling the Homeric idea that we could talk of other animals' having the pleasures of the senses in the same way that humans do. Aristotle remarks, in his usual deflating way, that Homer was wrong to think that the lion delights in the *sight* (or sound) of its prey: rather, he remarks, it delights in the prospect of a meal. But if even this is true, it clearly suggests that the lion has a fair degree of facility in practical reasoning and imagination; it also suggests that the lion's action in leaping on its prey will be not only meet for purposive explanation, but will actually be done for a purpose.)

There is then a *prima facie* clash in the evidence, between those passages (such as Texts A, B and C) which admit that animals act voluntarily, but deny that they act upon *proairesis*, and those passages (typified by Text D) which seem to suggest that (all? some?) animals *do* reason their way to what they do, or at least that what they do is explicable by way of reasons.

How are we to account for this clash? Must we simply say that Aristotle's attitude to animals is inconsistent between the ethical and the biological works? There might certainly seem to be a strong case for saying that: compare a dismissive passage like NE 1149b32–36 with the deep interest in animals evident in the quotations above and throughout the dMA (and cp. dA 432b23–25). (For more on Aristotle on animals, v. Sorabji (1993), esp. Part I.) But we might also suggest that there must be more to acting upon *proairesis* than just acting in a way that is explicable by way of reasons – so that the *prima facie* clash turns out to be merely *prima facie*.

How are we to spell this idea out? Here is an initial suggestion, based simply on what Aristotle himself says about action on *proairesis* at NE 1112a16–17: that it is to be defined as action which has been deliberated on. From this it may be inferred that the difference between merely voluntary action and action on *proairesis*, such as human beings perform, is that the latter involves deliberation and the former does not.

But then the problem is not how to distinguish the merely voluntary from action on *proairesis* in respect of the rationality requirement, but how to distinguish the merely voluntary from the *in*voluntary in that respect. Consider some behaviour X which is not action on *proairesis*. Although X is in fact done without pre-deliberation, still X may be explicable, with reference to some piece of predeliberation, as if that predeliberation had actually occurred. Then if X is so explicable, is X a case of rational action? Not necessarily, since (as I said in Ch.1) the difference between rational action and irrational behaviour is that, in the case of rational action, it is not merely that relevant belief and unhindered appetition *are present* when the behaviour occurs; it is rather that the agent performs the behaviour *because of the combination of* relevant belief and unhindered appetition. But X could perfectly well be explicable with reference to some piece of predeliberation as if that predeliberation had actually occurred, without it being true that X occurred because of the combination of relevant belief and unhindered appetition.

What we want, as the midway case between action which just looks like action which has been done for a consciously pre-deliberated reason, and action which really has been done in that way, is action which is genuinely done for (because of) a reason, but not a reason which is actually and consciously thought out by the agent. In this case, I suggest, the merely voluntary may be distinguished from the involuntary, with respect to the rationality requirement, in the following way.

The merely voluntary is behaviour performed because of the combination in the agent of relevant belief and unhindered appetition. The involuntary is any other behaviour which is not action on *proairesis*.

And the merely voluntary must be distinct from action on *proairesis*, with respect to the rationality requirement, in the following way.

Action on *proairesis* is voluntary behaviour performed because of the combination *in predeliberation,* in the agent, of relevant belief and unhindered appetition.

Thus merely voluntary action is like action on *proairesis* in that it is also behaviour performed because of the combination, in the agent, of relevant belief and unhindered appetition. But it is unlike it in that, in the case of merely voluntary action, that combination does not involve predeliberation.

These definitions might seem to raise the question of how it is possible for there to be behaviour which is performed because of the combination in the agent of relevant belief and unhindered appetition, yet which does not involve at least some predeliberation. Had this question arisen for him, I think Aristotle could have answered it by positing a distinction between *actual* and *potential* predeliberation. Given this distinction, we may amend the latter half of the last definition to read: 'except that, in the merely voluntary, that combination involves potential, as opposed to actual, predeliberation'.

It is not too hard to see what potential, as opposed to actual, predeliberation will be. Compare Aristotle's distinction between actual and potential knowledge (NE 1146b31--33). According to this distinction, I will not, e.g., give the answer 'Canberra' to the question 'What is the capital of Australia?' if nobody asks me that question. No actualisation of that knowledge occurs, but this does not mean that I have no such knowledge. Rather I have potential knowledge of that fact if I would answer 'Canberra' if I were asked; and I am ignorant of it, if I would give any other answer if I were asked.

Likewise, then, regarding actual and potential predeliberation. I might not actually say to myself, for example, 'Children drowning in weirs should be rescued; that child is drowning in the weir; I must jump in and save her'. It may be true that no actual thought process of predeliberation occurs, but this does not mean that I simply act without any reason or predeliberation. Rather, I act on potential predeliberation if I would give an account of my action by reference to such a train of thought if I were asked; and my behaviour is (or may be) irrational if I could refer an inquirer to no such train of thought if I were asked.

Two objections may be voiced at this point. First, perhaps my description of what counts as rational action is too narrow. My account has it that predeliberation may be either actual or potential; in the case of potential predeliberation, the agent could supply a reason for their action if asked. But to supply a reason is a linguistic task, so to able to supply a reason is a linguistic capacity. Animals other than humans have no such capacity – or no adequate capacity. So, it seems, we are bound on my account to say that animals and infants cannot even achieve potential predeliberation. Hence their actions are not rational at all, and therefore not voluntary. But we wanted to say they *were* voluntary.

It is proper to respond, shifting our ground somewhat, that the best reason for ascribing rationality to animals and infants is just that there is a quite obvious purposiveness about much animal and infant behaviour. We can see perfectly well what the monkey or the baby is aiming at in sticking its hand into the biscuit tin – a biscuit, of course. But of course this response invites a second objection: that my description of what counts as rational action is too wide. If all that is needed for the rationality requirement to be satisfied is evident purposiveness, then surely Aristotle's completely general doctrine of the evident purposiveness of all nature (v. dMA 700b15– 18, quoted above) is going to guarantee that even falling stones act rationally in the required sense!

Here I refer the reader back to the points established in Section 2.1, about the differences between various sorts of process- originating principles. It is in fact quite true, in Aristotle's opinion, that there is a striking analogy between natural tendencies and human appetitions; nonetheless appetitions are not tendencies, and tendencies are not appetitions. When someone acts voluntarily the principle of their action is contingent in a way that the principle of a stone's falling is not; and the principle of their action is 'within them' in quite a different sense from that in which the principle of the stone's falling is, according to Aristotelian physics, 'within' the stone. Between full human voluntary action (i.e. action on *proairesis*), where the principle of and the reason for one's deed is actually evident to self-awareness and hence subject to the agent's own con- trol and modification, and the totally mindless behaviour of simple physical bodies, there are many transitional cases: and these include infants and animals. Insofar as infants and animals approximate to the paradigm case of rational and voluntary action, the mature human being, they too can be considered rational and voluntary agents; insofar as they act like simple physical bodies, they cannot. Hence the ambiguities of their position, evident in Aristotle's hesitation about (e.g.) whether to say that animals and children share in *praxis*.

I have, then, suggested how it may be that behaviour which is not action on *proairesis* nonetheless can involve a kind of deliberation, and so be rational, as well as uncompelled and performed without ignorance, thus counting as voluntary action (as I define that); and how merely voluntary action differs from actually involuntary behaviour in respect of the rationality condition. One thing that this account makes plain is the logical dependence of the category of the merely voluntary on the category of action on *proairesis*. It does not follow, from my rationality requirement, that the only genuinely voluntary action is action on *proairesis*. But it does follow that the form of explanation for all genuinely voluntary action is that form dictated by the nature of the paradigm case of voluntary action – action on *proairesis*.

3.3.　DELIBERATION

What we want to know about next, then, is the nature of actual deliberation or predeliberation – the item which is not actually present in merely voluntary action, but which gives all voluntary action, especially the focal case of action on *proairesis*, its characteristic form. The natural starting-point for this inquiry is Aristotle's discussion of deliberation, *bouleusis*, in NE III.3. What this discussion establishes is, first, the very close connection between *bouleusis*, *proairesis* and action on *proairesis*; and, second, that the possibility of giving a full and non-provisional account of deliberation (which Aristotle does not give) is dependent on the possibility of giving a full and non-provisional account of practical reasoning and 'the practical syllogism' (which Aristotle does not give either). Thus discussing deliberation will lead me on to the detailed discussion of the syllogistic of practical reasoning which takes up the rest of this chapter.

First, note six close parallels between Aristotle's remarks about *proairesis* and about deliberation.

(i) *Proairesis*, we heard (a), is not shared with irrational creatures; it is characteristic of practically wise adult human males (*phronimoi*). Likewise, the discussion of deliberation is dominated by the phrase '*we* deliberate', the subject of which, if Aristotle's examples are anything to go by, is again practically wise adult human males: 'We should say, no doubt, that what deliberation ought to decide is what the deliberations of a man of good sense (*ho noun ekhon*) would decide, not what a fool or a madman would decide' (NE 1112a20–21; cp. 1141b10).

(ii) There is no *proairesis* either of what is impossible *tout court*, or of what is impossible for me (e). Likewise 'we deliberate about those things that are up to us and do-able' (1112a31).

(iii) Wish (*boulesis*) is of the end, *proairesis* of the means (f). Likewise 'we deliberate not about objectives, but about the means to attain those objectives' (1112b13). Perhaps, however, there could be a wide and a narrow sense of 'deliberation' too.

(iv) *Proairesis* cannot concern any matter at all, as wishing can, but only 'what is up to us' (g). Likewise (1112a21) the range of deliberation does not include what is eternally unchanging or (1112b1) 'the objects of precise and self-governing sciences'; nor (1112a24) things that change with complete regularity (the objects of contemplative wisdom, 1141b1–3); nor (1112a26–27) irregular or chance changes (the objects of some sorts of rather chancy expertise, 1140a19–20). By exclusion of the subject-areas of the other intellectual excellences, it follows that the range of deliberation must coincide with that of the only remaining form of intellectual virtue, practical wisdom (1139l5–16). (That this is so is clear from 1112b8–10 and 1140a24–b6.)

(v) Belief is qualified as either true or false, but *proairesis* as right or wrong (h and k); *proairesis* makes our characters good or bad – not moral belief (i). Likewise Aristotle's *bouleusis* is that kind of deliberation employed in settling practical problems of the general form 'What is best?' (1140a25–26).

(vi) '*Proairesis* concerns pursuit or avoidance, but belief, what things are, and how advantageous, and for whom' (j: 1112a4–5). Likewise 'Particulars do not provide matter for deliberation, e.g. whether this is a loaf, or has been properly baked' (NE

1113a1); deliberation is more characteristically about what to pursue or avoid.

It is evident from this comparison that *proairesis* and deliberation are intimately connected. So intimately connected, in fact, that Aristotle actually feels it necessary to tell us how to distinguish them:

> What deliberation settles on is the same as what *proairesis* settles on, except that when *proairesis* settles on something, it is already predeterminate. For what one's deliberating has already adjudged, that is what *proairesis* settles on. (NE 1113a2–5)

The same point is made in a different way by 1139a32 ff.:

> The first principle of action is the *proairesis*: it is the cause in the sense of being where the movement that is the action comes from, though not in the sense of being the reason why the action happens. And the first principle of the *proairesis* [presumably in the same sense] is an appetition plus reasoning about something for the sake of which [the action is done].

The point of these passages is twofold. First: that the efficient cause of the *praxis* – the action on *proairesis*, as I have been calling it – is the *proairesis*. And second: that there is something which precedes the *proairesis* as its efficient cause, just as *proairesis* precedes action on *proairesis*. NE 1113a2–5 implies that this is deliberation; NE 1139a32, that this is 'an appetition plus reasoning about something for the sake of which the action is done'.

This suggests that deliberation is *equivalent* to 'an appetition plus reasoning about something for the sake of which the action is done'. Bear in mind the NE III.2–3 doctrine that *proairesis* and deliberation are of means, not ends, and compare NE 1112b13–14, 16:

> A doctor does not deliberate about whether he should heal, nor an orator about whether he should be persuasive… but positing (*themenoi*) a certain objective, they look to see how and by what means it can be brought about.

(I translate *themenoi* here as 'positing' because (as I have argued in Section 2.2b) the establishment of first principles for reasoning is not necessarily itself an irrational process, as might be suggested by such translations as the Loeb's 'taking for granted'. The doctor *qua* doctor does not deliberate about what end to seek to bring about; the objective of his actions is already settled for him by the very fact that he is a doctor. But a human being, *qua* human being, might well deliberate about whether to be a doctor; or indeed about whether to act, in some situation, *qua* doctor or (say) *qua* soldier.)

We may, then, gloss NE 1139a32 ff. as meaning that what happens in deliberation is that an end which the agent has already decided upon (by some other process which is not strictly deliberation, or at any rate not *this* deliberation) is converted into a *proairesis*, a decision to act. This happens by way of the process which is, strictly, deliberation. By a mental searching, means to the end in question are found.

The best and most detailed description of this process is given at NE 1112b16–27. Deliberation, says Aristotle, is a process of working from a first term, namely the objective which has been posited, to a final term, namely the beginning of the action: 'the last term in the analysis of what to do is the first term in the genesis of what is done' (1112b24).

(Note that, on this account, the deliberation includes the *proairesis*, and is the efficient cause, not of the *proairesis* as at 1139a32–33, but of the action on *proairesis* itself. The cause of the trouble here may be the ambiguity of Aristotle's use of *proairesis* between 'decision to act' (so 1139a32) and 'action on a decision to act' (so, apparently, 1112a13–16).)

The deliberator, in 'examining how and by what means [the end] will be brought about' (NE 1112b16), works from a first term, the objective, to a last term, the action or the beginning of the action, by the quickest method possible – if any method is possible. If several methods are available, the deliberator asks herself 'Which is the easiest and best of these methods?' (1112b17); in the case where only one method is available – and, presumably, in the case where the deliberator has decided which is the best of several methods – the deliberator asks two further questions: 'How will this method bring about the end? How is this method itself to be brought into operation?' (1112b18): and in this manner the deliberator works back to some performance or movement within her power which is immediately available for her to do without doing anything else first – and does it. But if at any stage in this process it becomes clear that in fact no method is available, the deliberator abandons the project (1112b19, b27).

There is then a performance or movement which is the last term in the deliberation, and the first cause of the doing of the action (1112b24). The use of the word 'cause' at 1112b24 reminds us again that this account can be seen as explaining the 1139a32 remark, that the deliberation is the efficient cause of the action. The process of deliberation terminates in something which can be done as the beginning of a process of action: what Aristotle calls 'the first cause', and what David Charles (1984, Ch. 2), following Melden (1961), calls a 'basic action'. The same point is suggested by Aristotle's formula (NE 1139a5) about *proairesis*, that it is 'both appetitive rationality and rational appetition'. He repeats it in another form at 1113a5–6:

Each person stops considering how to act once he has traced the first principle back to himself, and to the leading part of himself: and this is the part that chooses (*kai touto to proairoumenon*).

This analysis of Aristotle's account of deliberation suggests three points.

First: to give an account of deliberation, as I have just done, is itself to give an account of the combination of unhindered appetition of some objective with relevant knowledge (awareness of the appropriate method for obtaining the objective, and of the best means to put that method into practice). It was, of course, this combination which I suggested was what constituted the rationality of a voluntary action – whether the deliberation in question is actual, as in action on *proairesis*, or merely potential, as in the merely voluntary.

Second: we now have an account of something which may have seemed obscure thus far, namely what it means to say that some behaviour is performed 'because of' a combination of unhindered appetition and relevant knowledge. 'The last step of the deliberation is the first cause (*proton aition*) of the action' (1112b24): the 'first cause' is both the termination of the process of deliberation, and the commencement of the process of action. Hence it is itself the causal link between thought and action. Thus to say that some behaviour B is performed 'because of' the combination of unhindered appetition and relevant knowledge in deliberation is to say no more and no less than that B satisfies the rationality condition of voluntary action.

And third: if this is what deliberation is, then it would seem that a more precise account of the nature of deliberative reasoning might be obtained by closer examination of the notion of the 'practical syllogism'. To this I now turn.

3.4. PRACTICAL REASONING AND THE 'PRACTICAL SYLLOGISM'

The suggestion is that an account of practical reasoning in the form of the 'practical syllogism' is at the heart of Aristotle's account of deliberation, which itself is central to Aristotle's account of action on *proairesis*, which is in turn the most fully explicit form, and the focal case (cp. NE 1157a30–32, Mph 4.1), of voluntary action. What, then, is the Aristotelian 'practical syllogism'? In particular, how far is it inference in the strict sense? Answering this question will involve me in a brief examination (4a) of standard Aristotelian syllogisms, so as to compare them (4b) with practical syllogisms.

First, a note on the name 'practical syllogism'.

The expression ['practical syllogism'] is not a translation or transliteration of any expression Aristotle ever uses…. The Greek words *syllogismoi ton prakton* [NE 1144a32] are taken as the Aristotelian authority for the use of the expression…. But to take [these words] as a unit of expression is to misread the Greek.

Kenny (1979), p. 111

In Greek, NE 1144a32 reads *'hoi gar syllogismoi ton prakton arkhen ekhontes eisin, epeide toionde to telos kai to ariston…'*. As Kenny says, *arkhen ekhontes eisin* cannot possibly be, as some have thought, the Greek for 'are such as to have first premises'. Hence these words should not be taken together; and so neither should the three words which precede them, namely the words which started the controversy, *arkhen ekhontes eisin*. The right division of the vital words here gives us not this:

hoi gar syllogismoi ton prakton // arkhen ekhontes eisin, // epeide toionde to telos kai to ariston…'.
('Practical syllogisms are such as to have first premises [which state that] "Since such and such is the objective and the best…"').

But this:

hoi gar syllogismoi // *ton prakton arkhen ekhontes* // *eisin, epeide toionde to telos kai to ariston...*'.
('Those syllogisms which contain first principles of things-to-be-done run: "Since such and such is the objective and the best..."').

Which noted, I shall nonetheless follow the usual practice in using (*faute de mieux*) the phrase 'practical syllogism' – henceforth without scare quotes – to describe the particular pieces of inference which Aristotle, clearly enough, believes to be the basic components, or at any rate a basic component, of the phenomenon of practical reasoning in general.

4a. The Standard Aristotelian Syllogism

To understand Aristotle's account of what we are going to call the practical syllogism, then, we need to compare it very briefly with his account of the standard, 'theoretical' or 'abstract', syllogism. Aristotle's account of the standard syllogism is part of his account of general abstract reasoning, which in turn is part of his account of argumentation: i.e. his account of how to give persuasive arguments (dAR 1354a16) or demonstrations (APr 24a11). At dAR 1354a1 ff., he distinguishes two types of argument:

(i) Logical arguments (which can be either 'demonstrations' or 'dialectical arguments'), which depend on appealing solely to reason.
(ii) Rhetorical arguments. These depend on appealing to 'the moral character of the speaker, [by] some way of making the listener feel, and [by] the speech (*logos*) itself, through its proving or seeming to prove its thesis' (dAR 1356a1–4).

Aristotle divides logical argumentation into demonstration and dialectic (APr 24a23 ff.), or, perhaps equivalently, into syllogism and induction (APr 68b13–14; NE 1139b26: 'All teaching is either through induction or through syllogism').

What is Aristotle's contrast between induction and syllogism? Induction can be characterised as narrowly and tightly as it seems to be at APr 68b15–29 (and NE 1098b4), or more loosely so that it includes definition, habituation, perception, imagination and intel-

lect (dMA 701a32–33). But, in general, it seems safe to say that
Aristotle thinks that (in some sense of induction) it is induction's job
to supply the first principles of syllogism:

> Some first principles are seen (*theorountai*) by induction [in the
> narrow sense], some by perception, some by some sort of
> habituation, and others in yet other ways. (NE 1098b4)

Now Aristotle does not believe that any sort of induction (in the
strict or in the loose sense) is rationally justifiable in the argumentative form of the syllogism, to which induction is epistemo-
logically prior (though not logically prior: cp. Phys 184a17–21) and
by which induction is presupposed. But this does not commit him to
saying that induction is not, in any sense, rationally justifiable.
Consider the Aristotelian syllogism: it is the paradigm of rational
justification, and yet it is not self-supporting. For the formation of its
principles, and hence for its very existence, the syllogism depends
crucially on other forms of rational justification.

The syllogism is the complete or perfected (*teleios*) form of
theoretical reasoning: i.e. what all reasoning 'aims at being' (or cre-
ating) is the syllogistic form (APr 24b23–25). Only syllogisms are or
can be completely and rigorously valid. So induction lacks the formal cogency of syllogism. Yet what induction lacks in formal
cogency, it makes up (says Aristotle) in immediacy and subjective
certainty: 'If [a reasoner] is not more certain of his first principles
than of his conclusion, he will have his scientific knowledge
accidentally' (NE 1139b34–35). 'By nature, the syllogism by the middle term [sc. the standard syllogism] is prior and more knowable
(*gnorimoteros*, which also means 'nobler'). But to us, the [syllogism]
by induction is more obvious (*enargesteros*)' (APr 68b36–37).

Aristotle saw that induction too plays a crucial role in human reasoning, a role which syllogistic inference could not possibly fill. That
role is the establishment, whether by perception, definition, or
induction strictly so called, of the first principles of those syllogisms.
This is a necessity prior to the establishment of any syllogisms at all.
'Induction has to do with the first principle and the universal pre-
miss, whereas deduction *begins from* the universal premisses' (NE
1139b28–30). Admittedly some syllogisms derive their first principles from other syllogisms. But at least some syllogisms must,
Aristotle thinks, be dependent on first principles arrived at not by
syllogism but by induction. Eventually, in any reasoning, 'there will

be a stop' (NE 1142a30) – the syllogising will come to rest on a first
principle known by induction not syllogism.

The doctrine of the *Analytics* is that we can classify all fully
rigorous logical arguments as what Aristotle calls 'full' or 'perfect'
syllogisms (*teleioi syllogismoi*). Less rigorous arguments, but which
are still clearly logical or pseudo-logical in character, will be
'imperfect' (*atele*) syllogisms – degenerate types of syllogism. (Syllogisms of proper form can be less than fully cogent too, of course.
They may involve falsehoods and improper transitions.) Other less
than perfect forms of argumentation are the two rhetorical forms,
enthymeme (APr 70a11–23) and 'argument by analogy' (*paradeigma*,
APr 68b38–69a13): from a logical point of view, these turn out to be
imperfectly formed syllogism and induction respectively.

Full syllogisms are either simple syllogisms; or they are what are
called sorites, involving a series of transitions from one simple
syllogism to another, in which one premise of the second syllogism
is the conclusion of the first, of the third, the conclusion of the
second – and so on. Aristotle believes that all sorites are resoluble
into simple syllogisms (APr 42a32–b26 seems to suggest this,
without actually saying it; cp. Lear (1980), pp. 10–11).

There is on Aristotle's view a definite number of argumentative
forms, some of which will always be valid and some of which will
always be invalid (provided, of course, that we are dealing with
well-formed examples of these forms). Aristotle's project, in the
Analytics, is to classify these argumentative forms. If he succeeds,
anyone who wants to show that a given dialectical argument is
rigorously valid will need only to establish that it is a well-formed
example of a rigorously valid form of syllogism. Aristotle wants to
give us a 'look-up table' of all the kinds of good argument there
are – and some account of why only these kinds of argument are
good.

4b.   Comparison with the Practical Syllogism

How far, then, does this general account of the syllogism apply to
the practical syllogism? To quote Anthony Kenny again:

> Practical syllogisms are not, and most of them do not even look
> like, syllogisms. A syllogism should consist of two premises and
> a conclusion, all three grammatically of subject–predicate form; it
> should contain three terms, one of which ('the minor') occurs in

subject place in the conclusion, one of which ('the major') occurs in predicate place in the conclusion, and the third of which ('the middle') occurs in both premisses but not in the conclusion.... A traditional syllogism of this kind is something very unlike the patterns of non-theoretical reasoning in Aristotle.... We find practical inferences involving two, three and four premisses; the conclusion is never a straightforward subject-predicate sentence; the premisses are often of conditional form so that the whole looks more like an exercise in propositional calculus than in syllogistic... one must realise that a 'practical syllogism' is something even in appearance very different from a syllogism in Barbara or an inference of the form 'All Xs are Ys; A is an X; therefore A is a Y.' (Kenny (1979), p. 112)

It is certainly true that Aristotle's remarks on and examples of practical syllogisms, when compared with his remarks on and examples of abstract syllogisms, seem puzzling and unhelpful. The sustained and intricate account of the abstract syllogism in the logical works stands in stark contrast to Aristotle's scattered and informal remarks on the practical syllogism, and his desultory and apparently carelessly-chosen examples. It does not look easy to extract a single canonical form, or even as few as two canonical forms (v. Allan (1955)), from these.

Nonetheless, although the practical syllogism is undeniably unlike other Aristotelian syllogisms in some respects, it is not totally unlike. There is room for doubt that the practical 'syllogism' is truly a syllogism, when we consider Aristotle's definition of 'syllogism' at APr 24b19-20: 'A syllogism is an argument in which, given that some things are posited, something other than the posits follows by necessity from their being as they are.' On the other hand, there is no doubt at all that Aristotle thinks that the practical syllogism expresses *some* kind of logic.

My line will be that Aristotle viewed the relation between standard syllogisms and practical syllogisms as no more, and no less, than an analogical relation (v., once more, Mph 4.1). That the relation between them is not simply identity of kind, but not simply dissimilarity either, seems to be expressed by Aristotle's language about practical syllogisms. If the relation was identity of kind, we might expect Aristotle's commonest term for 'practical syllogism' to be the heavily theory-charged term *syllogismos*. But, in fact, he uses *syllogismos* of practical reasoning on only two occasions in the NE

(1142b23, 1144a31; but cp. also 1149a33 *hosper syllogisamenos*). Again, if the relation was anything approaching simple dissimilarity, we might expect Aristotle to prefer the very neutral, non-committal term *logos* (which he uses of practical reasoning in five places: 1112a16, 1149a26, 1149b1–3, 1150b28, 1151a29). But neither of these terms is Aristotle's commonest term for the type of reasoning called in English the 'practical syllogism'; this is *logismos* (NE 1111a34, 1117a21, 1119b10, 1141b14, 1142b19, 1145b11–12, 1146a33, 1149b35, 1150b24). Moreover, unlike *logos*, *logismos* never seems to have any other sense in the NE. (The only possible exception is 1141b14, but even this seems dubious.)

This terminological survey has a moral: the reasoning of practical syllogisms is not so loose as to deserve no more than the prosaic name *logos*; but not so rigorous as to deserve the special name *syllogismos*. It is somewhere in between. Adding the scientific-looking suffix *-ismos* promotes *logos*; dropping the intensive prefix *syn-* demotes *syllogismos*. By either route, or both, one arrives at *logismos*. (The word was not of course an Aristotelian coinage; but its shape was very convenient for expressing what he wanted.)

I will now substantiate my suggestion that the relation between the standard syllogism and the practical syllogism is an analogical one. The right place to start this account is with the examples of practical syllogisms which Aristotle actually gives. So here, in my own very literal English, are twelve of Aristotle's formal or specific examples of complete or readily completable practical syllogisms, stripped as far as possible of the commentaries in which they are embedded.

(1) '[Belief and reasoning about the universal say] that such a person should do such a sort of thing; [belief and reasoning about the particular fact say] that this thing now is a thing of that sort, and that I myself am such a person' (dA 434a17–20).

(2) '...As when he thinks that every man should walk, and that he is a man, he at once walks...' (dMA 701a14).

(3) '...or if he thinks that no man should walk now, and he is a man, he at once is still' (dMA 701a15).

(4) '"I should make something good"; "A house is something good"; he makes a house at once' (dMA 701a16–17).

(5) '"I need a covering"; "A cloak is a covering"; "I need a cloak". "I should make what I need"; "I need a cloak"; "I should make a cloak"' (dMA 701a17–20).

(6) '"I should drink", says desire. "This is a drink", says perception or imagination or intelligence. At once he drinks' (dMA 701a32–33).

(7) '"Since this is health, it is necessary, if the patient is to be healthy, that so and so should be the case, such as 'homogeneity'. If there is to be 'homogeneity', there must be heat..."– and so he always continues thinking until he arrives at the last term, what he himself can do' (Mph 1032b7–9).

(8) '"If he is to be healthy, he must be made homogeneous." – "So what counts as homogeneity?" – "This; and this will come about if he is heated." – "What counts as being heated?" – "This; and this is present in potential [i.e., is possible] and is already up to him"' (Mph 1032b18–22).

(9) '[One can be wrong] either that all "heavy water" is unwholesome, or that this is "heavy water"' (NE 1142a23).

(10) '...He may know that dry foods are good for every man, and that he himself is a human, or that Food X is a dry food; but that this is Food X, he may either not know or not actualise' (NE 1147a5–7).

(11) 'If every sweet thing should be tasted, and this thing is sweet – being some particular item – it is necessary for a person, who is able and is not prevented, at once also to taste it...' (NE 1147a29–31)

(12) 'So when the universal premise is present which forbids tasting [whatever is sweet], but also the [universal premise] that "every sweet thing is pleasant", and [the particular premise] that "this thing is sweet", and this latter is operative when desire happens to be present; then the [first universal premise] says that one should flee this, but the desire leads one on' (NE 1147a31–34).

What are we to make of these examples of practical syllogisms, when we compare them with standard syllogisms? There are five main problem areas, which I will consider in turn:

(a) Do practical syllogisms have only two premises, one major and one minor?
(b) What is the 'major premise' of a practical syllogism?
(c) What is the 'minor premise' of a practical syllogism?
(d) What is the conclusion of a practical syllogism?
(e) Are practical syllogisms, in fact, formally valid?

(a)   Do practical syllogisms have only two premises, one major and one minor?

This question divides into two sub-questions: (a1) How many premises does a practical syllogism have? (a2) Of what sorts?

On (a1), dMA 701a12 ('from the *two* premises') is clear enough; but dMA 701a23–25 ('the premises about what to do come to be in *two forms*') clouds the picture by not telling us for sure that only one premise of each form comes to be in any single practical syllogism. My examples (1–4), (6), (9), and (11) support the dMA 701a12 view; but (5), (7), (8), (10) and (12) go against it. (And NE 1147a4–10 apparently argues that there are two universal premises in each practical syllogism: 'There is one universal premise regarding himself, and another regarding the matter in hand...' (1147a4–7).)

Consider, however, the difference between standard 'syllogisms' which are simple syllogisms and those which are actually sorites. It is, I suggested, Aristotle's conviction about standard syllogisms that all sorites can be analysed as compounded out of simple syllogisms. Why not apply this idea to practical syllogisms also? Suppose we had formalised example (5) as follows:

(5′) 1.   (X thinks:) X needs a covering.
      2.   (X thinks:) A cloak is a covering.
      3.   (X thinks:) X needs a cloak.
      4.   (X thinks:) What X needs, X must make.
      5.   (X thinks:) X must make a cloak.

Given the point about sorites, we might renumber (5′5) as (5′6) and add a new (5′5), of identical content to (5′3):

(5′) 5.   (X thinks:) X needs a cloak.

(5′1–3) and (5′4–6) can now be seen as the two simple syllogisms out of which (5′) is compounded as a sorites. For clarity, we may write the sorites out, showing the transferred conclusion, and with its constituent simple syllogisms marked off, like this:

(5′) 1.   (X thinks:) X needs a covering.
      2.   (X thinks:) A cloak is a covering.
      3.   (X thinks:) X needs a cloak.

4. (X thinks:) What X needs, X must make.
5. (X thinks:) X needs a cloak.
6. (X thinks:) X must make a cloak.

A similar treatment can be applied to the other cases which show just the same problem, (7), (8) and (10); with, however, the added complication that these are three-stage, not two-stage, sorites. Given that (7) and (8) are essentially the same piece of reasoning, we might formalise that reasoning thus:

(7') 1. (X thinks:) The patient Y is to be healthy.
   2. (X thinks:) Health is 'homogeneity'.
   3. (X thinks:) X must increase Y's 'homogeneity'.

   4. (X thinks:) X must increase Y's 'homogeneity'.
   5. (X thinks:) Y's 'homogeneity' will be increased if Y is heated.
   6. (X thinks:) X must heat Y.

   7. (X thinks:) X must heat Y.
   8. (X thinks:) If Y is massaged, Y will be heated.
   9. (X thinks:) X must massage Y.

Example (10), likewise, will give us this sorites:

(10') 1. (X thinks:) To be healthy, X must eat what is digestible and wholesome.
    2. (X thinks:) Light meat is digestible and wholesome.
    3. (X thinks:) X should eat light meat.

    4. (X thinks:) X should eat light meat.
    5. (X thinks:) Chicken is light meat.
    6. (X thinks:) X should eat chicken.

    7. (X thinks:) X should eat chicken.
    8. (X thinks:) This is chicken.
    9. (X thinks:) X should eat this.

If this sort of analysis is accepted and generalised, there is no obstacle to saying, as I wish to say, that *individual* practical syllogisms have two premises, just like standard syllogisms. Though certainly such individual practical syllogisms can form part of chains of reasoning, the same is true of standard syllogisms.

(a2) What sorts of premises does a practical syllogism have? It appears from the *Analytics* that standard syllogisms have one minor premise or premise 'of the particulars' (*ton kath' hekasta*), and one major premise or premise 'of the universal' (*tou katholou*). Aristotle regularly uses these terms when referring to the premises of practical syllogisms in the NE (1143b3–4, 1147a1–10, 27 ff., and cf. 1135a6–8) and in the dA (e.g. 434a17–18). But in the dMA, Aristotle uses a different pair of terms for practical syllogisms:

> The practical premises appear in two forms, namely premises *of the good* and premises *of the possible*. (701a23–25)

A division of premises into 'premises of the good' and 'premises of the possible' seems to suggest a rather different picture. For clearly a premise of the good need not be universal; equally clearly, a premise of the possible need not be particular (though it might be said that it is no good knowing that actions of a certain type are *usually* possible: what we need to know about is whether *this* action is possible). Despite these reservations, it seems clear that Aristotle is here using two different pairs of names for the same pair of phenomena. And, of course, that in itself should tell us something about his views about such questions as whether there are any universal moral principles: cp. Section 2.2a.

(b)   What is the 'major premise' of a practical syllogism?

This brings me to (b) an examination of the practical syllogism's major, or universal, premise, or premise of the good – whichever we should call it. The term 'major premise' should, perhaps, be reserved for standard syllogisms, so that practical syllogisms have neither major nor minor premises. But considering some of the 'universal premises' in the examples above, neither of the other two pairs of names seems to fit either. In what sense are 'I need a covering' (5), or '"I should drink", says desire' (6), premises of the good? And what does their inclusion as examples say about the other, perhaps less problematic, examples?

Nor, when we consider the name 'univeral premises', is it at all clear how general or specific Aristotle takes such premises to be. On the one hand, dA 434a17–20 offers us a precise, situation-relative sense: 'The one apprehension and argument (*hypolepsis kai logos*) is of a universal, the other is of a particular. For the one says that such a man ought to do such and such, and the other that this here is a case of such and such, and I am such a man...'. On the other, there is the apparently extreme generality of NE 1144a31–33. Indeed the latter passage seems at odds with the idea that anything but a very basic (and so, perhaps, very widely universal?) moral first principle could be the first premise of a practical syllogism. To turn to our examples, the first premises of (4) ('I should make something good'), (5) ('I need a covering'), (6) ('"I should drink", says desire'), and (7, 8) ('The patient is to be healthy'), may fit the pattern laid down by dA 434a17–20, but are, it seems, too narrowly specific to be examples of the sort of very general statements that NE 1144a31–33 apparently requires them to be. Whereas, on the other hand, the first premises of (2, 3) ('Every/ no man should walk'), (9) ('All "heavy water" is unwholesome'), (10) ('Dry food is good for every man'), and (11) ('Every sweet thing should be tasted'), might fit the NE formula, but are surely too broad to be a statement 'that such a man should do such and such...' as the dA requires. ((2,3) and (11) at least are also, as Anscombe (1957) remarks, 'insane' assertions; how could any credible first-order moral theory include these views?)

The reconciliation of this conflict is, however, fairly simple, given what we have already established. Perhaps unsurprisingly, it turns on a correct interpretation of 1144a31–33, which I quote once more:

> Those syllogisms which contain first principles of things-to-be-done run: 'Since such and such is the objective and the best...'

The correct interpretation depends on two conditions. First, that 'the goal and the best' should not be given too exalted an understanding (and certainly nothing which deserves the Kantian capitalisation which Rackham's Loeb translation gives it); for Aristotle carries on: – whatever the best may be – for the sake of the argument let it be any old thing' (33–34). Second, that it be understood that the kind of practical first principle with which Aristotle is concerned is, very often, not some absolutely primary moral principle, but 'the first principle of a thing to be done'.

Thus 1144a31–33 does not, as Rackham's translation suggests, mean that every individual practical syllogism must start with a completely general and completely basic statement about what is good. Rather, one need only start one's actual reasoning with a statement of the relevant good which is to be sought in some particular case of action. Everything that precedes that statement, going back to some or other moral first principle, may in a given case be merely potentially present. The whole chain of reasoning which leads to a particular action is a sorites, with premises of the good of increasing specificity as one works down it; but there is no need to suppose that the agent who does the right thing and does it for the right reason must have actually worked through the whole of that practical sorites. His actual reasoning can begin at a very late stage in it indeed: as Aristotle's examples suggest.

This then is how this account applies, say, to the first premises of (5) ('I need a covering') and (6) ('"I should drink", says desire'). Aristotle wants us to assume (actual or possible) sorites in which these are intermediate conclusions, as for example:

(i)   When it rains, all men should avoid getting wet
(ii)   It is raining here and now
(iii)   All men here and now should avoid getting wet

(iv)   All men here and now should avoid getting wet
(v)   I am a man here and now
(vi)   I should avoid getting wet here and now

(vi)   I should avoid getting wet here and now
(viii) If I have a covering, I will avoid getting wet here and now
(ix)   I need a covering

(ix) emerges from this sorites, and one can see that 'I should drink' might emerge from something similar. It is now clear, therefore, how such statements might be brought back to depend on statements of the good at some earlier stage in what will be a rather complex sorites.

The upshot of this analysis, then, is that the first premise of any normal practical syllogism is typically a statement of the good which is to be sought in that particular case of action. It is not usually, in spite of the appearance of 1144a31–33, a completely general statement about a sort of good. In any case of practical reasoning it must be possible to work back to such general statements; but it is not necessary actually to do so.

(c)   What is the 'minor premise' of a practical syllogism?
Given that this is the nature of the first premise of an Aristotelian practical syllogism, and given what was established in (a) about the number and kind of the practical syllogism's premises, it should now be plain what the second premise, the 'premise of the possible', will typically be like. I have cleared the way for the view of dA

434a17–20 concerning the first premise of the practical syllogism. But there is far less conflict about the nature of the second premise: it is not as hard to reconcile (for example) the claims that the second premise is a 'belief about the particulars controlled by perception' (NE 1147a26) and that it is the premise which says 'that this now is a such and such, and I am such a man' A 434a20).

The second premise of the practical syllogism is concerned with the application of the moral belief or other pro-attitude expressed by the first premise. It is the second premise which does the vital work in making reason practical, in getting us from a moral belief (the first premise) to an actual deed (the conclusion). Aristotle's stress on the means, not the ends, side of practical reasoning in NE III.2–3, and his remarks that it is the last premise which determines or controls the actions we do (1147b10), and that 'The understanding in itself motivates (*kinei*) nothing; it is the practical understanding which aims at some end which motivates' (1139a35), are all different ways of pointing to the crucial importance of the second premise of the practical syllogism.

(d)   What is the conclusion of a practical syllogism?

It is a much-debated question whether the conclusion of a practical syllogism is an action or a proposition. For example Charles (1984), Ch. 4, argues that it cannot be an action; the conclusion of a practical syllogism is a proposition, and only the presence of desire in addition to the presence of that conclusion can render the conclusion operative. Anscombe (1957) famously argues that the conclusion of the practical syllogism was (or ought to have been, had Aristotle had this notion) an intention, not an action; and other writers have followed this sort of line. Other philosophers again (e.g. von Wright (1978)) have argued that the conclusion of a practical syllogism is not a proposition, but an action. But the evidence which Aristotle gives us does not obviously favour any of these views over the others. Indeed, if one accepts that one must take either the 'action' view or the 'proposition' view (I leave aside the 'intention' view), Aristotle seems to contradict himself.

In the dMA, he apparently argues for the view that the conclusion of a practical syllogism is not a proposition, but an action: 'From the two premises, the conclusion that results is the action. Thus, if someone thinks that "Every man ought to march", and that "He himself is a man", he marches at once (*euthus*)' (dMA 701a14–15). In the NE, moreover, he adds that 'When one [opinion] results from these, it is necessary for the soul to affirm the consequent there [sc. in the standard syllogism], and [likewise necessary here], in practical [deliberations], immediately to perform the consequent' (NE 1147a27–29).

On the other hand, there is the doctrine of NE 1139a32–33, that 'appetition and reasoning for the sake of something' is the cause of the *proairesis*, and *proairesis* in turn of the action. I have argued that 'appetition and reasoning for the sake of something' is equivalent to deliberation, and that the practical syllogism is the form of deliberation. Hence what the practical syllogism causes (or at any rate, causes directly) – where 'what it causes' means 'what it terminates in', 'what its conclusion is' – will not be the action but the *proairesis*.

The evidence, then, conflicts. I suspect there are good reasons for this. As we have already seen (Section 3.3), Aristotle equivocates between (a) saying that the deliberation includes the *proairesis*, and is the efficient cause of the action on *proairesis* (so 1112a13–16), and (b) saying that the deliberation is separate from the *proairesis*, and is directly the efficient cause only of the *proairesis* (so 1139a32–33). Likewise, therefore, he also equivocates between saying that the practical syllogism (which *is* the deliberation) leads to the *proairesis*, which in turn leads to the action, and saying that the practical syllogism itself leads directly to the action.

Aristotle evidently *wants* to sit on this particular fence. He does not want to be forced into saying either that the conclusion of a practical syllogism is a proposition and therefore cannot be an action, or that it is an action and therefore cannot be a proposition. What he wants to establish is that the conclusion of the practical syllogism is a hinge, a causal link, between thought and action. So NE 1112a24–25 ('The last step in the analysis [made by reason] is the first step in the genesis [of action]') and Mph 1032b7–10: 'And thus he will always continue thinking until he arrives at what he himself can do – the last term.' But attempts to classify the conclusion of a practical syllogism as either simply a proposition, or simply an action, beg the question if they assume in advance that there can be no such link, that the movement from thought to action cannot be smooth and continuous.

For Aristotle, the conclusion of the practical syllogism is, or can be expressed in, both a proposition (such as an intention might give rise to) and an action. And why not? Generally speaking, it surely makes sense to suggest that an action can embody, incarnate, a proposition, just as much as a proposition can give an interpretation of, a 'read-out' from, an action. (Think of mime artists, for instance, or the action that 'says' as clearly as any verbal remark 'I am disgusted by the taste of this water'.)

The conclusion of the practical syllogism will appear most obviously as an action in cases of action where there is little need to run through one's reasons for acting in a specific way – that is, where the deliberation involved in the action remains implicit, and the rationality of the action is potential rather than actual (cp. Section 3.2). It will appear most obviously as a proposition rather than an action in cases where the expression of the action form of the conclusion is thwarted, e.g. by compulsion or by akrasia, so that only the propositional form remains:

> It is normally only in the case where decisions are not acted on (in the case, for instance, of the incontinent) or where action is postponed that there is any point in distinguishing between the act and the decision.
>
> Kenny (1979), p. 143

But there is, of course, nothing impossible about cases where the conclusion of the practical syllogism is expressed simultaneously as both action and proposition ('You need help,' I say to the tramp, giving him a fifty-pound note). Certainly Aristotle sits on the fence on this question, but perhaps he was right to want to sit on it, if he is to succeed in presenting a full account of 'how it is that a thinking agent sometimes acts and sometimes does not' (dMA 701a7).

(e)Are practical syllogisms, in fact, formally valid?

Much has been written about this. One notable contribution is Hare (1971). Hare distinguishes between the necessary and sufficient logical or causal conditions of satisfying an imperative, meaning a universal imperative (which is what he thinks any moral statement amounts to). He applies this distinction to such imperatives as (A1) 'All men must march' (dMA 701a13) and (B1) 'I must make what is good' (dMA 701a17). Then (A3) 'I must march' gives us a necessary, but not sufficient, condition for the satisfaction of the imperative (A1). It is a necessary condition that I should march, if (A1) all men are to march and (A2) I am a man. But if I am the only one who marches, then this is not a sufficient condition for the satisfaction of (A1), 'All men must march'.

On the other hand (B3), 'I must make a house', gives us a sufficient, but not a necessary, condition for the satisfaction of the imperative (B1). If (B1) 'I must make what is good', and (B2) 'A house is a good thing', then my action expressing (B3) is sufficient to satisfy (B1). But

there are indefinitely many other good things I could have made –
daisy chains, romantic novels, box girder bridges – any one of
which would have satisfied (B1), as it stands, equally well. So (B3)
expresses an action the performance of which is a sufficient but not a
necessary condition for the satisfaction of (B1).

Hare's point is that Aristotle cannot have it both ways. The
necessary conditions of some moral imperatives can be satisfied by
action; the sufficient conditions, of others; the necessary and
sufficient conditions, of none. What makes the difference is where
the universality comes in the first premise.

This is a neat argument, which would surely succeed, if Aristotle's
practical syllogisms, in canonical form, began with a universal
imperative of either of the two types that Hare envisages.
Unfortunately, however, as we have already seen, they do not. The
validity of a practical syllogism will not be subject to Hare's kind of
lacuna if (in line with dA 434a 17–20, and as I have argued in (b–d))
its first premise states simply that, for such a sort of person, this sort
of conduct is right and appropriate, and that this action here would
be a case of that sort of conduct, and that I am that sort of person; so I
should do it. At least if it concludes in a proposition, this kind of inference, as a piece of imperative logic, seems difficult to fault on logical
grounds, loosely phrased though it may (necessarily) be. But even if it
concludes in an action, my suggestions about how actions can express
propositions might be brought to bear, to give the conclusion that it
can still be sensible to talk about the 'validity' of practical syllogisms –
provided it is recognised that this is analogical talk.

3.5.　CONCLUSION

In concluding this chapter, I bring to a close the first part of my
exposition of Aristotle's theory of the voluntary. By now it should be
plain what, on my account, Aristotle thinks voluntary action is, and
how the nature of the voluntary is, for him, relevant to the problem
of human freedom.

On Aristotle's view, we may say of voluntary action that it is
action which is not compelled or done under duress; not done in
ignorance; and not irrational. More informatively, we may also say a
good deal about what an action must be like for it to satisfy these
three conditions. It must originate within the agent, the agent being
able to do otherwise. It must be action on well-founded information

and moral belief(s) or other pro-attitudes, where 'well-founded' means that the agent who has the information and holds the moral belief(s) has, and has employed, the appropriate epistemological expertises for gathering information and formulating moral belief(s). And the action must be rationally explicable by means of a process of practical reasoning which is at least potentially, and in the ideal case actually, occurrent in the agent.

If there are any actions which do satisfy these three conditions, then in Aristotle's view there is voluntary action. And if there is voluntary action, then there is free action; for to talk of free action could mean no more than to talk about voluntary action.

> Virtue is up to us, as likewise is vice. For in those cases where it is our choice if we act, it will also be our choice if we do not act; in cases where consent is possible, so is refusal. Thus if it is up to us to act, where acting would be good, it is also up to us to refrain, where refraining would be bad; and vice versa. Now since it is up to us to do good or bad things, and likewise to refrain from doing them; and since how we act was the criterion of whether we are good or bad people; it follows that it is up to us whether we are worthwhile or worthless people. For the saying that "No one's a willing scoundrel, nor yet unwillingly blest" – the latter part of this seems true, the former false. It is true that no one is unwillingly blessed; but wicked-ness is voluntary – unless we are to contradict what has just been said, and man is not to be called the origin and progenitor of his con-duct, just as of his children. But if that seems right, and we cannot trace back our conduct to other sources than those within us, then what has its origins in us is up to us and voluntary. (NE 1113b6–22)

In line with what I have been arguing, Aristotle holds that 'free action' is nothing else but voluntary action as he defines it: so the NE III.1 account of the voluntary and involuntary covers all the states which count as either. His theory of voluntary action is meant to be exhaustive as an account of free action. There is no free action which is not voluntary action in the sense which Aristotle gives that term.

But here there arises, for Aristotle's account, a question which the phrase 'No one's a willing scoundrel' (1113b15, above) might seem to presage. What about the case of akrasia? How does this fit into Aristotle's theory of the voluntary; is *it* not a case of voluntary or free action which does not fit his theory? To that question, lastly, I turn in Chapter 4.

4

The Varieties of Akrasia

In this chapter, I will first try to show that, if my account and development of Aristotle's theory of the voluntary in Chs 1–3 is right, then there is a way of dealing with a problem which the phenomenon of akrasia presents for his theory (4.1). I shall develop this line of argument by reference to the modern debate about akrasia, and then relate this debate to my account of Aristotle. The line of argument which I develop was, in principle, open to Aristotle, but he did not use it, because, among other reasons, he did not develop the notion of a third condition of voluntary action which I have claimed is implicit in his work. Then (4.2) I will consider Aristotle's actual treatment of akrasia in NE VII; and point out that, intentionally or not, Aristotle nowhere in this account discusses *full* akrasia. He could have offered a deductive proof of the impossibility of full akrasia; but what he actually offers is an inductive demonstration of the non-occurrence of full akrasia. Finally, in 4.3, I will point to some instances of the great variety of kinds of partial akrasia (or akrasia-like conditions) which exist. This chapter aims to show that, to the Aristotelian account of voluntary and free action which I have presented in Chs 1–3, the existence of these partial akrasias which Aristotle does discuss not only is no threat; it actually provides an interesting supplement to that account.

4.1. HOW TO SOLVE THE PROBLEM OF AKRASIA

At a time t someone, N, is confronted with two courses of action X and Y; N believes N can do either X or Y at t, but not both; at t N judges, unconditionally, that N should not do X and not Y at t; and nonetheless N, acting fully voluntarily, does X and not Y at t.

If this description is satisfied, then there is *akrasia*, as I shall call it, following Aristotle. (As with *proairesis*, and for the same reasons, I shall resist the temptation to translate the Greek term. Though the phenomenon has had various English names in recent discussion –

88

e.g. 'backsliding' or 'hypocrisy' or 'moral weakness' (Hare (1952), (1963)), 'weakness of will' (Davidson (1980), Charlton (1988)), 'incontinence' (Davidson (1980)) – these English names beg important questions.)

Does akrasia occur? Some philosophers, more or less following Aristotle (NE 1145b28), have taken it to be a rather obvious truth of experience that it does. Other philosophers, more or less following Socrates (*Protagoras* 355c), have taken it to be a rather obvious truth of logic that it does not. For the former school, the problem of akrasia is the problem of explaining how akrasia is possible. For the latter school, it is the problem of explaining why akrasia is not possible.

Richard Hare's and Donald Davidson's celebrated treatments of akrasia display this contrast very well (Hare (1952) and Hare (1963); Davidson, 'How is Weakness of the Will Possible?', in Davidson (1980), pp. 21–42). And, as Justin Gosling has recently observed (Gosling (1990), pp. 196–7), modern discussions of akrasia have mainly taken their cue from one or the other of these treatments. Re-examination of the alternatives which Hare and Davidson offer us suggests a way of reconciling the attractive, but apparently incompatible, intuitions on which they work. It also suggests a way of doing justice to a third intuition.

Hare's explanation why akrasia is not possible, at least not in the full-blooded sense in which many think it is possible, follows directly from his account of what moral beliefs are. On Hare's account, any belief is a moral belief if and only if it displays two features, prescriptivity and universalisability. The idea of prescriptivity is that 'Moral judgements, in their central use, have it as their function to guide conduct' (Hare (1963), p. 70). And the idea of universalisability is this: If I make judgement J1 in situation S1, then J1 is a universalised judgement if and only if, when I make J1, I thereby commit myself to making the relevantly similar judgements J2–Jn in all relevantly similar situations S2–Sn.

Hare thinks that these two requirements are together necessary and sufficient to characterise moral beliefs. To require of moral beliefs only that they should be universalisable, and not also prescriptive, would let in as a moral belief, e.g., 'This thing is red' (Hare (1963), p. 11). To require only that they should be prescriptive, and not also universalisable, would let in as a moral belief, e.g., 'I will jump/ want to jump this queue'.

So Hare can dismiss the possibility of full-blooded akrasia like this. If akrasia means that I act against a moral belief in Hare's sense, then Hare can simply deny that any belief against which I in fact acted could be a moral belief. It must be 'off colour' in 'one of the many ways that are possible' (Hare (1963), p. 68). For if a belief of mine is both fully universalisable and fully prescriptive, then necessarily, I will act on it unless something prevents me. For Hare it is a point of logic, a point about the use of words, that any case where I appear to have a fully-formed moral belief, but act against it, must be a delusion. In a sense then there is no akrasia, but there are some kinds of case which look like it:

> So difficult is it, in fact – so great is the strain between pre-scriptivity and universalisability in certain situations – that something has to give: and this is the explanation of the phenomenon of moral weakness.
>
> Hare (1963), p. 73

Davidson, on the other hand, means to explain how akrasia is possible. Though he does not put it quite like this, his method is, in effect, to distinguish three (not two) kinds of practical judgements: (i) *sans phrase* judgements, (ii) *prima facie* judgements, and (iii) 'all things considered' judgements.

(i)   *Sans phrase* judgements are practical judgements which are indefeasible, final, and unconditional; an example would be the unqualified 'N should do *A* at *t* and not *B*', where this decision does not fail to lead to action. For it is *sans phrase* judgements which stand in direct causal relation to actions.

(ii)   *Prima facie* judgements, on the other hand, are qualified or, as Davidson says, 'relational' practical judgements. Their persuasive force depends on their relation to evaluative generalisations about actions which can only provisionally be assumed to hold good (Davidson (1980), p. 39). Thus, e.g., the judgement that '*Prima facie*, N should do *A* at *t* and not *B*' would depend on the generalisation that actions of *A*'s action-type are as a rule preferable to actions of *B*'s action-type. *Prima facie* practical judgements, then, lack the practical cogency of *sans phrase* judgements.

(iii) Davidson's third kind of practical judgement is the 'all things considered' judgement, the judgement based on all (or is it: the majority of?) the evidence available.

Now it might seem that the judgement 'All things considered, N should do *A* at *t* and not *B*' can simply be equated with the *sans phrase* judgement 'N should do *A* at *t* and not *B*'. But the nub of Davidson's argument for the possibility of akrasia is to deny this equation. Despite some equivocation on the point (Davidson (1980), p. 40, para. 2), it seems fairly clear that his central claim is that (iii) 'all things considered' judgements are equivalent, not to (i) *sans phrase* judgements, but to (ii) *prima facie* judgements. Hence Davidson can say that the 'all things considered' judgement, against which the akrates acts, is not a *sans phrase* judgement, but a *prima facie* judgement. For Davidson, this counts as establishing the possibility of akrasia because there is no logical contradiction between the akrates' two judgements. For an 'all things considered' judgement, being logically equivalent only to a *prima facie* judgement, cannot conflict with a *sans phrase* judgement.

Hare and Davidson seem to me to represent two extremes, between which I want to find a mean. For in important respects I find myself agreeing and disagreeing with both of them.

Hare's central intuition that there is something logically wrong with the very idea of akrasia is one which many have found suspiciously aprioristic. So Lemmon:

> Hare should not have defined value judgements in such a way that sincere assent to them entails an imperative leading to action, since in quite normal senses of the word a man precisely does assent to a value judgement sincerely and still fails to act accordingly, in the situation of akrasia.
>
> Lemmon (1962), p. 144

But, *contra* Lemmon, I think Hare was on to something here. I think that there is a sense in which there is something logically incoherent about the very notion of akrasia. My disagreement with Hare is only about where this incoherence is to be located. For I agree with Davidson that what is in question in the problem of akrasia is not the nature of moral belief as such, but the nature of practical rationality: 'Incontinence is not essentially a problem in moral philosophy, but a problem in the philosophy of action' (Davidson (1980), p. 30, n. 14). (This is a point which might also be suggested by a reading of Philippa Foot; v., in particular, her essay 'Are Moral Considerations Overriding?' in Foot (1978).)

On the other hand, Davidson seems to argue against (Hare's?) idea that akrasia is a logical impossibility via an argument that the practical reasoning which leads to akrasia involves no logical contradiction. Thus Davidson seems happy to admit that the akratic agent acts against 'rationality' (in Davidson's sense of that word):

> Why would anyone ever perform an action when he thought that, all things considered, another action would be better? ...What is special in [akrasia] is that the actor cannot understand himself: he recognises, in his own intentional behaviour, something essentially surd.
>
> (Davidson (1980), p. 42)

But, though Davidson admits that the akrates acts against 'rationality', what he will not admit is the idea that the akrates' practical deliberation might involve a formal contradiction. No doubt akrasia is unreasonable behaviour, but (Davidson thinks) it cannot, quite, actually be illogical behaviour, in the sense of being based upon a logical mistake. Davidson considers his job done once he has shown that 'the *logical* difficulty has vanished because a judgement that *a* is better than *b*, all things considered, is a relational or [*prima facie*] judgement, and so cannot conflict logically with any unconditional judgement' (Davidson (1980), p. 39, my emphasis).

Two comments here. The first one is incidental: namely, that Davidson seems to take it that *any* case where I do one action when I think that, all things considered, another action would be better must be a case of akrasia. (Indeed, perhaps he even thinks that any case where I do one action when I think that, all things considered, another action is the *best* is a case of akrasia.) But this seems wrong if there can be supererogatory action, as there evidently can. In this case, we should say that akrasia is not concerned with cases where the agent merely does something other than what he sees as the best alternative, but cases of actions that are seen by the agent as *actions he should not do*. My definition aims to reflect this point.

Second, and less incidentally, showing that akrasia is not based on a logical mistake is not the same as showing that akrasia is not logically impossible. After all, anyone who says sincerely that three and three make eight is making a logical mistake, but this does not show that it is logically impossible to make that mistake. *Contra* Davidson, it seems an attractive and plausible suggestion to say that what we are trying to describe, when we deal with akrasia, is a logically confused process of practical reasoning. Of course it would not follow that any description of that process was bound to be confused.

In fact, I will not argue here that (full-blooded) akrasia is based on a logically confused process of practical reasoning. Full-blooded akrasia is not based on anything, because it cannot possibly occur: this is the first point I want to argue. But I will argue one quite similar point, viz. that one important species of akrasia involves a logical incoherence, not between different parts of the same practical reasoning process, but between the practical reasoning process which actually occurs and the practical reasoning process which we might want to infer on the basis of the akrates' actual behaviour. It is just because this is so that I am also inclined to agree with Hare that there is at least one important kind of akrasia (though not the same type) which cannot satisfy without logical inconsistency the description of akrasia with which this chapter begins. And this leads us to the third intuition to which I want to do justice: the sense that there are many different cases which we might be inclined to call 'akrasia': an intuition which, it seems to me, is basic to Aristotle's account of akrasia.

First, my argument that full-blooded akrasia cannot occur. Two preliminary points:

1. In line with my discussion in Section 2.2, I will say that there are such things as practical imperatives. These, very generally, are motivations to act of any and every conscious type. Practical imperatives are of two sorts: some are conditional (CPIs) and others are unconditional (UPIs); and any CPI formulated at time *t* is logically overridden by any UPI formulated at t. The reason for this is that any CPI formulated at a given time is 'contained in' any UPI formulated at that time in the sense that the UPI is formed precisely by the aggregative consideration of all CPIs (or at any rate all CPIs which occur to the reasoner). So the agent might reason, in a very simple case, like this:

(a) I want to go to the pub tonight.
(b) But I said I would visit my aunt tonight, so I ought to do so.
(c) One should keep one's promises unless there is good reason not to; and there isn't.
(d) So, all things (i.e. (a–c)) considered, it is best for me to visit my aunt tonight.

(Notice that while (d) is, in the circumstances, *unconditional*, we need not suppose that (d) is, in any circumstances, indefeasible; cp. Kenny (1975), pp. 91 ff. Practical imperatives are unconditional when I decide that there is in fact no more reasoning to be done, and it is time to act on that practical imperative which has already been formed. But they could only be *indefeasible* if, *per impossibile*, a case could occur in which there could not *possibly* be any more reasoning to be done, any more considerations to be taken on board. Cp. Lucas (1994), p. 290: 'Moral arguments do not proceed *more geometrico*. A geometrical argument is no argument at all unless it is absolutely watertight; a moral argument... is full of possible holes, but nevertheless holds water unless someone succeeds in picking an actual hole.')

In the sequence (a–d), (a) mentions a desire, (b) an obligation, (c) a moral principle and its application. But none of (a–c) is any more than a CPI. The only UPI here is (d). My point is that (d) is arrived at simply by taking into account all the factors conceived by the agent as relevant, which in this case means (a–c).

This piece of practical reasoning, which goes to form the UPI (d), is not, of course, a practical syllogism. It is a practical induction, a dialectical process which issues in the definition, or specification, of (d) as the first premise of a subsequent practical syllogism. The unconditionality of (d) is then 'transmitted', by that practical syllogism, to its conclusion: if the practical syllogism says that getting on the bus is a necessary means to fulfilling the UPI (d), then 'I must get on the bus' will itself become a subsidiary UPI for the agent.

It follows that only some practical imperatives, viz. the UPIs, are directly causes of actions, in this sense: the agent acts upon a UPI because he recognises it as a (sufficient) reason for action. Thus if some agent who acts formulates only a CPI, then something is missing from the explanation of his action as a voluntary action. For, while a CPI does provide some sort of motivation to action, it alone cannot have provided the agent with a sufficient motivation to act. For that we need to postulate that there was also a UPI, even if this UPI differs from the CPI in no respect except that of having been made unconditional (perhaps merely by the agent's decision to see it as unconditional).

2. A recapitulation of the points already made about the conditions of voluntary action in Chs. 1–3: to understand a piece of behaviour as a voluntary action involves three assumptions about that behaviour: (i) that the agent was not compelled to do what she

did; (ii) that she acted without ignorance of any important relevant consideration; and (iii) that her behaviour was rationally explicable, by which I mean that we may assume that it was done as a result of a piece of practical reasoning based on the combination of true belief and unhindered appetition, in the way already described in the last chapter.

Now, given these two points, I can show in what sense akrasia involves a logical incoherence between thought and act; and in what sense the concept of akrasia is itself a logical incoherence. Let us ask: what are the necessary and sufficient conditions for a case of akrasia? I suggest that they are six in number. Three of them together stipulate that the akratic behaviour be a voluntary action. Three of them concern the akrates' beliefs at the time of action, and together stipulate that the akrates must knowingly do what she simultaneously believes it would be better not to do. The latter three conditions are, of course, based on the three conditions of voluntary action which I have argued for. The former three conditions of akrasia bring into play the contrast between UPIs and CPIs which I have just established. These then will be the severally necessary and jointly sufficient conditions for full akrasia:

Beliefs: For X's doing *A* at the time *t1* to be a case of akrasia, X must do *A* at *t1*, and consciously hold at *t1* beliefs which could be expressed in these words:

C1. 'Unconditionally, *A* is not to be done by X at *t1*.'
C2. 'Conditionally, *A* is to be done by X at *t1*.'
C3. '"Unconditionally, *A* is not to be done by X at *t1*" overrides "Conditionally, *A* is to be done by X at *t1*".'

Voluntariness: For X's doing *A* at *t1* to be a case of akrasia, X must also do *A* at *t1* in these three ways:

C4. without compulsion of any external or internal kind,
C5. without important relevant ignorance, and
C6. in a way that is not rationally inexplicable.

Taking these to be the necessary and sufficient conditions of full-blooded akrasia allows me to draw the following three conclusions.

(i) There is a kind of akrasia, namely full-blooded akrasia itself, the very idea of which does indeed, as Hare says, involve a logical confusion – though not the confusion Hare had in mind. The point is that C1–3 are logically incompatible with C6. If C1–3 are satisfied, then it follows that C6 is not satisfied, and vice versa.

How so? Consider again the notion of the rational explicability of a voluntary action. Explaining a voluntary action (I have suggested) means giving an account of the causation of the behaviour which it involves, in terms of the agent's seeing himself as given sufficient reason to do what he does by the unhindered pro-attitudes and true beliefs which he has. The presence in the agent's thinking of such (to the agent) sufficient reasons for action is the essence of any action's rational explicability. Now a sufficient reason for action can only be provided by an unconditional practical imperative. Hence properly to explain any piece of behaviour as a voluntary action is to cite the UPI which provided the sufficient reason for that action's performance.

But consider the fully akratic action, *A*, as just characterised by my C1–6. Upon what unconditional practical imperative is *A* performed by X at *t1*? There is (of course) only one UPI which X, as described above, entertains at *t1*. But not only is this not a UPI to do *A* at *t1*; it is actually a UPI to do *not-A* at *t1*!

By the canons of rational explicability which I have suggested here, the only voluntary action at *t1* of which the beliefs given in C1–3 could be explanatory is any voluntary action or abstention from action which counts as not doing *A* at *t1*. But, in the case of full akrasia, such an action is precisely what we do not have. X does the practical reasoning which, for the purposes of rational explicability, ought to go with voluntarily not doing *A* at *t1*; and yet the action which X does at *t1* – is *A*. It follows that *A*, so performed, cannot satisfy C6. Hence *A*, so performed, is not a voluntary action. And – since full-blooded akrasia is supposed to be voluntary action – *A* is not a case of full-blooded akrasia either.

Thus the sense in which the very notion of akrasia is incoherent is nothing to do with the nature of moral judgement. It is rather the confusion of thinking that a piece of behaviour could be rationally inexplicable in the sense I have defined, and yet still also be a fully voluntary action. A case of full-blooded akrasia, satisfying all of C1–6, would have to be like that. But it is impossible for any case to be like that because unless it is rationally explicable, a piece of behaviour does not qualify as a voluntary action at all, but remains merely unexplained behaviour. About the causation of such behaviour we do not know what we must know to be able to count it as a voluntary action.

(ii) There is also a kind of akrasia – though it is not 'full-blooded' akrasia, like the kind just discussed which is of a logically incoherent form – which does indeed involve what Davidson calls 'something surd', and even an actual logical inconsistency. The inconsistency in question is not so much in the agent's practical reasoning, as between the agent's actual practical reasoning and the practical reasoning that ought to go, but does not, with the agent's action. Take the case where C1–5 are satisfied, though C6 is not (for brevity, call this case (12345)). The agent's thinking leads, or ought to lead, the agent not to do the akratic action; yet the agent does the akratic action. There is nothing logically impossible about the occurrence of this sort of akrasia, even though it seems to involve something very like a logical inconsistency. Such a case is simply puzzling; one is inclined to say of it, with Davidson, that 'In the case of incontinence the attempt to read reason into behaviour is necessarily subject to a degree of frustration' (Davidson 1980, p. 42).

(iii) My third conclusion is an intuition about akrasia shared by such diverse recent writers on the topic as Hare, Davidson and Gosling. This is that there is a great *variety* of cases which look like akrasia:

> We are dying to say: remember the enormous variety of ways a man can believe or hold something, know it, or want something, or be afraid of it, or do something.... These half-states and contradictory states are common, and full of interest to the philosopher.
>
> Davidson (1980), p. 28

> In practice many different kinds of behaviour are commonly described as showing weakness [of the will] which do not feature, or not largely, in traditional accounts. Consideration of some of them suggests a criss-cross of overlapping problems....
>
> Gosling (1990), p. 167

> There are many different methods of backsliding without appearing to.
>
> Hare (1963), p. 76

This intuition seems to have been shared by Aristotle too, to judge by the very various phenomena which he discusses under the rubric of akrasia. How many kinds of behaviour? And how are we to classify them? If there are six severally necessary and jointly sufficient conditions of full-blooded akrasia, then perhaps the way to classify the varieties of akrasia and non-akrasia is by means of the statistical array generated by considering the permutations of the six conditions of akrasia. Since there are 2^6 (= 64) ways in which any six conditions can be either satisfied or not, there will be 64 different types of case answering to all the varieties of partial, full-blooded and non-akrasia which exist, might exist, or demonstrably cannot exist. Examining this array may make it clear which types of akrasia logically cannot occur; what the range of possible partial akrasias is; and what kinds of cases are not akrasias at all.

However, consideration of some of these partial akrasias, near-akrasias and non-akrasias will be deferred until 4.3; what I want to do next, in 4.2, is consider Aristotle's account of akrasia.

4.2.   ARISTOTLE'S ACCOUNT

If full-blooded akrasia existed, it would pose a threat to Aristotle's doctrine of voluntary action. For, as we have seen, Aristotle's account of the origination of action is (leaving aside variations which do not matter here) that practical reasoning generates a *proairesis*, or (in the case of merely voluntary action) some less explicit form of decision to act, by the combination of belief and appetition; and the (actual or potential) *proairesis* in turn generates a voluntary action, unless it is prevented from doing so by the conditions which make for involuntary action (which do not include akrasia). Now akrasia, apparently, is voluntary action (EE 1223a37–b3); yet akrasia is 'against the *proairesis*' (NE 1148a18). From Aristotle's definition of voluntary action it ought to follow that there is no voluntary action which is not caused by (explicit or implicit) *proairesis*. The threat is that full-blooded akrasia may provide a counter example to this claim.

Aristotle could deal with this threat by employing something like my distinction between a CPI and a UPI to deny that anything which could be called full-blooded akrasia ever occurs. He could equate *proairesis*, or the implicit decision to act based on the combination of desire and belief, with the UPI, and the various kinds of conditional motivations with the CPI. Then suppose that a piece of behaviour B occurs in which the agent acts 'against the *proairesis*'. Expressed in my terms, what Aristotle could say is that, because B is not action on any UPI, and hence is not rationally explicable, B is not a voluntary action at all; hence B is not a case of akrasia either.

Aristotle does come quite close to equating *proairesis* with what I call the UPI, and the three kinds of appetition and other kinds of conditional motivations with the CPI. Consider Aristotle's account of the nature of *proairesis* (and deliberation) in NE III.2–3. The central point of this is (Section 3.1) that *proairesis* is neither merely belief nor merely appetition. We can now see that the reason why *proairesis* is not just belief is because belief is, in itself, at most only a conditionally motivating factor – a CPI, in other words; but *proairesis* is unconditionally motivating, because a *proairesis* expresses a UPI. Again, *proairesis* is not just appetition, because the three forms of appetition, although they are motivating factors, are not unconditional motivations – but *proairesis* is, because it expresses a UPI.

Proairesis, then, is a form of motivation which (whether actually or only potentially occurrent) provides a sufficient condition of the occurrence of the action to which it leads. In the terms which I am arguing for, we might say that a complete deliberation gives an unconditional motivation to act – a UPI. It gives such a motivation because (going forwards) a deliberation is incomplete until it actually causes an action (1112b25); and also because (going backwards) a complete deliberation involves not only CPIs but also a UPI.

So, if the real problem about akrasia which Aristotle's account must deal with is the question: 'Can there be voluntary action on what Aristotle classes as a conditional motivation and against what he classes as an unconditional motivation?', Aristotle could have had a neat response to this question. He could have allowed for the possibility of behaviour which goes against an unconditional motivation, and is apparently action on a conditional motivation. But he could also have argued that such behaviour is not explicable by reference to the agent's actual or potential deliberations. For the combination of an unconditional motivation to do X and a conditional motivation to do *not-X* yields an unconditional motivation to do X; but the akratic agent is the person who, in this situation, does *not-X*. Hence there is nothing in the agent's actual or potential deliberations which explains his actions. Hence his behaviour is not rational; and hence in turn his behaviour is not voluntary action.

But this is not, in fact, anything like the account of akrasia which Aristotle does give us in NE VII. Aristotle's account of akrasia in NE VII is dominated by the drawing of distinctions about different senses in which an agent can be said to 'have the knowledge' of something when acting. These distinctions are brought out in response to the Socratic challenge recognised at 1145b23–26: 'It would be strange if, when knowledge was present in the agent, something else could conquer that knowledge and drag it about like a slave.' Aristotle thinks he has met this challenge by 1147b15: 'It seems that what Socrates sought has come about...'.

For Aristotle to treat 'the problem of akrasia' in these Socratic terms is for him not to address head-on what I say is the real problem raised for his doctrine of voluntary action by akrasia – the problem of whether the possibility of akrasia provides a counter-example to that doctrine. Aristotle never takes the swift way with the problem that I have just suggested. What his account does do is itemise a series of phenomena, none of which (plainly enough) is akrasia of a sort that could provide a counter-example to the doctrine of voluntary action. Aristotle's argument against the possibility that some form of akrasia might be a counter-example to that doctrine is, then, inductive where it might have been actually deductive: it has the form '*This* is not an example, and neither is *this*, nor *this*...'. Aristotle therefore has not played the strongest card he might have done to deal with the problem of akrasia. Nonetheless his inductive account is successful, so far as it goes, and full of interesting material, which I shall now examine.

Given the way Aristotle's account of akrasia stands (most of it) between the raising of a Socratic question and that same question's laying to rest, we ought to find a certain unity in the account. And so we do. Nonetheless, we may discern six separate phases in Aristotle's treatment of akrasia, marked out by introducing-words almost as if the phases were meant as separate accounts:

1146b31   'But since we speak in two ways of understanding...'
1146b36   'Again, since there are two sorts of premises...'
1147a4   'But there is a distinction about the universal premise...'
1147a11   'Again, men's having of knowledge occurs in a different way from those we have just now spoken of...'

1147a24 'Again, one may examine the cause in the following scientific way...'
1150b19 'One form of akrasia is impetuosity, the other is weakness...'

These are the six phases so marked:

1. 1146b31–36: the potential/ actual knowledge distinction. (§2a)
2. 1146b36–1147a4: application of this. (§2b)
3. 1147a4–10: the 'syllogism breakdown'. (§2c)
4. 1147a11–24: the conscious/ unconscious knowledge distinction. (§2d)
5. 1147a25–b18: the combined account. (§2f)
6. 1150b19–28: the impetuosity/ weakness distinction. (§2e)

Five of these (given between 1145b24 and 1147b15) have an obvious unity. The relation of the sixth phase to the other five is less clear. And, if Aristotle meant even these first five phases to relate only to the Socratic question, he did not succeed in keeping the issue that clear-cut.

The most complex of these, 1147a24–b18, in which he seems to be trying to bring into play together all the ideas he has raised in phases 1–4, is apparently Aristotle's most full and considered exposition on akrasia. (The sixth account looks like a bit of an afterthought.) As the fifth account is an attempt to combine elements of the first four (and other elements too), it is probably best left till last. The place to start is with the first account, for this seems to be involved in all the others except the sixth.

2a. Potential/ Actual Knowledge

At 1146b33–35, Aristotle distinguishes two ways in which someone can be said to 'have knowledge':

Someone who has knowledge, but is not using it, is said to know; so is someone who is using that knowledge. So the case where a [wrongdoer] has knowledge [that what he does is wrong] but is not considering it will be different from the case where a man is considering what he ought not to do. It would indeed seem strange [if he did wrong when he was considering that knowledge]; but not if he was not considering it.

I have already invoked EE 1225b11–12 as evidence for a potential/actual knowledge distinction in Aristotle (Sections 1.3, 3.3). That distinction is this: I actually know P at $t1$ if I state, to myself or someone else, that P at $t1$; I potentially know P at $t1$ if I could state, to myself or someone else, that P at $t1$, but (for one reason or another) do not do so (and I do not know that P at $t1$ if I neither do nor could state, to myself or someone else, that P at $t1$). Likewise (I said), I formulate, at $t1$, a practical syllogism S actually if I state S, to myself or someone else, at $t1$; potentially if I could have stated S, to myself or someone else, at $t1$; and not at all if I neither do nor could state, to myself or someone else, S at $t1$.

This state of affairs makes it impossible that any case of akrasia the description of which hinges on the actual/potential knowledge distinction could be a case of full akrasia. For the point which Aristotle wants to make about potential knowledge here is that the action which should be performed is not performed because the agent's knowledge is only potential. Evidently this could happen. When, for example, I forget to meet John at the station for an afternoon's trainspotting, I could make the statement 'I said I'd meet John at the station at 2 p.m.', if I was suitably prompted ('Where are you meant to be at 2?'). So I do know the fact, considered simply as a piece of knowledge, potentially but not actually.

But, as far as the explanation of action goes, such knowledge does not count even as potential knowledge. Potential knowledge *which explains action* is knowledge which I act upon, although I make no actual statement of the knowledge (but could if prompted). Thus, if I went to the newsagent's at 1.45 and went straight on, without thinking, from there to the station, this action would display potential knowledge which was motivating the action: although I have not formulated the thought 'I said I'd meet John at the station at 2 p.m.', this is what makes me go to the station. Potential knowledge which explains action is the kind of thing which one could mention – if one were to formulate it – in answer to the question 'Why are you doing that?' But if there is no action to which some potential knowledge K is relevant as explanation, then, as far as the explanation of action goes, I do not potentially know K; I am actually ignorant of K. Thus any case of akrasia which involves such 'forgetfulness' will not be a case of full akrasia (123456), but of akrasia mitigated by ignorance: that is, at most, (1234). Therefore Aristotle cannot appeal to potential knowledge as being part of the description of some sorts of akrasia unless he means that the potential knowledge in question has no influence upon what the akratic does. For if the knowledge is potential in the sense that is not inconsistent with its having a role in the causation of action, then this does not militate against the action in question's being voluntary, and so does not militate against its being full-bloodedly akratic. If Aristotle wanted to show that *that* sort of action is not full-blooded akrasia, he could not do it by pointing out that the knowledge involved is not actualised. However, this is not a problem he discusses: he contents himself with pointing out the possibility that knowledge which ought to be seen as relevant to an action may not be seen at all. And when this happens, of course, we do not have full akrasia.

2b. The Application of this Distinction

Aristotle goes on to apply this idea of akrasia as involving 'forgetfulness' at 1146b36–1147a4:

> Again, since there are two forms of the premisses [sc., both universal and particular], nothing prevents someone who has both from acting contrary to knowledge when his knowledge of the universal is actual but his knowledge of the particular is only potential. For action has to do with particular things.

If someone's knowledge of a particular premise fails to get actualised, and remains only potential (in a form that has no bearing on the explanation of the action), then, as we have just seen, there is no good reason to say that the agent really knows the premise. If it is forgotten information, then it is not (in the relevant sense) knowledge at all.

(Why, incidentally, must it be the knowledge of the particular premise which fails to get actualised? Couldn't the knowledge of the 'universal' fail to get actualised too? Because, as we saw in Ch. 2, the more general, and the more explicitly moral, a principle seems, the less easy it is to envisage it being forgotten.)

2c. 'Syllogism Breakdown'

Aristotle next gives us a second, more complicated, example of his actual/potential knowledge distinction:

There is also a distinction as to the universal. For one universal relates to the agent and one to the thing [cp. NE 1105b309 ff., distinguishing the mean of the thing from the mean relative to us]. Thus, the agent may know that dry food is good for every human, and that he himself is a human, or that foodstuff X is dry food. But that this is foodstuff X – either he may not be exercising this knowledge, *or he may not have it at all*. [My emphasis]

Again, as the emphasised words are meant to show, it is impossible that any case of akrasia the description of which hinges on this sort of breakdown of the syllogism should be full akrasia. If any piece of particular knowledge simply isn't there, as opposed to being *in potentia* only, then something vital is missing from the description of the agent as an akratic. For the agent is ignorant of something which is vital to the syllogism. And (as we have seen) to be ignorant is to be less than fully voluntary; and to be less than fully voluntary is to be less than full-bloodedly akratic.

If there are two 'universals' here, Aristotle does not tell us what the second 'universal' is, which presumably is the one relating to the agent, not the thing. 'Dry food is good for every human' is evidently the 'universal of the thing'. 'He himself is a human', 'Foodstuff X is dry food', and 'This is foodstuff X' are all, surely, particular premises. So what 'universal' is missing? It seems that Aristotle wants us to picture a practical sorites which, made completely explicit, goes like this:

A. Dry food is good for humans to eat.
B. I am a human.
C. Dry food is good for me to eat.

D. Dry food is good for me to eat.
E. Foodstuff X is dry food.
F. Foodstuff X is good for me to eat.

G. Foodstuff X is good for me to eat.
H. This is foodstuff X.
I. [He eats the bit of X.]

Here 'the universal of the agent' is, apparently, (D). (There is also (G): Aristotle must be conflating the second and third syllogisms of this sorites if he thinks that (D) is the only 'universal of the agent'.)

But now what point is Aristotle making by drawing our attention to this 'second' universal? For the premise that he suggests is the mischief-maker in a practical sorites like this is, as we might expect, none of the universal premises (A), (D), and (G). It is one of the particular premises (presumably either (E) or (H)). So what Aristotle really means to do, by drawing our attention to the distinction between the two (or rather three) *universals,* is to make a point about the two (or rather three) *syllogisms* which compose the sorites – and specifically about the *practical* premises of these syllogisms. The point is then that having merely potential knowledge of a practical premise can be a cause of akrasia too. Once again it is appropriate to point out that this sort of merely potential knowledge is for all practical purposes equivalent to ignorance.

2d. The Conscious/ Unconscious Knowledge Distinction

Aristotle has not finished making fine distinctions about the various ways in which actions alleged to be voluntary (and fully akratic) actions can be 'off-colour' because the knowledge they involve is 'off-colour'. Not only (he thinks) is there a type, potential knowledge, opposed to actual knowledge; there are two types of potential knowledge.

> In the state of having knowledge but not exercising it [= potential knowledge], we can see a distinction as to how it is had, so that a person can as it were both have [potential] knowledge and not have it – like a sleeper or a madman or a drunkard. But persons under the influence of emotions are like this.... It is clear then that we can say that akratic agents are like this too. The fact that they speak the words which come from knowledge means nothing... akratic agents speak like actors playing parts. (NE 1147a11–24)

Aristotle is working on reducing the meaningfulness of saying that 'akratic agents have knowledge' till it has come almost to the vanishing point – but is not quite there; except when he reverts to talk about akratic agents as not having certain kinds of knowledge at all. What then is the sense of this distinction which, for want of a better name, I call the 'conscious/unconscious knowledge distinction'? Since Aristotle gives us no particular hints about what it means, apart from his examples, we have to shift for ourselves. One would like to say that the point is that sleepers, madmen and drunkards are under a double counterfactual where the possessors of ordinary (only) potential knowledge are under a single one. That is, a possessor of ordinary only-potential knowledge is in a state where this proposition is true of him: He would normally have been able to tell you the answer to your question if he were asked; but is not so able for the duration of his akrasia. Whereas a possessor of unconscious only potential knowledge is in a state where this proposition is true of him: He would normally have been in the state of the possessor of ordinary only potential knowledge; but, for the duration of his akrasia, is not in that state, even.

This suggestion is at least partly supported by the examples. Drunkards and madmen are afflicted by kinds of abnormal mentality that put them at a double disadvantage when it comes to avoiding akrasia. In the first place, they might be akratic anyway, when not also maddened or drunk. In the second place, madness and drunkenness, whether or not enkratically entered into, certainly do not help us to remain enkratic. Madmen and drunkards will also provide good examples of knowledge that appears to be being 'used', in Aristotle's sense, but in fact is not being: for the causal connections between stimulus and response, and information and knowledge, are all wrong in their cases. The drunkard who repeats the verses of Empedocles (1147b13) is indeed producing 'the words that come from knowledge' (1147a29), at least if you take Empedocles' verses to contain knowledge, but producing them fortuitously. However, this suggestion of a double counterfactual remains only a conjecture. And still the central point to make about this section of Aristotle's account is, once again, the distinction between potential but action-guiding and potential but action-irrelevant knowledge. It is the latter to which Aristotle can appeal to demonstrate that none of the cases which he discusses is a case of full akrasia which might contradict his theory of the voluntary.

2e. The Impetuosity/ Weakness Distinction

Some akrasia is impetuosity, other akrasia is weakness. Some [the weak] deliberate, but through emotion do not abide by the [decisions] which they have reached by deliberation. Others [the impetuous] are led by emotion because they have not deliberated.... The excitable [*hoi ekstatikoi*] are better than [the weak], those who have reason but do not remain in it. For the

[weak] succumb to smaller temptations, and they have previously deliberated, unlike the other sort. (1150b19–22, 1151a1–5)

Aristotle here seems to suggest two ways of accounting for akrasia. Akrasia A, impetuosity, occurs when an agent seems to act voluntarily against an unconditional motivation which she never actually formulates. Akrasia B, weakness, occurs when an agent seems to act voluntarily against an unconditional motivation which she does actually formulate, but does not act upon.

This last distinction, as I say, looks very like an afterthought. The focus of the rest of the discussion is on the status of the akratic with regard to knowledge and ignorance; but this distinction focuses on the akratic's status with regard to appetition and compulsion. Does this distinction, then, raise the possibility of any form of akrasia which would be more threatening to Aristotle's account of voluntary action? I think not. Neither of these 'akrasias', A or B, is in fact a genuine case of full-blown akrasia, and so neither are these counterexamples to Aristotle's account of the voluntary.

If (A) an agent seems to act voluntarily against an unconditional motivation which she never actually formulates, then there are two possibilities. Either (i) she formulates it potentially, in which case her behaviour will be irrational and so, as it does not satisfy condition (6), will not in fact be voluntary action. Or else (ii) she does not formulate it at all, in which case there is no sense in which she holds the belief mentioned in my condition (1).

But if (B) an agent seems to act voluntarily against an unconditional motivation which she does actually formulate, then, again, there are two possibilities. Either (i), if that motivation is unconditional, then her 'action' against it involves her holding the beliefs which satisfy my conditions (1–3); hence her behaviour, while it is a form of partial akrasia (12345), is not voluntary action because it is not rational. Or else (ii) that motivation is not unconditional, in which case her behaviour is either irrational, and therefore not full akrasia, or else is voluntary action (on some other unconditional motivation), but not any sort of akrasia.

2f. The Combined Account (1147a24–b18)

The combined account, as its name implies, contains intimations of at least six quite distinct ways of accounting for akrasia as less than full-blooded, some of which are not compatible with the others:

(i)   'Biological' or 'compulsive' akrasia (a24, b4–9, and cp. 1151a20–24);
(ii)   'Syllogism conflict' akrasia (and
(iii) moral dilemma) (a25–36);
(iv)   'Unconscious' akrasia (b11–13, and 1146b31–36);
(v)   'Not real knowledge' akrasia (a36–b4, b9–11, b13–18);
(vi)   'Syllogism-breakdown' akrasia (one hint in b11, and cp. 1146b36–1147a10).

(i) The passage begins with words that we might translate, though I have never seen them so translated, as follows: 'Or again, one could view the cause of akrasia as being biological – in this way...'. This tendency to account for akrasia in a biological, or physiological, manner is quite marked in Aristotle:

> Fits of rage, and sexual desires, and certain other similar passions, quite evidently alter even the body, and in some cases actually cause kinds of madness. It is clear, therefore, that we should say that akratic agents are in a similar state. The fact that they say the kind of things that come from knowledge proves nothing. Men in these states I have mentioned recite proofs and the words of Empedocles. New students chant together arguments that they do not yet understand. But knowledge [, to be truly understood,] has to grow into your very nature (*dei gar symphuenai*) – and this takes time. We might say that akratic agents' words are like those of actors. (NE 1147a14–24; cp. 1151a20–24)

Reason decides what to do, but is swept away by some compulsive passion. Its direction remains right; but its movement in that direction is about as effectual as it would be for me, once embarked on an express train, to start walking down the train back towards the station where I got on. In a case like this, human rationality is no more than a veneer. To talk of it merely obscures what is really going on. The claim to want to do the right is just talk, even if sincere talk. The real and effectual power in the agent is some urgent desire or passion which drags the agent about like a slave – an internal compulsion, in fact (cp. Section 1.2c). The idea is one that would have appealed strongly to the Euripidean Romantic Irrationalists Aristotle seems so against (NE 1110a28).

If the cause of this kind of akrasia is biological, is in one's nature, then this kind is not full akrasia. It is a kind of partial akrasia which resembles 'subhumanity' (*theriotes*) – for objectionable behaviour which results from nature is, by definition, subhumanity (NE 1148b15–1149a20; cp. the description of animal 'motivation' at dMA 701a29–36). The similarity to actions done in drunkenness and sleep of this kind of akrasia is noted by Aristotle (NE 1147b7–9). But this very similarity suggests more a pathological state in which normal rational decision is impossible, than anything like the clear and conscious decision to do wrong which would have to be a constitutive part of full akrasia.

The victim of such a pathological state is not clearly a voluntary agent at all, at the time when he is such a victim. Aristotle would say that it was up to the agent not to become this sort of person (NE 1114a4–7), or in the one-off case, not to get drunk on this occasion (1113b33–35), or otherwise to avoid situations of temptation. The cases where the agent made the decision to get drunk, or to become the kind of person he now is, are clearly closer to full akrasia than anything the agent does while in the fit of passion or booze. It follows that action on such internal compulsions is not itself full akrasia. In my schema, it will at most be either (1235) or (123).

(ii) There seems no necessary connection between this biological argument presented at a24 and b4–9, and the very different argument about the form of the practical syllogism involved presented at a25–36. The 'two syllogisms' idea helps us see how close to being rational partial akrasia can be. But it is not obvious why this 'two syllogisms' shape, where one of the syllogisms is simply overridden by the other through the action of desire, should always or necessarily fit together with a biological compulsion. It is hard to imagine a case of akrasia where there were two conflicting syllogisms but no compulsion. Such a case would not really be a case of (even partial) akrasia. But it is not hard to imagine a case where there was a compulsion, but no 'two syllogism' form. Such a form would obviously be less like full akrasia, inasmuch as the akratic action is not rationally chosen. But my point is simply that the 'two syllogisms' explanation and the compulsion explanation are not necessarily parts of the same explanation.

When there are two syllogisms present to me, either I will recognise that I agree with the universal premise of one but not the other, yet still end up acting on the one I disapprove of. This will be a very strong form of akrasia like (12345) – but it will not be full akrasia, for it cannot satisfy the rationality requirement. Or

(iii) I will not be sure which universal premise I approve of, and vacillate. While I vacillate, I am not in a state which is very like even partial akrasia. My position is, rather, one of moral dilemma (such as (3456) or (456)). I am confronted with two alternatives (or more? –Why not?), both of which may seem good to me, or (for that matter) bad, by different and perhaps incommensurable-looking standards. If I resolve this dilemma, and act accordingly, I am no kind of akratic. If I resolve it, yet act against my resolution of it, then what I will be undergoing is likely to be (12345) again. If I act while this dilemma is still unresolved, then again it is unclear that I am any kind of akratic agent, for condition 1 is not satisfied: I am not clear that I disapprove of what I do, even if I am not clear that I approve of it either. Such a case will be (3456), (456) or the like.

(iv) 'Unconscious' akrasia (b11–13; cp.1146b31–36 and EE 1225b11–13). This, again, is not inconsistent with biological akrasia; but it is not a necessary concomitant of it either. A physiological compulsion may cause me to lose sight of what I normally know to be right; but, as I said, it may also carry me protesting on. Getting myself in a state, like drunkenness, where I 'forget myself' is often combined in practice with getting into a state where I cannot control myself; but need not be.

As I have already argued, full akrasia could not involve anything like what Aristotle means by merely potential knowledge, or unconsciously held knowledge, of the sort that does not guide action. While I am unconscious in *this* way of an item of knowledge, I am, for all practical purposes, ignorant of it. So there is no counter-example to Aristotle's theory here, either.

(v) 'Not real knowledge' akrasia (a36–b4, b9–11, b13–18). The suggestion is that there are two grades of knowledge possible, and that the type which gets 'dragged about like a slave' is only the lower grade, so that no such case is a case of full-blooded akrasia. It seems inconsistent of Aristotle to pursue this idea. He himself has already rejected the (Platonist?) suggestion that, in akrasia, it is only belief, and not knowledge, which gets dragged around: 'Many who only have beliefs yet have no doubts, but think themselves to have exact knowledge' (1146b26–27). But at b16–18 he seems to be arguing for something very like this suggestion himself:

It does not seem to be the true sort of knowledge that is present when the fit (*pathos*) [of akrasia] occurs; nor is it true knowledge that is dragged about by the fit, but perceptual.

Supposing that perceptual awareness is somehow second-rate as knowledge, how does this help explain how such akrasia as this is not full-blown akrasia? Aristotle's reply might be that full-blown akrasia would have to be action against principle, not factual knowledge, and moreover against knowledge of principle, not mere surmise about principle: see below, 4.3, third distinction. This seems implausible: the man who pretends that this biscuit he steals is not anyone else's seems just as full-bloodedly akratic as the man who pretends that stealing biscuits is not wrong. But I pass on.

(vi) 'Syllogism-breakdown' akrasia (one hint in b11; cp. 1146b36-1147a10). The hint I mean is:

This opinion the akratic either does not possess or possesses it only so as to be able to repeat Empedocles like the drunkard does....

Once again: to possess some knowledge, but 'only potentially' in the sense that Aristotle means, and not to possess it at all are not, where the explanation of action is concerned, distinct. Aristotle himself seems to blur the distinction here, in spite of the fact that the 'unconscious akrasia' argument depends on it.

If the akratic does not have the right particular premise at all, not even potentially, then the syllogism breaks down. Either the akratic will have no opinions on the object of perceptual awareness in question, in which case (a) he is ignorant and (b) no syllogism, right or wrong, is possible; therefore his case is not one of full akrasia. Or else he will have a wrong opinion, in which case a wrong syllogism is possible. But since the wrongness of this syllogism derives from a particular piece of ignorance, this is not full akrasia either.

Thus 'syllogism-breakdown' akrasia is action in ignorance too, and so no closer to full akrasia than (1234).

Here then is how Aristotle discusses various forms of akrasia, and proves, case by case, that no such form is the full form of akrasia. On the one hand, his argument establishes that no example of full akrasia has yet been produced. On the other hand, it fails to establish, as any inductive argument is bound to, that no case of full akrasia *could possibly* be produced. I have pointed out that there is a way of doing this. But this is my thesis, not Aristotle's.

4.3. THE VARIETIES OF AKRASIA

On the other hand, the way Aristotle argues does show how very profuse the sub-species of partial akrasia are, and how many ways we might explain some psychological phenomenon and still call it (partial) akrasia. His catalogue, despite its problems, is full of interest; but perhaps it is not anywhere near complete. And so from Aristotle's catalogue to mine. As a coda to this essay, I will list some interesting forms of partial akrasia, and conditions more or less like partial akrasia, drawn from my array of the 64 permutations of C1–6. It will be obvious that none of these conditions (some of which, though not all, Aristotle mentions) counts as full akrasia in my sense, since none of them satisfies all of C1–6.

(Remember first that we know that some forms of akrasia, viz. those involving the satisfaction of both C1–3 and C6, are logically impossible: which rules out not just (123456) but also (12346), (12356), and (1236).)

I.   Failure of Condition 1
((23456), (2345), etc.)

1. Plain and simple ignorance that one is doing wrong, (a) when one isn't, (b) when one is.

Whether the others who think that I am doing wrong are right to think so or not, still I am plainly not acting against my own moral beliefs in this case. Ignorance is worth mentioning mainly because there are often cases where apparent akrasia can be explained by ignorance.

2. Incommensurability dilemmas.

If I genuinely accept the claims both of filial duty and of patriotism, I may face a dilemma when my choice is to fight with the Free French or care for my aged mother. I may truly not know what I should do, and hence form no unconditional practical imperative. But if (a) I resolve my dilemma, and act accordingly, then this is straightforwardly not akrasia. If (b) I resolve my dilemma by forming a UPI, but act contrary to my UPI, then this is a form of akrasia which does not satisfy C6. And if (c) I fail to resolve my dilemma and form no UPI, but still act on one or the other of my CPIs, then again my action cannot satisfy C6, since I act on no UPI.

(I do not act against my better judgement; I haven't got a (firmly held) better judgement.)

The subject of moral dilemmas and incommensurability is very interesting, but I doubt that that subject is central to the study of akrasia. (Apart from the above considerations, the study of akrasia is a study of so many different phenomena that, in a way, nothing is central to it.)

3. Uncertainty about a moral principle, which plays the part of an unconditional practical imperative, leading one to act against it. (Mere belief being mastered.)

Contra Aristotle (NE 1146b24 ff.; but cp. 1147a36–b4, discussed above), there seems no good reason why the difference between (mere) belief and (supposed) knowledge should not make a good deal of difference to how easily I slip into akrasia. Of course Aristotle is right that 'Some men hold no less firmly to what they only believe than others to what they actually know – as Heracleitus makes clear' (NE 1146b29). But this is just a statement of the difference between objective certainty (here OC) and subjective certainty (here SC); and there are some other interesting distinctions around.

SC is feeling sure that *p*, the certainty found in some kinds of religious faith, and not necessarily supported by anything outside itself. OC is having good reasons to be sure that *p*, the kind that was supposed by Logical Positivists to be most characteristic of the certainties of mathematicians and scientists. OC and SC are not mutually exclusive. OC often engenders a sense of SC; SC is not inconsistent with a hunt for reasons, which if we find them may lead to OC as well.

Aristotle argues that we can't say that the difference between SC alone and SC + OC is significant for akrasia, because akrasia is a matter of what goes on in the agent's own deliberations. Therefore what matters for akrasia is SC. This, no doubt, is correct; but what about the possible degrees of SC? I am (let us say) strongly tempted to go to bed with my neighbour's wife. But I also have a firm conviction, a matter of complete SC, that it would be wrong to do so. In these conditions, it is (*prima facie*) most unlikely that I will go to bed with my neighbour's wife. But suppose that my conviction that I should not bed my neighbour's wife is weaker than complete SC. Surely it is plausible to say that, the weaker my anti-adultery conviction, the more likely I am to end up an adulterer? So, in the sense of 'believe' that we oppose to 'know' ('You don't know that, you just believe it'), it does seem that a distinction between moral knowledge and moral belief is relevant to some forms of partial akrasia. So, for example, with Pierre Bezuhov in *War and Peace*:

> 'It would be nice to go to Kuragin's,' he thought, but immediately recalled his promise to Prince Andrei not to go there again. Then, as happens to people who have no strength of character, such a passionate desire came over him for one last taste of the familiar dissipation that he decided to go. And the thought immediately occurred to him that his word to Prince Andrei was not binding because before he had given it he had already promised Prince Anatole to come. 'Besides,' he reasoned, 'all these "words of honour" are mere convention and have no precise significance, especially if one considers that by tomorrow one may be dead, or some extraordinary accident may happen to sweep away all distinctions between honour and dishonour.' Arguments of this kind often occurred to Pierre, nullifying all his intentions and resolutions. He went to Kuragin's.
>
> Tolstoy, *War and Peace*, Ch.1

4. Failing to see that this action is covered by a moral principle of which one is aware.

I may hold a UPI that actions of type *P* are to be avoided; but I fail to see that action *p* is of type *P*. Hence my UPI is not 'transferred' to the conclusion of my practical syllogism. But this is just a kind of ignorance of a particular premise necessary to a correct syllogism of the type favoured by Aristotle.

5. The suppression of one's awareness of the truth of the belief expressed in Condition 1.

This is the first reference I have made directly to another interesting phenomenon which deserves, and receives (but not here), massive treatment of its own: the phenomenon of self-deception. The phenomenon was evidently known to St Paul (v. Romans 2:28). In more recent centuries the idea of self-deception has been of importance to thinkers as important as Butler, Marx, Freud and Sartre. As Patrick Gardiner is not the first to have pointed out, the idea is paradoxical:

It is surely odd to suggest that somebody could try to make, and succeed in making, himself believe something which he, *ex hypothesi*, at the same time believes not to be true.

(Gardiner (1969/70))

The logical perplexities of self-deception seem remarkably similar to those involved in some kinds of partial akrasia. Perhaps we could call it doxastic akrasia, when someone deliberately sets about giving himself new and less inconvenient beliefs: persuading himself that adultery isn't really wrong, or alternatively that this isn't really a case of adultery, etc. (see cases 36a–i).

But if we say that I do this, fully consciously, to myself, and am successful and hence become akratic in my action, an obvious rejoinder follows: 'No, the action was not a case of (full) akrasia, but simply done under a delusion. What was (full, or fuller) akrasia was the act of persuading yourself to hold false beliefs.' (Gardiner: 'One way out… consists in arguing that self-deception is really a form of other-deception…. On such a hypothesis, I am prevented (I do not prevent myself) from recognising certain things about myself…. [But the] difficulty merely re-emerges…. If [the censor] is to perform the functions asssigned to it… it must presumably be aware of its own activity…. But this implies that the censor in its turn is in "bad faith".')

When I consciously make myself unconscious of certain facts of which I am conscious but wish to be unconscious, is this full akrasia? If I choose to suppress facts, then presumably I formulate a UPI to do so, and do so. But this does not necessarily involve me in acting against a UPI. If I do act against a UPI in self-deception, then clearly my act of self-deception cannot satisfy C6 (since this specifies that my act should not be inexplicable, in the sense of being counter to a UPI). But if I do not act contrary to a UPI, then my act cannot satisfy C1 (which specifies the UPI against which any akratic action must go to be fully akratic). Either way, self-deception cannot involve full akrasia.

Doxastic akrasia, I suggest, is an important form of partial akrasia; but (as with moral dilemmas) the temptation should be resisted to make this account the model for all forms of explanation of akrasia. For there are plenty of cases where my akrasia has nothing to do with my suppressing my own beliefs. 'Partial akrasia' can mean being dragged unwillingly about by passion, or denying with complete sincerity the truth of some crucial premise of the syllogism, just as well as it can mean self-deception.

6. Problems of various sorts about the distinction between actual and potential knowledge (sufficiently discussed in 4.2).

II.   Failure of Condition 2
(156) (?)

7. Behaviour with no actual or potential conditional motivation towards the action which expresses akrasia.

This, surely, will only occur when one is behaving completely compulsively. Examples of completely compulsive behaviour are examples of full subhumanity; but they are also examples of partial akrasia.

7*. Not: 'Deliberate suppression of one's awareness of the truth of the belief expressed in Condition 2'.

To do X while actually suppressing one's belief that 'Conditionally (in one way or another), X is to be done by A at $t1$', would be a very strange psychological phenomenon; but it would not count as akrasia.

III.   Failure of Condition 3
(12456 and others)

8. Making an exception.
Cases like that of the person who can't resist the cream cake 'just this once' are often cases where a belief about the relationship between unconditional and conditional motivation is suspended or claimed not to apply on every occasion. One may make an exception (a) of this occasion; or (b) of oneself or a partner in crime, of this agent; or (c) of the dirty deed, of this action.

9. Amoralism.
Wherein one simply denies in general, without trying to make excuses, that the UPI of C1 does override the CPI of C2; and, normally, rejects the UPI. Just as type 7, on the one hand, is very close to full subhumanity, so this kind, on the other, is very close to full-blown wickedness.

10. Deliberate suppression of one's awareness of the truth of the belief expressed in C3.
V. my remarks on type 5.

IV. Failure of Condition 4

11. External duress.
12. External compulsion.
13. Internal duress.
14. Internal compulsion.

The difference between duress and compulsion was explained in Section 1.2d–f.

15-18: Pretending to be under one of these, or (19–31) more than one of them.

If the pretence (a) only fools others, the pretence itself is a kind of wickedness. If (b) it even fools me, the remarks about self-deception for case 5 apply.

V. Failure of Condition 5

32a–i. Total ignorance of different parts of the practical syllogism.
  This, of course, is never anything like full akrasia.
33a–i. Effective ignorance of different parts of the practical syllogism due to the relevant piece(s) of knowledge being only 'potential' (in Aristotle's sense).
34a–i. Effective ignorance of different parts of the practical syllogism due to the relevant piece(s) of knowledge being only 'unconscious' (in Aristotle's sense, whatever that is).
35a–i. Effective ignorance of different parts of the practical syllogism due to deliberate suppression of the relevant piece(s) of knowledge.
  V. case 5.
36. Failure to formulate a practical syllogism correctly because of a fault in the reasoning: i.e., by drawing a wrong inference from good premises by committing any one of the kinds of fallacy that apply to practical reason (for these, see Section 3.4).
37. Formulating a practical enthymeme (a merely rhetorically persuasive argument) instead of a practical syllogism.
  If rhetorical arguments aim (subjectively) at persuading us rather than (objectively) at establishing the truth (dAR 1356a1–4), it is possible that what happens, quite often, in akrasia is that I listen to and act on an emotionally appealing argument because it is easier to

do so than to listen to a logical argument. But if I act on it fully voluntarily, then I do not act on it fully akratically.

VI.   Failure of Condition 6

38. Irrationality is due to only one cause: the lack of an explanation which applies to one's behaviour. See above, 4.1.

And that completes my catalogue. Of course, some of these categories overlap; but on the other hand, several of them are subdivided into different alternatives. I started by showing that, in a defined sense, there is no full akrasia, and hence no great threat to Aristotle's theory of *the voluntary*. This last catalogue, my catalogue, is my final demonstration that partial akrasia is a far more complicated affair than many philosophers give it credit for – though Aristotle's own catalogue shows that he is an honourable exception to this. My original suggestion was that the subspecies of akrasia were to be found among a class of up to 64 types. That is an idea I have not deserted. But this last catalogue suggests strongly that, for each condition except C6, there is not just one way in which it might fail to be satisfied.

If we bear in mind that many of the 38 states of partial akrasia described in my catalogue are mutually compatible, and that many of these states are subdivided into different sub-possibilities, we will see that many of these states could occur together. Which will give sense to my final suggestion. The subspecies of akrasia were to be found among a class of up to 2^6 types; but evidently the sub-sub-species of akrasia are to be found among a class with something of the order of 2^{38} members. If we accept Aristotle's opinion that the akrates is, at least sometimes, at least 'half-wicked' (*hemiponeros*) (1152a18), we will then be in an even better position than Aristotle himself was to appreciate how very applicable to akrasia is the untraced line of verse which he quotes so approvingly at NE 1106b35:

The good are all of a sort, but the bad are many and various.

Part II

Augustine

5
Voluntariness and Responsibility in Augustine

The concept of 'free will'... is the most infamous of all the arts of the theologian for making mankind 'accountable' in his sense of the word, that is to say for *making mankind dependent on him*... the doctrine of will has been invented essentially for the purpose of punishment.

Nietzsche, *Twilight of the Idols*, tr. Hollingdale, p. 53

If it is not by the exercise of will that we do wrong, no one at all is to be censured or admonished. If you take away censure and admonition the Christian law and the whole discipline of religion is done away with. Therefore it is by the will that sin is committed.

Augustine, *de Vera Religione* 27

We in remorse are a radical minority within the social work community. We believe that not every wrong in our society is the result of complex factors such as poor early learning environment and resultative dissocialised communication. Some wrong is the result of badness. We believe that some people act like jerks, and that when dealing with jerks one doesn't waste too much time on sympathy. They're jerks. They do bad things. They should feel sorry for what they did and stop doing it.

Garrison Keillor, 'The Current Crisis in Remorse', 1989

5.1. INTRODUCTION

My analysis of Augustine's doctrine of human freedom to act begins in the same way as my analysis of Aristotle's: with an account of the negative conditions which Augustine thinks necessary for voluntary action. The same beginning, for the same reason: because – as I argue – the philosophical 'problem of freedom' is no more and no less than a

121

problem in the theory of action. To be able to give the full conditions of voluntary action is to be able to give those of free action also.

First I argue (5.2) that Augustine's interest in voluntariness stems from his concern, as an apologist, with responsibility for evil. Then (5.3) I survey (some of) his conditions for voluntary action. It will appear that, like Aristotle's, Augustine's theory of the voluntary has an important negative aspect. For him too the voluntary is at least partly defined by exclusion. Does his theory, again like Aristotle's, also have a positive aspect? I address this question in Ch.6.

As I note in 5.4, fallen humans' actions, being vitiated by what Augustine calls *ignorantia* and *difficultas*, fail to satisfy his own negative conditions for voluntary and responsible action. Nonetheless such actions are, apparently, responsible. I explain this (5.5) by noting Augustine's crucial distinction between culpable and non-culpable ignorance and compulsion.

5.2.   THE LINKING OF VOLUNTARINESS AND RESPONSIBILITY

First, why should a Christian pastor and apologist be interested in an arcane philosophical question like the nature of the voluntary? Augustine himself tells us why. In his youth he was much troubled by the evergreen question 'Where does evil come from?' (Conf. 3.7, dLA 1.4). This question led him into Manichaeism. It was only when he had a satisfactory answer to it, in Christian Platonist terms, that Augustine returned to the Catholic Church.

The problem which Augustine refers to by his question 'Where does evil come from?' is this one:

> We believe that everything that is comes from the one God: and yet that God is not the author of sins (*peccatorum*). But, if the sins arise from those spirits (*animabus*) which God created, and those spirits arise from God, one wonders why those sins cannot be referred, by one small step (*parvo intervallo*), to God. (dLA 1.4)

Nietzsche's barbs, in my first epigraph to this chapter, are aimed at Augustine. For it was Augustine's efforts to solve this problem, the problem of evil, that induced him to develop his 'free will defence', his version of the Biblical argument (Gen. 3, Mk 7.14:23, Jas 1:13–15) that evil results from the exercise of creatures' God-given autonomy, not from God's own action: 'Each evil person is the author of his own evil-doing' (dLA 1.1). Hence Augustine, and his commentators, are usually quicker to spot the difficulties he makes in theodicy in the dLA than those he makes in the theory of action. This, of course, is for the good reason that theodicy, not theory of action, is what Augustine thinks he is up to: it does not follow that his remarks are not interesting for the contribution they (perhaps unwittingly) make to the theory of action.

Consider the first argument in the dLA:

> If we believe that God is just – and it would be blasphemy to deny it – then we must believe that he rewards the good with prizes and the evil with punishments…. If no one pays a penalty which they do not deserve to pay (which we are bound to believe, since we believe that this universe is governed by divine providence), then God is the author of those evils which are punishments, but absolutely not the author of those evils which are not punishments [i.e. sins]…. Evil deeds are punished by the justice of God. For they would not be justly punished unless they were done voluntarily. (dLA 1.1; cp. dVR 27)

The argument is this:

1. God punishes some actions.
2. God is just.
3. God's punishment would not be just unless the actions punished were sins.
4. Therefore some actions are sins. (1, 2, 3)
5. But no action is a sin unless it is voluntary.
6. Therefore some actions are voluntary. (4, 5)

The argument shows clearly enough why Augustine is interested in voluntary action: because he sees a necessary connection between voluntariness and responsibility. If there are no creaturely voluntary actions, then the only voluntary agent in existence will be God. But if God is the only voluntary agent, then (Augustine thinks) he is, necessarily, also the only responsible agent. In that case everything, good or bad, must result directly from divine agency; and so God himself must be directly responsible for everything, including all the evil in the world. Augustine thinks this an impossible position for a Christian. Hence, as he argues repeatedly throughout his career, Christians are committed to believing that God is not the only voluntary agent.

However, we must distinguish two claims about the relation of voluntariness and responsibility:

1. Any piece of behaviour is a responsible action if and only if it is a voluntary action.
2. Any piece of behaviour is a responsible action if and only if it is either (i) a voluntary action or (ii) a relevantly connected consequence of the right sort (e.g. an easily foreseeable, directly intended, and not disproportionate causal consequence) of a voluntary action.

When Augustine writes, for instance, that 'A sin is so much a *voluntary* evil, that it would not even be a sin at all unless it *were* voluntary' (dVR 27), we might think that he was arguing for (1). But (1) is an unsophisticated and implausibly strong thesis. We have already seen that Aristotle rejected it (NE 1114a4–13): the person who kills someone while blind-drunk is responsible for that killing, not so much because he chose to kill them, as because he chose to get blind-drunk. This distinction between (as we might say) direct and indirect responsibility is also defended by Augustine, both in his early and in his late works. However, the importance of that distinction, as supporting a more fully developed doctrine of original sin, is clearer in his later work:

> Man deserted God and came to deserve eternal evil, for he betrayed the good in himself that could have been eternal. This is the reason why the human race is one whole condemned mass (*universa massa damnata*); for he who first did this has been punished along with the stock that had its root in him, so that no one should be freed from this just and deserved punishment except by undeserved grace and mercy. (dCD 21.12)

So Augustine's 'free will defence' is never simply (1), that the human agent is responsible directly for each and every sin he commits, because each such sin is itself a voluntary action. It is, more subtly, (2): that one original sin by a human agent was a voluntary and hence responsible action, and that all human sins since have been related to that responsible action as relevantly connected consequences of the right sort (what sort?).

5.3.   TWO OF AUGUSTINE'S CONDITIONS OF VOLUNTARY ACTION

It is an important claim to say that voluntariness and responsibility are necessarily connected – whatever it may mean (v. Williams (1993), p.66 ff.). Augustine never abandons this claim, at least not in the qualified form (2). But the claim is not very informative without an answer to a prior and more important question, namely: What is 'voluntariness'? That is: Under what conditions is action properly called voluntary?

Augustine's responses to that question tend, as the dLA illustrates, to be unsystematic. Hence it is that, particularily in Augustine's later work, crucial ambiguities and contradictions on that question pass (conveniently?) unnoticed. Augustine's attention, as we have seen, is on theodicy, not on action theory. Anyway, even the young Augustine usually sees no need to spell out the conditions of voluntary action because he thinks that they are intuitively obvious. Typically, his remarks about them are flanked by bold phrases like 'Who would doubt…?' (dDA 1.15), 'Since nature itself proclaims…' (dDA 1.14), 'Isn't this the view that is repeated by the very shepherds on the hills? By poets in the theatres? By the ignorant at the shows and the learned in their libraries?' (dDA 15). At dVR 27 we have an appeal to the authority of common sense strongly reminiscent of Aristotle's appeals to 'the many and the wise' (v., e.g. NE 1095a18):

> Indeed this is so manifest that none of the few wise or the many ignorant would dissent from it. (dVR 27)

This tone of airy confidence might encourage an unwary commentator to take Augustine's conditions of voluntary action for granted too. But a clear account of these is of the greatest importance for an adequate understanding of the strengths and weaknesses of Augustine's position. And, in spite of Augustine's tendency to gloss over them or only mention them in passing, it is not impossible to give an account of what these conditions are, as represented in the early works. I will base this account on the dLA (Augustine's fullest treatment of the issues) and the dDA (his ablest treatment).

The picture that emerges is remarkably Aristotelian (cp. Ch.1). For a start, the early Augustine agrees with Aristotle in believing that any behaviour, to qualify as voluntary action, must (at the least) satisfy two negative conditions, with which I will deal in this chapter. It must be:

(i) not compelled,
(ii) not done in ignorance.

These conditions are evident, for example, at dDA 14, which gives us one of Augustine's most adequate formulations of the definition of voluntary action: *Voluntas est animi motus, cogente nullo, ad aliquid vel non amittendum, vel adipiscendum*: 'Voluntary action is a movement of the soul, without any compulsion, towards something either not to be lost or to be attained.'

I call this a definition of *voluntary action*. It may fairly be objected that, strictly, what Augustine is defining at dDA 14 is not voluntary action but *voluntas*, the obvious translation for which is generally said to be 'will'. I pause to ask: how are we to translate *voluntas*?

3a. How to Translate 'Voluntas'

Does *voluntas*, as used by Augustine, mean 'voluntary action' or the cause of such action, i.e. 'volition'? The simplest answer is: 'Both'. As many of his interpreters point out (most recently Dihle (1982)), Augustine certainly does use *voluntas* sometimes to mean 'volition' or 'will' rather than 'voluntary action':

> For what is it that makes the *voluntas* bad, when it is the *voluntas* that makes the deed (*opus*) bad? It is this: a bad *voluntas* is the efficient cause (*efficiens*) of a bad deed... (dCD 12.6)

> I feel nothing so surely and intimately as that I have *voluntas*, and by it I am moved to the enjoyment of particular things. (dLA 3.3)

Certainly the presence of *voluntas* is always seen by Augustine at least as a necessary condition for, and the defining mark of, the presence of voluntary action. But Augustine often uses *voluntas* in another way: to distinguish, not volitions from actions, but voluntary actions from other behaviour. When, for example, he writes (dLA 1.30) that humans come to merit the good life *'voluntate'*, he does not mean that they merit it simply by choosing well, but by both choosing and doing well. Likewise, those condemned for bad *voluntas* are not being condemned for evil volitions, but for evil voluntary actions.

Notice, again, that when Augustine makes a distinction between *voluntas* and action which expresses that *voluntas* – as we shall see him doing in the next section – he never says, in Abelardian mode, that what counts for moral assessment is the *voluntas*, and the action is (as good as) immaterial. Rather he says that, if my *voluntas* fails to get actualised in my doings, then this is an insuperable impediment to our being able to speak of me as a voluntary agent at all. Hence a proposal, the usefulness of which will I believe become clear in what follows: that Augustine's talk about the *voluntas* be understood simply as his way of talking about the voluntary – whether that means voluntary action, or choice, or both – and not, as it often has been, as talk about a reified faculty of will constituting a substantial presence in the theatre of the psyche. (Although I myself shall have occasion to translate *voluntas* as 'will', I shall not thereby imply any such reifying doctrine.)

3b. Compulsion

To return to the two negative conditions of voluntary action. The definition that 'Voluntary action is a movement of the soul, without any compulsion, towards something either not to be lost or to be attained' is defended phrase by phrase in the dDA, and it covers nearly everything that the young Augustine believes about voluntary action (except, surprisingly, the question of ignorance). The role of the phrases 'A movement of the soul' and 'towards something either not to be lost or to be attained' in Augustine's positive theory of the voluntary will be discussed in Ch. 6. The words *cogente nullo* cover the question of compulsion. Why does Augustine think these words should be included in the definition of voluntary action? At dDA 14 he writes as follows (notice how this remark fails to cover the question of ignorance; see next page):

> Everyone who acts voluntarily (*volens*) is not compelled, and everyone who is not compelled, either acts voluntarily, or does not act at all.

Augustine thinks that his claim that voluntary action must be uncompelled action is evident, not just from Scripture, but even from nature:

These things we say when nature itself proclaims them within every human whom we may ask without absurdity, from children to the old, from infants' school to the very throne of wisdom.... (dDA 14)

In the dLA, Augustine relies repeatedly – though not always explicitly – on the premise that wrongdoing, to count as sin, must be uncompelled. I give three examples.

(*First example*) One point of Augustine's long argument (dLA 1.16–1.22), that nothing is superior in power to the virtuous soul, except Reason and God, is that it helps him to establish that the virtuous soul cannot be compelled to do evil. For if it was compelled it would not be acting voluntarily, and so not sinning.

> So since nothing, whether equal or greater in power, can make a governing mind, equipped with virtue, into the slave of its desires (*libidinis*)... it remains that nothing else can make a mind go along with desire (*cupiditatis comitem*) except its own *voluntas* and free decision (*propria voluntas et liberum arbitrium*). (dLA 1.21)

(*Second example*) 'Whatever the cause of the action may be, it is done without sin if the cause cannot be resisted. But if it can be resisted, then the agent must resist it if he is to avoid sin.' (dLA 3.50)

(*Third example*) In dLA 3.4–11, Augustine argues that his doctrine of God's foreknowledge of human actions does not endanger his theory of human freedom; what God foreknows is that the human agent will act freely (dLA 3.8). Foreknowledge presents the threat that God's foreknowledge be seen to compel our actions; and this would mean that they were not voluntary actions, nor relevantly connected behaviour. But 'God does not compel anyone to sin, but he does foresee that some will sin of their own voluntary choice (*propria voluntate*)' (dLA 3.10). So likewise there is no reason 'why God should not reward the just man for doing what he foresaw he would' (3.11).

To return to the dDA 14 passage with which I began my consideration of compulsion. The claim made there by Augustine is, apparently, that 'X acts voluntarily' entails 'X is not compelled'. This claim will be true if the absence of compulsion is either necessary, or necessary and sufficient, for voluntary action. Obviously, since I say that the absence of compulsion is not the only condition of voluntary action, my account requires that this condition should only be necessary. But Augustine's 'Everyone who is not forced, either acts voluntarily or does not act at all' is, apparently, a claim that the absence of compulsion is both necessary and sufficient for voluntary action. So where does this leave the negative condition of ignorance?

3c. Ignorance

In spite of this passage, there is in fact plentiful evidence that Augustine did not, in truth, normally neglect the idea that ignorance is a limiting factor on responsible action. Elsewhere in his early writings Augustine clearly does defend that idea, so that the remark of dDA 14 is probably best dismissed as an insignificant slip, and not representative of Augustine's usual theory of responsibility. I give, again, three examples of this defence.

(*First example*) In the dDA itself, at Ch.12, Augustine considers the example of a person whose hand is made to write something obscene while he is asleep. His being asleep exculpates him from the sin of writing rude words either (i) if he is compelled (as above), or else (ii) if he does not know that his hand is going to be used in this way while he sleeps. But if he does know, and does nothing about it when he could have, then 'his being asleep will not help to make him innocent' (dDA 12). Strictly speaking, he will then be indirectly responsible, like the drunken killer. His knowledge meant that he could have avoided getting in a state where his hand would write filth, but he didn't.

(*Second example*) In the early RomsIE, Augustine discusses the 'unforgivable' sin of speaking against the Holy Spirit (Mt. 12:32). He argues against the rigorous (Novationist) view that those who so sin after baptism cannot be forgiven, whereas those who speak against the Holy Spirit before baptism can be. The Novationists said that someone who speaks against the Holy Spirit after baptism could no longer be excused on the ground of ignorance. Augustine counters that it is perfectly plain that people can and do remain ignorant of such important teachings after baptism:

But what about those who received the sacrament of baptism when they were children or even babies, but later were badly brought up and conducted their lives in the shades of ignorance, totally unaware of what Christian discipline commands and forbids? Are we really to say [as the Novationists did] that their sins cannot be accounted sins of ignorance (*peccata ignorantiae deputare*) just because they sinned after they had been baptised? (RomsIE 16)

What is at issue between the Novationists and Augustine is: How wide is the scope of exculpating ignorance? What is not at issue, but is accepted on both sides, is that there is exculpating ignorance. (Note, however, that here Augustine seems prepared to agree with the Novationists that sins of ignorance are nonetheless sins. What he is arguing is that such sins are less culpable, not that they are not culpable at all.) Augustine was arguing that the Novationists' understanding of that notion was insufficiently generous.

(*Third example*) At dLA 3.50, Augustine considers the idea that the experience of deception can sometimes result in a form of ignorance which exculpates:

Or is he perhaps taken in unawares? Then let him beware of being taken in. Or is there some deception so great that it was altogether impossible to avoid it? If it is so, then nothing done through such a deception is a sin. But in this case there *is* a sin. It follows that he could have avoided being taken in. (dLA 3.50)

So, despite the apparent claim of dDA 14, the early Augustine does in fact believe that there can be exculpating ignorance, parallel in kind to exculpating compulsion.

5.4.   *IGNORANTIA* AND *DIFFICULTAS*

However, as early as the dLA there is evidence of the beginnings of a quite different attitude to ignorance and compulsion, an attitude which came to dominate Augustine's later theory of responsibility. For the classical tradition, and with it the early Augustine, the conditions of ignorance and compulsion were restrictions on culpability. But in Augustine's later writings on the subject, it often seems as if what he calls the conditions of *ignorantia* and *difficultas* have become the very *hallmarks* of culpability.

In his later works, Augustine often seems prepared to argue that sin, so far from being – necessarily – neither compelled nor done in ignorance, is typically one or the other, or both. Augustine never renounced any of the central points of his teaching on the subject of responsibility and voluntariness. Yet his emphasis changes so dramatically that it looks at first as if he has done a complete *volte-face*: from the view that *ignorantia* and *difficultas* are conditions which diminish responsibility; via the position that, as 'penal conditions', they are characteristic of fallen humanity; to the view that these conditions are actually culpable in themselves.

'For these two penal states are reserved for every sinning spirit, ignorance and compulsion' (dLA 3.52). As Augustine developed his theory of human nature, he came to think that fallen humans were not just thwarted from the achievement of their wishes by ignorance and compulsion in general. They were, rather, typically subject to specific forms of ignorance and compulsion. What were these forms?

In dLA 3.51–6 Augustine says that fallen man acts wickedly either because 'it is not in his power (*in potestate*) to be good', or by 'not seeing what sort of person (*qualis*) he ought to be' (3.51). It is already apparent that his *difficultas* and *ignorantia* are impediments to voluntary action of quite specific kinds. *Difficultas* characterises the agent who wishes to do what is right, but cannot. *Ignorantia* characterises the agent who does not even have the knowledge of the good that puts him in a position to wish to do what is right.

(Does this mean that Augustine's *ignorantia* is equivalent to Aristotle's 'ignorance of principle' rather than Aristotle's 'ignorance of particulars'? It seems that Augustine does not really take this distinction on board. He is more concerned to make out his own distinction, between voluntary and involuntary ignorance, which (he thinks) is the most morally important distinction. The Aristotelian question, whether there is any difference in moral status between voluntary and involuntary ignorance of principle, apparently does not occur to him.)

Augustine gives us an even more detailed account of the roles of ignorance and difficulty or compulsion in thwarting voluntary action in four works of the early 390s (EPRoms, Simp, 83DQ, EEGal). Here he sees human moral regeneration as proceeding through four stages, summarised by EPRoms 13:

Before the law we [willingly] follow the desires of the flesh, *under the law* we are compelled (*trahimur*) by those desires, *in grace* we neither willingly follow them nor are compelled by them, *in peace* there are no desires of the flesh.

'Before the law' there is complete *ignorantia*, but absolutely no *difficultas*. There is no struggle (EPRoms 14, *non pugnamus*), because the human is in a state of *concupiscentia*, in which he simply follows his natural inclinations, and even approves of so doing (EpRoms 14, 83DQ 66.3). There is nothing to prevent this, for the human has no conception that what he does is wrong (EEGal 46, *non est qui prohibeat*). 83DQ 66.4 gives four Biblical proof texts: Rom. 5:12–13, 7:8–9, 7:13, and 1 Tim. 1:8.

'Under the law' there is no important *ignorantia*, but plenty of *difficultas*, compulsion. The human experiences unsuccessful struggle (DQ 83: *victi peccamus*) against desires which are now perceived, by the recognition which the Law brings, as evil (EPRoms 15, 'We admit that the things we do are evil'; EEGal 46, 'He tries to hold off from sin, but he is overcome'). EEGal adds that the struggle is unsuccessful because the human agent 'does not yet love justice for God's sake and its own sake: he wants justice for himself, to enable him to win his earthly battles'. Hence (says EEGal 46) the sinner 'is dragged along by the weight of worldly desire, and deserts justice'. (This remark has a very Platonic ring; cp., e.g. Republic 439a–440d.) As proof texts 83DQ 66.5 cites Rom.5:20, most of Rom.7:5–25, and Ps. 18:13.

'Under grace' there is no ignorance, and less and less compulsion, since the agent's experience is now of successful struggle with sin (EEGal 46):

For in this life, even if there remain the carnal desires of the body which go with mortality, yet they do not subdue the mind into consent to sin.

Cp. 83DQ 66.3:

No longer are we conquered by the enjoyments of a bad character (*delectatione consuetudinis malae*)... and yet until now we do experience its interference, even if we are not betrayed by it.

This victory is, of course, the result of grace (EPRoms 16):

So comes grace, which is to give freedom from sin and to help the agent's efforts, and add love (*caritatem*) to justice.

Without this grace victory is impossible (EEGal 46):

This cannot happen except by the spiritual love which the Lord taught us by his example and gave us by his grace.

Augustine's proof texts are: Rom. 7:25, 8:1–10, 25 (83DQ 66.6).

'In peace' there is no *difficultas* and no *ignorantia*. There is now no struggle with sin, for sin is finally defeated and the agent is perfected: 'After this sin is extinguished from every part' (EEGal 46).

> The fourth is the state where there is absolutely nothing in the man which resists the spirit, but everything is harmoniously joined and integrated (*connexa*) together and keeps him in one sure peace. (83DQ 66.3)

This stage, of course, is only reached in the life of the Resurrection:

> This is what happens when the mortal body is made living. (83DQ 66.3)

> Then there is perfect peace, because nothing resists us who are not resisting God. (EPRoms 17)

As his scriptural warrant for this Augustine cites Rom. 8:11 (83DQ 66.7). All four of these stages are implicitly identified at Simp 1.2:

> The law is given so that… sin may be demonstrated. And by this very demonstration, the law changes the human spirit to culpability from its previous secure-seeming innocence. It does this so that this very grief [at sin] may turn the convicted human to perceive God's grace, for the sin cannot be overcome without the grace of God.

First, the state of 'carefree innocence'; or rather carefree quasi-innocence, for of course Augustine's theology makes it impossible for him to mean that the human is sinless before the coming of the law; it is, rather, just that his sins are unrevealed (Simp 1.6: 'Not because the law did not exist, but because it had not appeared'). Then the stage of a grief caused by the awareness of the law; then, less clearly here, the two stages of grace and peace.

(With this four-stage progress from wickedness to holiness, it is interesting to contrast four Aristotelian states: complete vice (*akolasia*), failure of self-restraint (*akrasia*), successful self-restraint (*enkrateia*), and the full virtue of temperance.)

Simp 1.11 gives us an opinion on the interesting question of whether *difficultas* applies just to the performance of good actions, or even to the willing of them. There Augustine notes, of the stage where one is under the law:

> Certainly the willing itself (*ipsum velle*) is in our power, for it is very close to us (*quoniam adiacet nobis*); but it is not in our power to perform the good act (*perficere bonum*). (Simp 1.11)

> The agent wills without difficulty, even though he does not so easily do what he wills. (Simp 1.12)

Perhaps we may say that, at the first stage ('before the law'), what the agent lacks, being in a state of ignorance, is both good intentions and good performances. Whereas at the second stage ('under the law'), the agent has good intentions, but he is (through *difficultas*) incapable of any corresponding (good) performances. The role of grace, at the third and fourth stages, is to connect willing with performance. In this area too Augustine's doctrine appears at first sight to have changed substantially during his career; for the later Augustine quotes repeatedly the dictum of Paul that 'God is at work in you *both* to will and to work according to his good pleasure' (Phil. 2:12–13), whereas the earlier doctrine would have fitted better with a pseudo-Pauline 'God is at work in you to work *what you will* according to his good pleasure.'

It is now pretty clear what Augustine means when he talks of *ignorantia* and *difficultas*. The next question is: How did these conditions, so far from being thought exculpatory, come to be seen by Augustine as typical or even diagnostic of culpability?

5.5.   FROM THE EARLIER TO THE LATER THEORY

What enabled Augustine to take this direction was his development, again from what was originally fairly uncontroversial classical material, of the distinction between non-culpable and culpable ignorance and compulsion. He came increasingly to stress the culpable and neglect the non-culpable, until by the late works we hear almost nothing of exculpatory ignorance and compulsion, and a very great deal indeed about culpable ignorance and compulsion.

But it should be noted that what was involved was more a change of emphasis than of doctrine. This is evident from the dLA, in which most of the doctrines usually supposed to characterise only Augustine's late theology can already be found. The dLA, it is true, teaches such typically 'early' doctrines as synergism, the view that God and human work together in the economy of salvation. (So, e.g. when Augustine says that grace is given to those whom God foresees will respond to it: dLA 3.33.) But side by side with this kind of teaching, often in the same breath, comes the 'later' stress on the total efficacy of divine grace and the total inefficacy of anything else. The fact that this emphasis is *not* only found in the later writings, but is there in the earlier works too (though no doubt less stressed), suggests that, by and large, Augustine, in the course of his career as a writer on freedom and the voluntary, did not so much change his position as his nuances – promoting now one side of what he saw as Biblical doctrine, and now the other. This can be nicely illustrated by showing how, for Augustine's 'late' and 'early' doctrines on the issue of culpable and non-culpable ignorance and compulsion, we need look no further than the dLA, where nearly all of them can be found jumbled together.

If we may cut through the attritions, we may suggest that Augustine's most basic teaching on this issue is that 'natural' ignorance and compulsion are not culpable, but 'voluntary' ignorance and compulsion are. Natural ignorance and compulsion are just where the soul begins its journey, even in an unfallen creation. So, at dLA 3.71, Augustine has to deal with a dilemmatic question: 'If the first human was created wise, how could he be seduced? But if he was created foolish, how is God not the author of his vices?' He responds:

> There is a kind of foolishness about what to pursue and avoid which is not just any sort of foolishness, but a corrupt (*vitiosa*) ignorance.' (dLA 3.71)

Which ignorance, then, is corrupt (and culpable), and which innocent (and blameless)? Augustine's answer is that the innocent form of ignorance is that which is not chosen by the agent, viz. natural ignorance. *Pari passu*, the innocent form of compulsion is natural compulsion. Actions done under natural compulsion or ignorance are not culpable for Augustine, for the agent cannot avoid doing them (cp. dLA 3.50, quoted above). This was still Augustine's view when he wrote the dGLA: 'For it is one thing not to know, and another not to want to know' (dGLA 5).

This is a perfectly straightforward view, in which no important ancient philosopher would have seen any problem. But what are 'voluntary' ignorance and compulsion, and why are they culpable in fallen humans? This is where Augustine's teaching in the dLA becomes confusing. Sometimes (an 'early' doctrine, consistent with the view of 'natural' compulsion just outlined) he tells us that they are culpable in fallen humans because fallen humans can themselves avoid them:

It is not accounted a sin on your part if you are ignorant unwillingly, but it is if you neglect to find out what you do not know. (dLA 3.53)

It is not counted as making the soul guilty that it should be naturally ignorant or naturally incapable of something. What matters is that a soul did not *try* to know, or that it did not give the necessary effort to becoming capable of doing right. (dLA 3.64)

At other times, however, we get the 'later' doctrine that they are culpable in fallen humans because Adam and Eve could have avoided them:

Whatever anyone does not aright through ignorance, and which he cannot do even if he wills aright – such deeds are called sins for this reason, that they take their origin from that sin of the free will [which Adam committed]. For that precedent deserved these consequences. (dLA 3.54)

It seemed most just to God on high, who puts all things in order, that we should be born in ignorance and in difficulty and in mortality. For Adam and Eve, when they sinned, fell into error, and into oppression, and into death. (dLA 3.55)

At other times again it is already beginning to appear in the dLA as if such conditions are culpable in themselves:

If these things [*ista*: sc. those which are done from ignorance and difficulty] are not penal conditions for humans, but come about by nature, *then they (ista) are not sins.*' (dLA 3.51)

The question raised by this apparent diversity of opinions is one of culpability. Is human responsibility for sin a matter of what, above, I called direct culpability, or of indirect culpability, or of a mixture? Which of these is Augustine's claim?

(a) Fallen humans are directly to blame for all the wrong actions which they perform.
(b) There are wrong actions which fallen humans perform for which they are directly to blame, and as a result of which they help-lessly perform other wrong actions for which they are indirectly to blame.
(c) Fallen humans are indirectly to blame for all the wrong actions which they perform.

When Augustine talks of ignorance and compulsion as penal conditions, as he often does even in the dLA, it seems at first as if he is defending (a) above. So, for example, dLA 3.52: 'For this is the most just punishment of sin, that he should lose what he was not willing to use well.' The person who fails to take the initiative for good in his own life is punished by the removal of the chance to take that initiative at all.

But then we notice that actions performed in 'ignorance' and 'difficulty' are themselves, sometimes, punishable:

Even some things done through ignorance are to be blamed... even some things done through necessity are to be blamed, in cases where a person wants to do well and cannot. Why else would we hear it said that 'The good that I would I do not, but the evil that I would not, that I do'? (dLA 3.51, quoting Rom. 7:15).

The idea (b) that the kind of culpability in question for such actions is often but not always indirect might seem to be supported by Augustine's contention, in at least two other places, that sins of ignorance are culpable, but culpable in a reduced degree. So in RomsIE 17 Augustine entertains the conclusion that the only venial sins are those committed in ignorance: all others, he seems to be arguing here, are mortal. In dGLA 5, Augustine quotes the same Lucan verses (Lk. 12:47–8) in support of a somewhat similar argument, that 'It is worse for a person to sin knowingly than ignorantly.'

But this argument too seems to be denied by the assertion above, from dLA 3.54, that all fallen human sinfulness is indirect and dependent on the wrong choice of Adam and Eve. So Augustine's position becomes still harder to elucidate: it now seems closer to (c).

But there is a logical problem with (c), inasmuch as indirect responsibility is 'parasitic', logically dependent, on direct responsibility. At least in the sense in which 'responsible' is normally understood, I cannot be indirectly responsible for any doing of mine B unless (i) I was directly responsible for some other doing of mine A, and unless (ii) B was a relevantly connected consequence, e.g. a foreseeable causal consequence, of A. But if Augustine's doctrine of responsibility is (c) then it seems to fall at both these hurdles. (i) If my culpability under the doctrine of original sin depends on what Adam and Eve did, then it does not depend on any doing of mine, responsible or otherwise. (ii) *A fortiori*, the consequences of what they did were not, and could not have been, 'relevantly connected' to their action(s) from my point of view, neither as 'foreseeable causal consequences' nor as anything else.

Augustine seems aware of this problem, and it leads his theory into one last contortion, not yet noted, but hinted at in one of the quotations above:

> If these things [which are done from ignorance and difficulty] are not penal conditions for humans, but come about by nature, then they are not sins. (dLA 3.51)

Augustine's last manoeuvre on this topic, only performed on the occasions when he thinks he can get away with it, is actually to claim that what we are punished for by God is *what we do in ignorance and difficulty*. The penal conditions themselves become their own punishment. To offer two examples of this rare, spectacular back-flip:

(a) dCD 14.11: Eve was guilty because she was 'seduced', i.e. deceived (and therefore ignorant). And Adam, says Augustine, 'was not less (!!) guilty because he was not deceived'.
(b) dGLA 5: 'When a man says, "I cannot do what I am commanded, because I am mastered by my own concupiscence", he has no longer any reason to blame God in his heart, but he recognises and laments his own evil in himself.'

If one is attempting, as Augustine is, to explain the performance of large numbers of evil deeds by humans, this last manoeuvre is, of course, a patently circular and self-defeating one; not so much a back-flip as a belly-flop. One might as well 'explain' the presence of large numbers of prisoners in jails by arguing (legitimately) that they were there because they were being punished, and then (crazily) that what they were being punished for was the offence of being prisoners.

5.6. CONCLUSION

I have argued in this chapter that Augustine quite often articulates a very standard classical view of ignorance and compulsion as exculpating or mitigating factors, and that nothing he ever says amounts to a serious denial of this standard view. But, as I have also pointed out, in certain moods Augustine can be seen as attempting, in effect, to stand the classical view on its head. For sometimes he argues that certain kinds of ignorance and compulsion not only are not exculpating factors: they are either standard features of the behaviour of agents who typically incur blame; or else standard features of blameworthy cases of action; or even good reasons for ascribing blame to actions in which they are evident.

This attempted reversal is a bold and interesting move, but, as Augustine presents it, it does not work. I have pointed out in his work some of the various theses about responsibility and voluntariness which Augustine sometimes seems prepared to endorse. But it is not satisfactorily clear exactly which of these he means, overall, to be arguing; and he cannot coherently combine them. Augustine starts from the tried and tested foundation of eclectic classicism, and launches zealously out on a highly revisionary programme in the philosophy of action. This heroic programme might have been more successful had Augustine paid closer and more sustained attention to those fine logical details and distinctions which, at his best, he himself delighted in drawing.

6

Voluntas and the Voluntary

If the action is not free, there is no *voluntas*.
Augustine, de Duabus Animabus, 15

6.1. INTRODUCTION

In the last chapter, I examined two negative conditions which Augustine gives for voluntary action, namely that such action should (i) not be compelled and (ii) not be done in ignorance. I also raised the question whether Augustine, like Aristotle, gives any positive conditions for voluntary action.

In this chapter and the next, I argue that Augustine does indeed give us at least two such conditions of normal voluntary action, as is already evident from the formula quoted in Ch. 5 from *de Duabus Animabus* 14:

Voluntary action is a movement of the soul, without any compulsion, towards something either not to be lost or to be attained. (*Voluntas est animi motus, cogente nullo, ad aliquid vel non amittendum, vel adipiscendum.*)

The two positive conditions to which I refer are these:

(i)   Voluntary action, for Augustine, is, or is action on, that 'movement of the soul' (*animi motus*) which he calls the *voluntas*, and as such is the very opposite of compelled behaviour.
(ii) Augustinian voluntary action is also action with the form of an aspiration to the good life (*ad aliquid vel non amittendum vel adipiscendum*). As that good life is, in Augustine's view, of determinate form, such aspirations partake of the 'measure, weight and number' of practical wisdom; which makes them anything but ignorant.

(i) is a converse of the negative condition about compulsion. (ii) is, as I will argue, a positive account of the rationality (in the sense of that word used in my study of Aristotle in Part I) of Augustinian voluntary action. Its existence suggests the existence also of a negative condition of voluntary action, that it should not be irrational; but no separate attempt will be made to draw this out. Nor will I discuss Augustine's theory of knowledge, the positive converse of his negative condition about ignorance, already discussed in the last chapter. No doubt such a converse can be found in Augustine's Platonist epistemology; but this subject is too large to discuss here, and (unlike Aristotle's theory of knowledge) is in any case not neatly separable from what Augustine has to say about practical rationality/wisdom.

In this chapter I will deal with (i) Augustine's account of the efficient causation or origination of voluntary action. In Ch.7 I will deal with (ii) Augustine's theory of *felicitas* – his account of such action's rationality, that is, of its final and formal causation.

6.2.   THE NATURE OF *VOLUNTAS*: TWO REQUIREMENTS

For Augustine, any behaviour which is to count as voluntary action must be positively describable as being:

(a) original to the agent in question; and
(b) such that the agent could have chosen to do otherwise.

These conditions might seem to be equivalent. It might be said that any action which is original to me (a), is one I am in control of; and any action I am in control of, is one I can either do or not do – a description which satisfies (b). But, in fact, (a) and (b) are quite separate conditions. To see why, consider these two triplets of claims:

1. A chooses to do X; A does X; A could have done Y, if A could have chosen to do Y, and had chosen to do Y.
2. A chooses to do X; A does X; A could have chosen to do Y.

(In (1), 'A could have done Y, if A could have chosen to do Y, and had chosen to do Y' is a more formal representation of the claim we make by the loose locution 'He could have done it if he had chosen to.' It might seem that an adequate formalisation of this would be: 'A could have done Y, if A had chosen to do Y.' But this leaves obscure the vital point about (1) and (2): namely, that actual choosing, unlike merely counterfactual choosing, entails ability to choose.)

If (a) were equivalent to (b), (1) would entail (2); which it does not, because of the third part of each triplet. 'A could have done Y, if A could have chosen to do Y, and had chosen to do Y' does not entail 'A could have chosen to do Y' (and/ or: 'A did choose to do Y'). The former does not entail the latter: any more than 'If Brownies were little boys, they would be Cubs' (which seems to be true) entails 'Brownies are little boys' (which is certainly false). Therefore (a) and (b) are not equivalent.

To specify some item A as the origin of a movement M is intended to mean that A was the cause of M: without A, M would not have occurred. Now in the case of a voluntary action, we say that the efficient cause of the movement M is the agent A, or (more precisely) A's decision to act and her execution of that decision. So M would not have occurred without A's decision to act and her execution of that decision. This in turn implies that, had A decided otherwise, a different movement, or no movement at all, would have been the outcome.

This is to say that A's production of M was such that A could have done otherwise, had she been able to choose to do otherwise, and had so chosen. But – and this is the vital distinction – it is not to say that A could have chosen to do otherwise. For it to be true that the cause of M was the agent A's decision to act and her execution of that decision, it only needs to be the case that if A had not taken that decision and acted on it, M would not have occurred. It does not (ever) need to be the case that A could have taken, let alone did take, a contrary decision.

Hence any behaviour M (it might be said) is coherently characterisable as a 'voluntary' action in two quite different senses. First, because M was caused by some agent A: i.e. M would not have occurred without A's decision to act and her execution of that decision. This weaker sense is coordinate with condition (a). And second, because – in addition to what the first sense specifies – M is also something that A could have chosen to do and could have chosen not to do: a sense in line with both conditions (a) and (b).

Condition (a) might be made the sole positive condition of voluntariness, yielding a *thin* account of voluntary action which is compatible with strict determinism. Or conditions (a) and (b) could be combined, to give a *rich* account of voluntary action, one which makes room (as the thin account seems not to) for a plausible theory of responsibility. I argue that Augustine's wider purpose of theodicy (among other considerations) commits him to argue, rightly, for the rich account. And he acknowledges that he is so committed; most often in his earlier writings, but not just there.

Nonetheless, the later Augustine seems, at times, to have been attracted by the thin account. In that mood he will, as we have seen, come close to arguing that one's inability to choose to do otherwise than sin is no reason for remitting one's culpability – and indeed may actually be evidence of one's culpability. But he himself presented good reasons for thinking this position untenable; as we shall now see, as we look at the evidence for Augustine's acceptance of (a) and (b).

(a) As we have seen, the condition that I should be the origin of those actions which truly pertain to me, simply means that it should be my 'movements of the soul', my volitions, which those actions, non-accidentally, express. Now there are, for Augustine, certain limitations, in the nature of things, on what shape my volitions could have.

Two in particular: first, my tendency to have good or bad volitions is governed by my habituation, my *consuetudo* as Augustine calls it (v., e.g. 83DQ 40). Second, a direct desire for something which I hold to be evil, desired because it is evil, could never be a volition of any agent created by a good God. In Augustine's view, all volitions, good or bad, aim at a single and particular good (however indirectly or inaccurately they may be aimed). However, to explore this side of the doctrine of *voluntas* is really the topic of Ch. 8; for this aspect of the doctrine has more to do with Augustine's teachings about practical rationality and wisdom than with his teachings about 'ability' or 'freedom' (as the converses of 'difficulty' or 'compulsion').

Although, as I have stressed, (a) and (b) are logically separate conditions, still Augustine would insist that they are contingently connected in human psychology. For him, a different way of defining what it means to require that voluntary action should be original to the agent, would be to say that to require this is to require that voluntary action should originate in that 'part of the agent' in which it could have originated otherwise. This leads us on to (b).

6.3.   ABILITY TO DO OTHERWISE

That Augustine does take (b), ability to do otherwise, to be a condition of voluntary action is clear in at least four separate ways. Namely:

1. the connection between this condition and another, about absence of compulsion, already granted;
2. the historical context of Augustine's choice of the phrase 'free choice', *liberum arbitrium*;
3. Augustine's definition of sin; and
4. Augustine's use of the language of the neutral will, or at any rate the morally ambivalent will.

I take these in turn.

1. Ability to do otherwise and absence of compulsion. As noted, positive condition (b), ability to do otherwise, is connected to the negative condition that voluntary action should not be compelled (v. Ch. 5). For, as Augustine points out, if it is not open to an agent to do otherwise than she actually does, then we usually call her a compelled agent, not a voluntary one.

But, of course, this might be disputed. Is it self-contradictory to claim both that 'A does X voluntarily at *t*', and that 'A has no choice but to do X at *t*'? It might seem not. To begin with, it may be said that 'has no choice' is an ambiguous phrase. A politician convicted of corruption or of breaking election promises 'has no choice' but to resign (at any rate, this used to be true); a sheep which falls out of a tree 'has no choice' but to plummet to the ground; but still we say that the politician resigns voluntarily and the sheep plummets involuntarily. So, it might be argued (say, by the kind of determinism sketched above), there are different senses in which A may have no choice but to do X at *t*, and not all of these are relevant to the question of voluntariness. In particular (it might be said), there is an important contrast between these situations:

(1) A has no choice but to do X at *t* because A is not acting voluntarily; that is, A's doing X at *t* is not 'original to A' in the required sense.
(2) A has no choice but to do X at *t* because A, although acting voluntarily at *t*, never has any choice to do or not to do.

To refer back to the distinction made above: on this view, 'A does X voluntarily at *t*' entails only that A could have done other than X at *t*, had she been able to choose to do otherwise, and had so chosen. It does not entail that A could have chosen to do other than X at *t*.

For Augustine, the main problem with this position would be, as I have suggested, the mere irrelevance of the proposed distinction. For if the reason why I have no choice but to do something is not that I am not acting voluntarily, but (say) that that thing is the only thing which is expedient, then there is no question of my being altogether excused from responsibility. (To go back to the resigning politician: our saying that he has 'no choice' but to resign does not entail that he will certainly resign. Nor does it even entail that we will not think less badly of him if he does resign than if he does not. The politician's responsibility and voluntariness are not diminished by his plight; what is (drastically) diminished is his room for manoeuvre.)

2. *The history of 'liberum arbitrium'.* Augustine's very phrase *liberum arbitrium* in the setting up of conditions about voluntary action implies the presence of a condition about ability to do otherwise, as is shown by the *Oxford Latin Dictionary*'s entry on the phrase (s.v. *arbitrium*). The phrase has legal origins: the *OLD* cites Livy's use of it at *Historiae* 32.37.5. There Livy is describing a meeting between the Roman general Quinctius and Philip of Macedon. He writes: 'So the royal ambassadors were dismissed without obtaining peace: Quinctius was given full discretion (*liberum arbitrium*) regarding peace and war.' Livy means that it was entirely up to Quinctius to declare or not declare war. No Roman law or regulation bound him to do either, and so the decision was deemed to rest with him. His action was such that he could have done otherwise had he chosen to.

Likewise, when the jurist Gaius wants to say that the court is not bound by any established rule to follow a particular procedure against a defendant, he says that the court 'has freedom of judgement (*liberum arbitrium*) either to make the defendant a defendant against a capital charge or to seek restitution' (Gaius, *Institutiones*, 3.213). The point is exactly that the court is free to do either.

This historical evidence gives us good reason to presume that Augustine's choice of the phrase *liberum arbitrium* was partly motivated by its legal sense of 'freedom of judgement' or 'discretion'. Augustine deliberately used a term which implied, to

Roman ears, that the kind of decision in question was the kind which can go either way – the kind where an ability to do otherwise than one actually does is present.

3. *Augustine's definition of sin.* At dDA 15, Augustine defines 'sin' as 'a voluntary keeping or pursuing what justice forbids, *and one is free to refrain from (et unde liberum est abstinere).*' This hardly seems compatible with the view that Augustine took the 'thin' view of voluntary action.

Of course, it might be objected that the italicised words give a constraint on what counts as a sin, not on what counts as a voluntary action. So how can this remark help establish that (b) is a condition of voluntary action? Does it not, rather, imply that there might be volitions from which one was not free to abstain? These objections are met when Augustine continues:

> If the action is not free, there is no *voluntas*. For no one deserves to be thought badly of or condemned who does not do what is contrary to the prohibition of justice, or does not do what they *cannot* do. But every sin deserves to be thought badly of or condemned. So who can doubt that sin is what occurs when it is both unjust to choose it, and possible not to choose it (*liberum nolle*)? (dDA 15)

Here Augustine gives two necessary conditions for any deed to count as a sin: (i) it must be a wrongdoing, (ii) it must be avoidable. Thus an agent who does what it is impossible for him not to do, even if this is 'prohibited by justice', cannot be said to have sinned.

NB the distinction, which will come up again in Ch. 8, between 'wrongdoing' and 'sin'. A 'wrongdoing' is anything that is 'contrary to the prohibition of justice', i.e. it is an infraction of the commandments of a legal or quasi-legal code. A 'sin' is such an infraction which is deliberate. Augustine's view on the relation between sin and wrongdoing switches back and forth between these four alternatives:

(i)   all sin (which is directly culpable) is wrongdoing, but not all wrongdoing (which may be either indirectly culpable, or not culpable at all) is sin;

(ii) all wrongdoing is either directly culpable (sc., when it is also sin) or indirectly culpable (sc., when it is merely wrongdoing);

(iii) the words 'sin' and 'wrongdoing' have exactly the same
extensions: all wrongdoing is essentially sin, and there is no
non-deliberate wrongdoing;

(iv) the words 'sin' and 'wrongdoing' have exactly the same
extensions: all sin is essentially wrongdoing, and there is no
deliberate (in the sense of avoidable) wrongdoing at all; but we
are nonetheless somehow to blame for our wrongdoings.

Augustine's best choice out of these four, and the position which
he most coherently presents and should most consistently have presented, is (i). But it cannot be denied that, on this question, there is a
noteworthy shift of emphasis – if not also of doctrine – in his
position that is evident when we compare the earlier and later
works. V. Section 5.5.

The action of such an agent as Augustine envisages at dDA 15
does not, according to (i), count as a sin because it does not count as
a responsible action. It does not count as a responsible action
because (v. Ch. 5) it does not count as a voluntary action. And why
does it not count as a voluntary action? Because – and this is the
central point which Augustine is making here – 'if the agent is not
free [sc. to abstain], there is no voluntary action'. Hence the
relevance of (b), the positive condition of avoidability, is not just to
sins but to voluntary actions in general.

*4. Augustine's notion of the neutral, or at any rate morally ambivalent,
will.* A fourth reason for thinking that Augustine did not take what I
have called the 'thin' view of voluntary action arises from what may
seem a problem for the account of Augustine that I am presenting.
This is that Augustine commonly seems to talk of *voluntas* as being
neutral between good and bad. I shall be arguing in Chs 7–8 that, on
Augustine's conception, *voluntas* is anything but neutral between
good and bad (although it is, somehow, able to turn to either). But
this argument might seem an uphill struggle when confronted with
some passages from Augustine. Such as these three:

(i)   Unless the movement by which the *voluntas* is turned this way
or that were voluntary (*voluntarius*) and had been placed in our
power, a person would not be blameworthy or praiseworthy
according to whether it was to higher or lower things that he
twisted away the hinge (so to speak) of his *voluntas*' (*cum...
detorquet quasi quendam cardinem voluntatis*).' (dLA 3.3)

(ii)   No one uses the virtues badly, but one can use the middle and
       the lesser goods both well and badly.... Therefore the *voluntas*
       is a middle good (*medium bonum*). (dLA 2.50, 52)

(iii) Free choice (*liberum arbitrium*), which was given to the rational
       soul naturally by its creator, is that middle power (*media vis*)
       which can either fix itself on faith or incline to infidelity. (dSL
       58)

The least these passages prove is that voluntary action, for
Augustine, involves the ability to choose to do *x* or not to do *x* –
that is, the ability to do otherwise – even when one of these alternatives is a morally bad thing to do. (That they do not, in fact,
establish very much more than this, will be argued in Chs 7–8.)
But these passages do at any rate show that Augustine requires
the ability to do otherwise as a condition of uncompelled action.
Given, further, that for him voluntary action must be
uncompelled, and that he thinks that no deed can be responsible,
worthy of praise or blame, unless it is voluntary (points I made in
Sections 2–4), this conclusion reflects interestingly on his much-
discussed doctrine that the original human freedom was an
ability not to sin, whereas the human freedom of the Resurrection will be an inability to sin: 'The first free choice was an
ability not to sin (*posse non peccare*), the latest will be an inability
to sin (*non posse peccare*)' (dCD 22.30).

Does Augustine's *non posse peccare* describe any state of real
freedom? If it does, then one wants to ask, with J. L. Mackie, why
God did not give Adam this kind of freedom rather than the
dangerous *posse non peccare* variety. But it would seem that this
eschatological freedom, as Augustine describes it, is not in fact
much of a freedom. It is not clear that someone who is unable to
sin is capable of voluntarily refraining from sinning. Hence it is
also unclear that such an agent is responsible, or praiseworthy,
for so refraining. After all, even a fallen human normally
displays inability to sin in some respect or other. In my present
state I cannot commit the sin of drunkenness, because I cannot
afford it; nor the sin of fornication (as opposed to adultery),
because I am married. Am I to be praised for my economically
enforced sobriety, or my logically enforced non-fornication?
Hardly; but then why should any such enforced sobriety be
praiseworthy?

6.4.   THE CAUSE(S) OF *VOLUNTAS* AGAIN

I began with the question: What, for Augustine, counts as an efficient cause of *voluntas*? I considered two sub-conditions which Augustine gives upon the origination of voluntary action: that it should originate with the agent, and that it should originate in such a way as to make it possible that it should have originated otherwise. But all this might seem insufficiently informative. How much does it tell us about how voluntary actions do in fact originate? We might now wish to come back to the opening question: What does Augustine think the efficient cause of voluntary action is (if there is one)?

Augustine's remarks on this question are ambiguous. In some places, his view is apparently that the *voluntas* is altogether uncaused. In others, he seems to take a second view: that the *voluntas* can be caused, but only by itself. In others still, he seems to argue for a third view: that there can, in fact, be causes of the *voluntas* other than the *voluntas* itself, and that an interesting theory of the causation of voluntary action can be elaborated. This third view is, I will argue in Chs 7–8, Augustine's most convincingly argued view about normal voluntary actions; although there is one special kind of voluntary actions to which the first and second views might seem to apply better.

For the first view, we might cite this evidence:

An evil *voluntas* is the cause of all evils... But what, in the end, could be prior to the *voluntas* as *its* cause? Such a cause would either be the *voluntas* itself – in which case we have not reached the root of the *voluntas*; or it will not be the *voluntas* – in which case there will be no sin. (dLA 3.48–9)

If we translate *voluntas*, in this context, as 'voluntary action', then we may say that Augustine seems here to be arguing thus:

1.   All possible causes of voluntary actions are themselves either voluntary actions or not voluntary actions.
2.   If a supposed voluntary action *A* had a cause *C* which was not itself a voluntary action, then *A* could not be a voluntary action, because [?] *A* would have been compelled by *C*. Therefore no possible cause of a voluntary action could itself be something which was not a voluntary action.

3. But if a supposed voluntary action *A* had a cause *C* which was itself a voluntary action, then the same question about its origin would arise about the voluntary action *C*. Therefore it is unhelpfully regressive to suppose that the cause of a voluntary action could itself be a voluntary action. Therefore the cause of a voluntary action cannot itself usefully be supposed to be a voluntary action.

4. But if voluntary actions have causes at all, these must either be voluntary actions themselves, or something other than voluntary actions. Now both suppositions have been shown to be vain. Therefore voluntary actions have no causes.

From elsewhere, however, it seems that Augustine cannot be arguing that *any and every voluntas* has no cause. Augustine's point at dLA 3.48–9 is not about all *voluntates*. He is not saying here that *voluntas* (in general) has no prior cause. He is saying that bad *voluntas* (in particular) has no prior cause – indeed, that it is only bad *voluntas* which has no cause: other kinds of *voluntas* do indeed have causes.

For the same reason, Augustine cannot be committed either to the second view, that nothing but one voluntary action or choice can cause any other voluntary action or choice; even though he himself might be read as giving a lot of space, particularily in the dLA, to developing the view that *voluntates* typically are the causes of *voluntates*; that voluntary action, reflexively, is *its own* cause. This form of the 'reflexive theory of the will' deserves a little further consideration – before its final rejection.

6.5.   A REFLEXIVE WILL?

For Augustine, the cognitive abilities of the human mind are reflexive: to know (or perceive) anything is also to know that I know it (or perceive it). A foundational epistemological certainty is had by simple consciousness of one's self-consciousness. That I am a self-conscious living existent can, it is claimed, be established by simple introspection (dLA 1.16). An interesting parallel to this in Augustine's philosophy of action has appeared in the dLA. There, and sometimes elsewhere (e.g. dTrin 14.10), the nature of the human psyche in its cognitive role is mirrored by its nature in its conative role. The structure of voluntary action and choice too is reflexive.

This claim can be taken in different ways. It might imply no more than that good *voluntas* is *necessary* for the good life because without it we cannot put anything else to good use. But it might also imply that good *voluntas* is *sufficient* for the good life. The idea would be that a power of good voluntary choice is had by simply choosing to have it. To want to have good *voluntas* is *eo ipso* to have good *voluntas*. Clearly it is the second, stronger form of the reflexivity idea that we are interested in if we are considering the idea that the *voluntas* is its own cause.

The second reading makes the *voluntas* its own cause in the sense that the explanation of my having a power of good voluntary action and choice of the first-order variety is that I made a (second-order) choice to have it. Presumably, if we are to look for an explanation of this ability to make a second-order choice, we will be deferred to the third order; and so on *ad infinitum*. *Voluntas*, on this picture, is something absolutely independent of everything outside itself; something free-standing, self-motivating, and even, in something a little like Aristotle's sense, self-moving.

The attractions of this theory to certain kinds of exegete of Augustine are obvious. If it is held that Augustine aims to argue for a quite general causal indeterminism as a necessary part of arguing for libertarianism, the reflexive theory of *voluntas* seems to be a way of achieving that end. For, according to this theory, nothing causes the will except the will itself.

Indeed, it seems to be quite commonly thought that Augustine's aim is to present us with a voluntarist (as opposed to rationalist) theory of the voluntary, i.e. a theory based on a *voluntas* which 'being anterior to reason, has at the most fundamental level no reason for its biddings' (MacIntyre (1985), p. 156). If the reflexive theory of the voluntary is Augustine's most developed thinking on the subject, then it seems possible to argue that, taking him all in all, Augustine is indeed a voluntarist in the sense required.

Of course, it would then have to be conceded that the explanation of the activity of the *voluntas* offered by this theory is essentially regressive and uninformative. First-order choices are referred to second-order choices; second- to third-order choices; third- to fourth-; and so on. If the *voluntas* is to be caused by nothing but the *voluntas*, then we cannot escape from this regress by saying (e.g.) that at some order there can be a *voluntas* which is not caused by another *voluntas* but by something else. But then the activity of the *voluntas* will remain unexplained, and apparently inexplicable.

As already suggested, the rejoinder might be that this inexplicability of the will is exactly what we ought to expect in a voluntarist world. If it is true (i) that the deliberations of the will are anterior to reason, and (ii) that the 'freedom of the will' means its being radically unconditioned by causes outside itself, then clearly (it might be said) a free *voluntas* is bound to be, at bottom, inexplicable.

But to say this is to admit that the reflexive theory leads us either into a regress or else into a circle. As I say, some might think that this is how it ought to be. Others, in the light of much else that Augustine says, will view this prospect with suspicion. In particular, it is not at all clear that the exegetical basis for attributing the strong version of the reflexivity thesis to Augustine is sound: it cannot be if Augustine means, in dLA 3.47, to talk only about *bad* will and not about *voluntas* in general. But it can be argued that Augustine means to talk only about bad will at dLA 3.47 ff.: indeed I shall argue this, in Ch. 8. Hence my reasons for rejecting the strong version of the reflexivity idea should be plain.

One last point in the strong version's favour, however, may be mentioned before leaving the topic. Such a recursive understanding of *voluntas* might seem to connect with, perhaps even to support, the circular idea of responsibility pointed to in the last chapter. The suggestion there was that fallen humans are culpable for the sins which they cannot help committing, because they are in a state of helplessness, which itself is the penalty of committing those same sins. The suggestion here is that the only possible cause of any nth-order *voluntas* is an (n+1)th-order *voluntas*. So the moral quality of any one *voluntas* of any person is fixed, if by anything, only by another *voluntas*, which will (*ipso facto*) share that moral quality. Ascriptions of praise and blame apply, therefore, equally to all the individual willings of a given person. Thus our account of responsibility has to be circular; for our account of motivation is circular. The moral state in which we find ourselves is not something to be explained; it is simply a given, just as one point of the Adam and Eve story (remarked by Ricoeur (1967)) is that the prevenient existence of evil is a given even in the Garden of Eden.

However, if there is a connection to be made here, Augustine never explicitly made it. Although it is never formally repealed, the idea of the reflexivity of will is only developed in the early works. The idea of reflexive responsibility, on the other hand, is most commonly developed in the later works. The only work in which both ideas may be found is, as we have seen, the dLA; but no tie-up is attempted by Augustine, which suggests that this was not what he had in mind.

Moreover, quite apart from its deep implausibility, there are other, crucial developments in his doctrine which stand in the way of a general ascription to Augustine of this kind of reflexive theory of the voluntary. A broader look at Augustine's philosophy of action shows that it is, overall, very far from the truth to say that he believes that typical voluntary action and choice are either uncaused or rationally undetermined. On the contrary: Augustine has a very definite and prominent theory of practical reasoning, according to which rational determination is in fact characteristic of voluntary action, and moreover is itself, in one important sense, the cause of voluntary action. To that theory I now turn in the next chapter.

7

The Good Will and the Good Life

> There is no reason for humans to philosophise except so as to be happy.
>
> Augustine, *City of God*, 19.1

7.1. INTRODUCTION

Augustine has much to offer us in the way of demarcation of the conditions of voluntary action, as has become clear in Chs 5 and 6. He develops a number of (not always consistent) lines of thought on the subject. But among his principal themes are the very Aristotelian ones that absence of compulsion and of ignorance are negative conditions for voluntary action; and that among the positive conditions for voluntary action are (i) that the action should originate with me and (ii) that I should be able to do otherwise.

For my analysis of these conditions I took as a starting-point the first two phrases of Augustine's description of voluntary action, at dDA 14, as a 'movement of the soul, without any compulsion, towards something either not to be lost or to be attained'. In this chapter I turn to the last phrase of this definition. The phrase 'either not to be lost or to be attained' points us, as I have suggested, towards the question of what Augustine might have to say about the rationality of voluntary action, that is about its formal and final, rather than efficient, causation.

Of Aristotle's theory I noted that his three conditions for voluntary action can most succinctly be expressed in their negative forms, as the requirements that voluntary action should not be (i) compelled, (ii) done in ignorance, or (iii) irrational. But I also noted that Aristotle says a great deal to fill out these negative conditions with a positive content. In particular, it is a positive consequence of Aristotle's negative condition about irrationality that fully voluntary action must logically follow from the combination of a premise of the good with a premise of the possible.

We have seen that there are clear analogues, in Augustine's theory of the voluntary, to Aristotle's conditions, positive and negative, about compulsion and ignorance. The question I ask in this chapter is: Does Augustine have anything corresponding (negatively) to Aristotle's 'no irrationality' requirement, or (positively) to his account of the role of practical reason in voluntary action?

7.2. PRACTICAL REASON AND PRACTICAL WISDOM IN AUGUSTINE

My answer is a very guarded 'Yes', with two caveats in particular, (i) and (ii) as noted below. Contrary to what many of his interpreters think, Augustine is no irrationalist: he does not believe that it is normal that nothing should motivate human choices except the sheer fiat of an inscrutable 'black box' called (in the usual version) 'the will'. Genuine voluntary action, for him just as for Aristotle, is action on a good reason:

> The peace of the irrational soul is an ordered quiet of the appetites; the peace of the rational soul is an ordered agreement of knowledge and action. (dCD 19.13)

> Because there is a rational soul in humans, it submits all of this that it has in common with the animals to the peace of the rational soul, so that the mind may contemplate and act in accordance with what it contemplates, so that there may be an ordered agreement of knowledge and action in it. (dCD 19.14)

Note the contrast between 'rational soul' and 'irrational soul': a contrast which might have been taken straight from NE 1102a29–30 (though more probably it came from a Platonist writer). If Augustine really believed, like David Hume, that the choices of a human soul were incapable of receiving the direction of reason – and that in fact the relation of control ran the other way – we might be surprised to find Augustine saying, as he so often does, that the human soul is, by nature, 'rational' (whatever precise meaning that word may have).

For Augustine as much as for Aristotle, genuine voluntary action involves the agreement or congruence (*consensio*) of one's action with one's knowledge and one's desire; or, to put it another way, it entails that one's action should, in some appropriate sense, follow from the combination of one's knowledge and one's desire. What is this if not an account, or at any rate the outline of an account, of practical reasoning?

However, (i) there is (as we shall see) one large problem with describing Augustine's account of practical wisdom as a condition of voluntary action, since Augustine emphasises that wilful wrong-doing, action directly against practical wisdom, is not necessarily involuntary in any sense. The complexities raised by this problem will be considered in Ch. 8.

Also (ii), unlike Aristotle in NE III and VI, Augustine nowhere fills in the outline with a detailed, explicit account of practical reason. This is not to say that he does not fill in that outline: it is to say that he fills it in with something else. Aristotle offers us the ingredients, at any rate, for a formal account of the mechanics and logic of practical reasoning. Augustine, on the other hand, concentrates on the other side of the picture. The mechanics and the logic of practical *reason* he leaves almost entirely implicit and unexplored, though this is no excuse for saying that he has no such concept as practical reason. On the more nebulous matter of practical *wisdom* Augustine has plenty to say.

Practical wisdom, for Augustine, means understanding what the good for humanity is so as to live it out. Discovering the good for humanity in one's own life is not just a result of deliberating well (which is why this kind of practical understanding is more appropriately called wisdom than reason). A kind of revelation, a kind of special knowledge, is needed. (V. dTrin 13.4, 'It was not that people did not wish for beatitude, it was rather that none of them knew what beatitude was'; cp. dFRV 1.)

On the other hand, Augustine often speaks of this special knowledge as if it were completely deducible on the grounds of self-reflective human reason alone (as in the argument for God's existence at dLA 2.7–39). This is an example of a standard tension in Christian apologetics, between natural and revealed theology; Platonic *gnosis* displays the same ambiguity of status between the natural and the revealed. It is in accord with that ambiguity that Augustine's quest for the good life begins with the transcendently metaphysical, in an appeal to revelation, just about as often as it begins with the frankly phenomenological, and an appeal to our own self-understanding. I consider both approaches.

2a.   The Good Life: Phenomenological Arguments

On the phenomenological side, the maxim of Augustine's practical wisdom is the Delphic 'know thyself'. The method of Augustine's work often suggests that practical wisdom is no more than self-awareness: becoming aware of what I really want, the better to pursue it. It means knowing what is the natural objective of all action and desire. We can arrive at practical wisdom by discovering what this objective is. And one way to discover that objective, since it is natural, is by simply examining what humans (for example, me) actually do pursue, what they intend to gain by this pursuit, and what the difference is, if any, between practice and underlying intention.

This examination is performed at the beginning of several of Augustine's works, e.g. the dBV, the cAcad, and the dLA. What such an examination finds is, unsurprisingly, a great variety of different objectives, and a great variety of degrees of success or failure in humans' attempts to achieve what they are seeking to achieve. But 'how can someone voluntarily (*voluntate*) live a miserable life, when absolutely no one wants (*velit*) to live miserably?' (dLA 1.30, cp. dTrin 14.4): how do we explain this gap between intention and performance? Augustine's answer is that it demonstrates that not just any route will lead one to the happy life:

> No one can reach the happy life (*beatam vitam*) by heading for what does not exist, or for what, even if it does exist, does not make one happy. (dLA 3.59)

This is where the need for practical wisdom appears. There is a gap between wanting the good and pursuing the good:

> All these people pursuing various things desire the good and avoid the bad. And yet they desire various things, because different things seem good to different people. So whoever desires what he ought not to desire goes wrong, even though he would not desire it unless it seemed good to him. (dLA 2.26)

It is right to pursue the good life, yet there are wrong, unwise, ways to pursue it:

> Therefore insofar as all people desire the happy life, they do not go wrong. But insofar as someone does not keep to the Way of Life, which leads to happiness, even as they claim and profess not to want anything but to arrive at happiness, thus far forth they go wrong.... And the more someone goes wrong in their way of life, the less they act wisely. (dLA 2.26)

Phenomenological examination of our natural desires shows that 'No one is happy who does not have what he wants' (dBV 10). Unhappiness is caused by seeking without finding (cAcad 1.6–8), or by finding and then losing again. One should therefore seek the objectives of greatest permanence for the maximal satisfaction of desire. Wrong objectives characteristically do not admit of that 'stable and permanent possession' which Boethius talks about as characteristic of eternal happiness (Boethius, *The Consolation of Philosophy*, Bk.V, Prose 6). So in the dLA Augustine argues, rather implausibly, that all and only bad objectives are transient:

> To long to live without fear is common, not only to all good people, but even to all wicked people. However, there is this difference: the good seek this objective by turning away their love from those things that they cannot have without risk of loss; whereas the wicked aim to enjoy these transient things, and so try to remove the obstacles to so doing. For this reason they lead a criminal and wicked life which is better called death. (dLA 1.10)

If Augustine can make out this step of the argument (more on which below), that the right objectives of action are the most permanent ones, that will bring us to the *metaphysical* form of his argument about the objectives of practical wisdom.

2b. The Good Life: Metaphysical Arguments

On the metaphysical side, practical wisdom is the possession of the highest good in virtue of understanding a certain kind of truth, the truth about what is really the *summum bonum*, independently of and antecedently to the various views of it which may be held. So dLA 2.36:

The truth shows those things all to be goods which are undeceptive (*vera*), and some or all of which intelligent people, in advance of their possession, choose to enjoy.

Action – which is to say pursuit of some perceived good – needs to follow from genuine knowledge of what is worth pursuit. Right cognition, cognition of the truth, is a condition of successful voluntary action. True to his Platonist roots, Augustine stresses the role of knowledge in practical wisdom. For him, as for Socrates, 'virtue is knowledge' – at least in the sense that knowledge is necessary for all virtue, even if it is not also sufficient.

Moreover, what we want for practical wisdom is not just the truth given by self-examination; it is truth in a rather loftier sense, a truth identical with wisdom and common to all humans:

> Can wisdom, do you think, be anything other than that truth in which the *summum bonum* is discerned and laid hold of? (dLA 2.26)

> If there is one highest good for all people, then that truth in which it is discerned and laid hold of – namely wisdom – ought to be one in common for all. (dLA 2.27)

(This last passage, incidentally, suggests a response to a likely objection to Augustine's doctrine of practical wisdom. It may be said that Augustine's argument is fatally flawed because he illegitimately infers from 'All humans seek some good thing in all their actions' to 'There is some (one) good thing which all humans seek in all their actions'. If Augustine argued like this, certainly he would be guilty of a logical fallacy. But in fact, he argues the other way round. He starts from the claim that there is one good at which all action aims. So the above passage begins from this assumption (*Si summum bonum omnibus unum est...*). He does not deduce this claim from the claim that all human action aims at some good or other. On the contrary, that latter claim is deduced from the first claim, by a logically unimpeachable transition.)

So lofty is Augustine's metaphysical conception of practical truth that, for him, practical truth turns out to be exactly the same in content as his theoretical truth. It is natural to all men to seek the (apparent) good and flee the (apparent) evil (cp. dLA 1.30, 'for even the wicked seek this'). But what is also necessary to the good life is exactly the same knowledge of transcendent and objective reality as forms the end of theoretical inquiry. In this sense Augustine's wisdom is as unitary as the objective truth which it contemplates: in fact, there is no neat division between practical and theoretical wisdom in his thought. Just as, for Augustine, talk of the conative (*voluntas*) and of the cognitive (*ratio*) relates to the same human person in the different roles of doer and understander, so also, for him, practical reason is only theoretical reason put to work, and theoretical reason is only practical reason in contemplative mode. The first principles of practical and theoretical reason are, in his view, one and the same.

> Thus when the sharpness of a strong mind, nourished with many and unchangeable truths, sees with sure reason, it directs itself into that same Truth which all those truths showed forth. (dLA 2.36)

This conjunction of metaphysics and phenomenology is also a conjunction of moral and factual claims. Augustine holds both that our desires naturally *have* a certain form, and that our desires *ought to have* that form. The vision of the good for humanity is, on the one hand, a kind of *theoria*, contemplation, of what is objectively the case. But, on the other hand, it is also action-guiding, indeed it is preeminently so. Augustine's endorsement of the idea that voluntary action is necessarily, in some sense, reasonable or rational behaviour is an endorsement of the claim, also made by Aristotle, that voluntary action has an intrinsic *directedness*, namely towards objectives which necessarily are always either actual or at least perceived goods.

7.3.   ARISTOTLE AND AUGUSTINE ON THE DIRECTEDNESS OF ACTION

This notion of directedness is a crucial one, and needs further elucidation. Before turning to Augustine's statements of this notion, I will briefly reconsider what Aristotle meant by it. (NB the similarities, and the contrasts too, between this notion of directedness and Aristotle's notion of the rationality of voluntary actions.)

We saw that, for Aristotle, a genuine explanation of an action must refer to some real (or supposed) good which is obtained (or thought to be obtained) by that action. Explanations which do not make any such reference are simply not explanations at all. It would not make sense to Aristotle for someone to say that the reason why they wanted, say, to drink a can of paint was 'because it seemed like a bad thing to do'. Thus, for Aristotle, it makes sense to explain 'John wants to drink a can of paint' by 'because he has made a bet about it'; or 'because he is being forced to at gunpoint by a maniac'; or 'because he wrongly imagines that the can of paint is a can of beer'; or even merely 'because he thinks it would be a neat thing to do'. Even this last could count as an explanation of an action, in the sense of 'explanation' which I have in mind. But it does not make sense to explain 'John wants to drink a can of paint' by 'because he hates the taste of paint', or 'because he knows that paint is poisonous', or 'because he thinks it would not be a neat thing to do'. As they stand, these 'explanations' simply are not explanations of John's behaviour at all. (Consider, for one thing, how much more naturally they would read if, in each one, 'although' were substituted for 'because'.)

Of course, we can easily adorn all three non-explanations so that they do read like pukka explanations. E.g., we can add to them, respectively, 'and wants to inure himself to horrible tastes', 'and is trying to commit suicide', and 'and is aiming to disgust his girl-friend into leaving him'. But what is the point, the attractiveness, of adding these adornments, if not that they restore intelligibility to our characterisation of John's behaviour precisely by indicating a conceivable good which it aims at? Which is simply another way of making the same point: that Aristotle's teaching is emphatically that 'whatever a human desires, he desires under the explanatory aspect (*sub ratione*) of some good' (as Aquinas puts it, *Summa Theologiae* 1a2ae.1.6c).

Augustinian voluntary action is 'rational' in the sense that, for Augustine, no behaviour is (fully) explicable as voluntary action unless we can give some account of the good at which it aims or is supposed by the agent to aim. For Augustine just as much as Aristotle, to explain a piece of behaviour in terms of reasons (as opposed to other types of causes) is to mention a good which the behaviour is supposed to be conceived as aiming at by the agent. That this is a belief of Augustine's, and such a fundamental one that much of the time it remains unexamined, is already evidenced by one casual aside I have quoted, from dLA 2.26: 'So whoever desires what ought not to have been desired, *even though he would not desire it unless it seemed good to him...'*. Here Augustine takes it absolutely as read that no one would pursue anything unless they held it, for one reason or another, to be a good objective to pursue.

If there is evidence of Augustine's endorsement of the thesis of the directedness of voluntary action, then a most important tie-up can be made in Augustine's moral theory: between practical rationality and practical virtue, between what it is rational or reasonable to do, and what it is good to do. But the evidence is no accumulation of slips of the pen; it is Augustine's consistent doctrine. Further evidence of that doctrine can be found by examining Augustine's expression of the thesis of the directedness of voluntary action in his theory of happiness, *felicitas* or *beatitudo*.

7.4. *FELICITAS*

The central importance to Augustine's thought of the question 'What is the good/best life for humanity?' is obvious from one end of his philosophical career to the other:

> Theodorus, we have inquired among ourselves about the happy life, and I do not see anything else that might more fittingly be called the gift of God. (dBV 1.5)

> Now we want to be happy, which cannot be unless either the truth is found, or diligently sought. So let us put off all other inquiries; if we want to be happy, it is the truth that we must inquire into. (cAcad 1.25)

> Socrates set his spirit to discover what was necessary to the happy life – that one question which the industry of every philosopher seems to have watched and laboured to answer.... (dCD 8.3)

> Why, is not Felicity a goddess [to the pagans]?... Then let her alone be venerated! For where she is present, what good thing will be absent? (dCD 4.18)

How does Augustine answer this question of the nature of the good/best life? Like Aristotle (NE 1097b22 ff.) and like Cicero in the *Hortensius*, he generally begins with what is often thought to be a truism: that the good for humanity is happiness, which all humans desire.

Certainly we all wish to be happy (*beati*). (dBV 10; cp. cAcad 1.5, Sermon 150.4, dTrin 13.4 and Cicero, *Hortensius*, Fr.36 Müller)

Since therefore all humans wish to be happy (*beati*).... (dTrin 13.4)

For who chooses one thing on account of another except so that he may be made happy (*felix*)? (dCD 4.23)

There is no one who does not wish to be glad (*gaudere*). (dCD 19.12)

Though at last we held on neither to piety nor to happiness (*felicitas*) because of our sinning, yet we did not lose our will for happiness even when we had lost that happiness. (dCD 22.30)

But what does it actually mean to say that *gaudere, felicitas*, or *beatitudo* is the good for humanity? Augustine has at least seven ways of approaching this question, which I will now run through. These seven approaches may or may not come down to the same thing, as they are intended to; and they may or may not depend circularly on each other, as they are not intended to.

4a. Peace

One standard image for the human good in the *City of God* is that of the final rest of the saints in *pax* or *quies*:

The completion (*fines*) of our goods is peace. (dCD 19.11)

For just as there is no one who does not wish to be glad, so there is no one who does not wish for peace. (dCD 19.12)

Is this peace the same to which Augustine had referred in the schema of moral progress noticed (Section 5.4) in his exegetical works on Romans and Galatians (*ante legem, sub lege, sub gratia, in pace*)? There is good evidence in the dCD that it is. The point about the peace referred to in the exegetical works is that such peace only comes after the end of the struggle between good and evil impulses – which itself is characteristic of unhappiness. The peace of the dCD is precisely this kind of absence of internal conflict.

(For one criticism of Augustine's doctrine of *pax* as the final good, v. Kirwan (1989), p. 222 ff.: 'It is striking that apart from the reference to worship this description at the end of *The City of God* is wholly negative'. But the absence of strife in heaven is an absence which, as we have seen, Augustine identifies in the dCD with something very positive, viz. the possibility of successful practical reasoning: 'The peace of the irrational soul is an ordered quiet of the appetites; the peace of the rational soul is an ordered agreement of knowledge and action' (dCD 19.13).)

One notable point about defining the human good as 'peace' in this sense is that, given Augustine's orthodox Christian belief in human non-perfectibility in this life, it makes that good essentially other-worldly. The point is clear already in the EPRoms and EEGal:

These carnal desires will not come to an end unless we have merited that transformation of the body which we are promised at the resurrection, when peace will be made perfect. (EPRoms 18)

After that indeed our punishing disposition (*poenalis consuetudo*) will be extinguished from every part, for the Spirit of Jesus... will give life to our mortal bodies. (EEGal 46)

Our lot in the present life is wretchedness and punishment, as is increasingly strongly emphasised as Augustine's thought develops:

All humans, inasmuch as they are mortal, must necessarily also be miserable. (dCD 9.15)

This life, which has been made so unholy by that sin which was perpetrated in paradise, has been made a punishment to us; and everything that is worked in us by the New Covenant pertains only to the new inheritance of the new age [to come]. (dCD 21.15)

God is only to be known in the hereafter. The *pax* or *quies* for which we long is only to be found in the perfected knowledge of God, which Augustine also calls

4b.   The Contemplation of God

There 'we shall see, and our heart shall rejoice' [Isaiah 66.14]. Isaiah does not explain what we shall see; but what can it be but

God? – So that the promise of the gospel shall be fulfilled in us: 'Blessed are the poor in spirit, for they shall see God' [Mt 5:8]. Here you believe; there you will see. (dCD 20.21)

Since this contemplation of God is happiness, the lack of it is unhappiness:

For that vision of God is a vision of such beauty, and so worthy of love, that without it, anyone who has a sufficiency and even an overflow of all other goods is someone whom Plotinus [*Enneads* 1.6.7] does not hesitate to call most miserable.' (dCD 10.16)

4c. Function

Very different in tone, and implicitly much more this-worldly, are Augustine's arguments about function, in the performing of which one's happiness is often, especially in the early works, said by him to consist. Like Aristotle, he takes 'human function' to mean 'activity/ state which sets humans "above" the animals':

'What do you think living happily can be,' I said, 'except living in accordance with what is best in humanity (*secundum id quod in homine optimum est vivere*)?... Who,' I asked, 'would doubt that the best part of a human is that part of the soul to the rule of which it befits him to subdue whatever else there is in his nature?' (cAcad 1.5; cp. Aristotle, NE 1113a5–9)

Whether it is more rightly called mind or spirit or both, this is what sets humanity above the beasts of the field.... When this part rules and commands whatever other parts make up the human, then is the human most in good order. (dLA 1.18)

It follows that not performing the human function is often taken to be definitive of unhappiness; as when one performs some other, lower animal's function:

A horse does well to go about on all fours; but if a human imitated it with his hands and feet, who would think that he even deserved chaff for food? In very many cases we disapprove of the imitation where we nonetheless approve of what is imitated. (dDA 20)

Or as when one's own body is disobedient to one's own *voluntas* – a phenomenon which seems to have fixated Augustine (dCD 14.23). In heaven the body will, he says, no longer disobey the *voluntas*, even though for now 'Man is enslaved by himself because he deserted God in pleasing himself; and not obeying God, he could not obey himself. Hence is that more obvious misery, whereby humans do not live as they choose to live' (dCD 14.24).

The obvious response to 'The happy life for humans is the life of living out the human function' is 'Yes, but what is the human function?' The above passages give some indications about what Augustine thinks the human function is. More evidence as to his beliefs on this may be gathered by examining another way in which he describes the good life, as

4d. Desire of the Right Things

The argument that the good life is a matter of having the right desires, and (if one has the right desires) of fulfilling them, is very clearly presented in the dBV. It is agreed there that happiness has to do with the satisfaction of desires:

> 'Does he seem to us to be happy,' I asked, 'who does not have what he wants?' – They said not. (dBV 10)

But not just of any desires:

> 'What then? Is everyone who has what he wants happy?' My mother replied: 'If he wants and possesses good things, then he is happy; but if he wants bad things, then he is unhappy, even if he gets them.' (dBV 10)

Compare the teaching of the *de Trinitate*:

> For it is the very height of misery to want what is unfitting (*quod non deceat*). It is even worse to want to get what one ought not to get (*quod non oporteat*) than not to get what one wants. (Cicero, *Hortensius, apud* dTrin 13.5; cp. the paradox of Plato's *Gorgias*, that it is better to be justly punished than unjustly unpunished.)

What, then, are the right things to desire? Augustine gives us these examples of wrong objectives of desire, desires which could not be given a central part in the constitution of the good life for humans:

> There are certain other things which do not appear in wild animals and yet are not the best things in the human, as for example joking and laughing. Anyone who judges most rightly about human nature will judge that these are human indeed, but the lowest reach of humanity. Then there is the love of praise and glory, and the passion for controlling others.... (dLA 1.18)

> A certain actor... promised to tell a whole theatre audience what was in their hearts and what they desired... on the appointed day a great crowd came together, full of expectation, and when all were silent and holding their breath he spoke: 'You want to buy cheap and sell dear.' (dTrin 13.3)

> We sin by loving the things of the body, because we are commanded to love the things of the spirit, and by nature we can do so. (dDA 20)

Augustine has three positive answers to the question of what right desire is. These answers seem different in content; different enough, at least, to supply two further ways of answering the earlier question, 'What is the good life?' First, in line with (7.4b), that the good for humanity is the contemplation of God, he argues that the right supreme object of desire is God himself. Second, it seems in many places that the right thing to desire is not the happy life, but

4e. Righteousness

> For those who are happy – who must also be good – are not happy because they wanted to live happily (for even the wicked want that); they are happy because they wanted to live aright, which the wicked would not. (dLA 1.30)

> No one except the happy person lives as they want to, and no one is happy except the person who is just. (dCD 14.25)

> The right life is to be lived: it is by that that one comes to the happy life. (dCD 14.25)

It appears that this right kind of life is defined as that life which exhibits all the emotions in a right kind of way, and a misdirected life is one which exhibits them in the wrong way (dCD 14.9): 'Since their love is right, they have all those emotions too.'

4f. Secure Goods

The third answer found in the dLA is: we should desire those things which we cannot lose against our will. This is the difference between the right desires of good people and the wrong desires of bad people: cp. dLA 1.11, as already quoted. And what, in turn, is it that we cannot lose against our will? In the dLA Augustine answers that what we cannot lose against our will is

4g. Good Will

– The good will (as I shall here translate *bona voluntas*) itself. This is the 'will by which we desire to live rightly and honestly, and to arrive at the highest wisdom' (dLA 1.25). Its value is greater than 'anything in the way of riches, or honour, or the desires of the body' for the simple reason that one has good will by choosing to have it, and can only lose it by choosing not to have it. This makes the good will the most secure of all goods, a good completely independent of the ravages of fortune and time:

> Thus you see that it is within our power of choice (*in voluntate nostra*) whether we should enjoy or lack so great and so true a good. For what is so much in the power of the will as the will itself? (dLA 1.26)

> Thus it is agreed that the happy person is the lover of his own good will, who for its sake contemns whatever else might be called good but the loss of which can occur even when the will to keep it remains. (dLA 1.28)

The same kind of thought is found in the dCD: 'Unless the happy life is not loved, it is not possessed' (dCD 14.25).

Now there are at least two important problems with defining the human good in this manner, as the good will. Firstly, the security of possession of the good will is no guarantee of its goodness as an object of possession. After all, by the same arguments that

Augustine gives for the security of possession of the *good* will, one could argue that the *bad* will, if there is such a thing, was a secure possession – and so a good thing? The argument from permanence of a possession to its goodness is implausible because, as Augustine himself points out as early as dBV 10, that desire for or possession of something is not a good state of affairs unless that something is a good thing. Indeed Augustine admits in the *Confessions* (6.16) that it is not (or not just) because the 'carnal' goods are impermanent that they are not the highest goods. For the implication of saying that would have to be that the 'carnal' goods *might* be the supreme goods, if they did last for ever; but Augustine hardly wants to concede that. (The tendency to appeal, irrelevantly, to the longevity of a good as evidence of its 'true' goodness is a chronic vice of Platonism, which Aristotle's tart medicine should really have cured once and for all: 'A thing which lasts for ever is not a better thing just for that reason, any more than a white thing which lasts a long time is whiter than a white thing which lasts a day' (NE 1096b3–5).)

Secondly: for a Christian bishop, there might seem a danger of some kind of unorthodoxy or idolatry in saying that the greatest good for humanity is good will, and that we should love this and scorn everything (!) else. After all, where does God enter this story? In the section of the *Retractationes* dealing with the dLA (Retr 1.8), Augustine does not explicitly repudiate this claim. But he does point out that even in the dLA the powers of the soul, including good will, are only 'middle goods', and that he there stressed the need for divine grace to assist human good will:

> Unless the will itself is freed by divine grace from the slavery which made it the slave of sin, and helped to overcome its vices, it is impossible for mortals to live rightly and reverently. (dLA 1.11)

This suggests that possession of the good will alone is not, in fact, sufficient for the possession of the good life. God's grace is also needed. But the supplying of that grace is clearly not within our power of choice, unless our possession of good will guarantees God's supplying of divine grace – a suggestion which Augustine and a host of followers have strenuously denied.

More usual answers to the question of the nature of the human good, in the later works especially, are the ones reviewed already, that it is (4a) peace or (4b) contemplation of God. Augustine's doctrine of the good will was never meant to be a denial of these answers, even if it looks rather like one at times. As more careful examination of the dLA shows, the good will is not so much the greatest good for humans as the desire for (or choice of) the greatest good for humans. It is therefore the best desire to have and the best choice to make, but this is only because it is desire/choice of the best possible objective – which in Augustine's view is of course God. Once again, we see the need to adopt a relatively modest view of the role of *voluntas* in Augustine's thought. The best interpretation of Augustine is not that the possession of good will is sufficient for the good life, but only that it is necessary.

Formally speaking, Augustine's way of reaching the conclusion that the best kind of *voluntas* is the desire for God is to revert to the 'function' style of argument. It is the human function to turn to what is good. What is good? What is eternal:

> Therefore the eternal law enjoins us to avert our love from temporal things, and convert it from worldliness to what is eternal. (dLA 1.32)

What is good is also, characteristically, not private, it is equally available to all. This is a principle of metaphysics in the dLA (2.29). In the dCD it is a principle of political philosophy too:

> In the city of God... there will be no love of anyone's own or private will; the city will rejoice in a common and unchanging good, making one heart out of many. (dCD 15.3)

Now what is common and eternal in this way, except for truth itself?

> I promised to demonstrate to you that there is something which is higher than our mind and reason. Look, it is truth itself! If you can embrace that, and enjoy it... what more would you seek for your happiness? And what could be happier than the person who enjoys the unshakeable and unchangeable and most excellent truth? Can we doubt that we are happy when we embrace the truth? (dLA 2.35)

In the very Plotininian *de Quantitate Animae*, the contemplation of truth is made the seventh and last stage in an 'ascent of the soul' from minimal vitality, via sensation, technical knowledge, the work of purgation, moral purity, and the hunger for What Is. It is 'the seventh and last stage', with nothing better to follow it, for there is nothing better than the 'complete enjoyment of the highest true good' (dQA 76). Truth is the chief good because (Augustine suggests) nothing could be put above its contemplation.

Truth is also the chief good because truth itself, in some mysterious way, is identical with God: 'This is our liberty, when we are under the rule of truth itself; and this truth is our God himself' (dLA 2.37). Hence 'There is no unchanging good except for the one true and blessed God' (dCD 12.1); and the good will which we cannot lose without choosing to is only a supremely good thing because it is identical with desire for this God.

This completes my presentation of Augustine's seven definitions of the human good. Perhaps it is clear now that they do in fact tie up, in this way. The highest human good is contemplation (4a) in peace (4b) of God because the beatific vision is the highest good that there is, the highest good that we can desire; such a good is also preeminently the right object of desire (4d) and a righteous desire (4e) or good will (4g), and (given that humans can attain to the very heights of the cosmic order) the natural thing for humans to desire (4c). Augustine also believes that God is that object of desire which (4f) it is supremely difficult to lose unless you choose to: that is the point of his argument (dLA 1.20–21) that no wicked power in heaven or earth, apart from the defection of the will itself, could be strong enough to overpower the good will.

The underlying motivation of all these arguments is the same. Augustine's central moral axiom is that there should be a match between the ordering of our desires and choices and the ordering of the world:

> The nature of the body puts it at an inferior level to the nature of the soul; *for this reason (ac per hoc)* the soul is a greater good than the body. (dLA 2.48)

> This is justice in each case: that God should command the obedient human, that the soul should command the body, that reason should command the vices even when they resist. (dCD 19.27)

> The perfect ordering of the volitions would reflect perfectly the perfect ordering of the goods which there are in the world; desire

would match up perfectly with desirability (in the gerundive sense). As may by now be clear, Augustine, in modern terminology, is an 'ethical naturalist'.

7.5.   GOOD WILL AND THE ORDER OF THE WORLD

In turn, the natural ordering of the world depends on God, on the one who has 'disposed everything in measure and number and weight (*mensura, numero, pondere*)' (Conf. 5.4). (Gosselin remarks (Gosselin (1949), p. 525) that in Augustine's writings 'Modus, species, ordo' *reviennent comme un refrain*': there are other similar, and related, refrains, as this passage shows.) The point of this refrain is that Augustine holds that God is the formal cause of that order in the world which is a necessary condition of its continued existence. This is argued at length in dLA 2.44–45.

The first step in the argument is the claim that all non-eternal things have form (as opposed to being form). They have this form inasmuch as they admit of numbers, i.e. are measurable, have proportions and quantities (a Platonic idea):

> Look at the sky and the earth and the sea, and at everything in them... these things have form because they have *numbers*; take those numbers away, and they will be nothing. (dLA 2.42)

> So if you regard any changeable thing, whether by bodily sense or the consideration of the soul, you cannot understand it unless there is some form of numbers present in it; which if you remove, the object will fall away into nothing. (dLA 2.44)

(Note here that, in both passages, Augustine says that what lacks this form is nothing. Likewise, at dNB 3 he writes that 'Where there is no measure, kind and order (*modus, species et ordo*), there is no nature.' Some writers, such as Gilson, have attempted to distinguish divine making and forming in Augustine's thought about creation, a 'faire' and a 'parfaire', as if God created matter first and only then imposed form on it, like water poured into a jug or a seal pressed into wax. But, at least from passages like these, it seems rather as if the creative operations of making and forming are, to Augustine's mind, identical. For him, what was (*per impossibile?*) only made and not also formed would not be anything actual at all.)

Hence Augustine does not go along with the Manichaeans in saying that matter is essentially evil. For him it is unclear that matter has any essence, evil or not. On the other hand, he does not deny the existence (in some sense) of matter. Rather, what he says about it is that there is an inherent inaccessibility, both perceptual and conceptual, about matter considered in itself:

> Nor should we say that this matter (*hyle*) is bad, which cannot be sensed through any appearance, but can, by the privation of any appearance (*per omninodam speciei privationem*) can just barely be thought of. (dNB 18)

Matter is something mysteriously poised on the brink of being nothing; its only reality is so much in potentiality, and so little in actuality, that it is barely anything real at all. There is an important analogue to all this in Augustine's theory of action – as we shall see in Ch. 8.

The second step of the argument is the claim that the forms recognisable in mutable things must have been imposed on those things from outside:

> But nothing can give itself form (*formare seipsam*); for nothing can give itself what it itself does not have. (dLA 2.45)

And where does this imposed form come from? From an eternal form:

> So it turns out that both body and soul are given form by some eternal and unchanging form. To this form it is said 'You shall change them, and they shall be changed; but you are the same, and your years will not run out' [Psalm 102: 26–7]. (dLA 2.45)

This eternal form is identical with *providentia*, providence, a word which Augustine chooses with an eye on Plotinus's *pronoia* (*Enneads* 3.2–3):

> Hence it can be seen that all things are governed by providence. For if everything that exists will be nothing at all if the form is taken away, then that unchanging form whereby all mutable things so subsist that the quantities of their forms are fulfilled and

made actual – that form is their providence; for those things would not exist, if that form did not. (dLA 2.45)

Providentia, in turn, is identical with God's wisdom (dLA 2.45), and God's wisdom is itself identical with God, specifically with the second person of the Trinity (dLA 2.39). God, then, is the formal cause of the order of the world. That is part of what it means to talk of him as creator. There is no other possible source for the existence, life and intelligence manifest in the world (dLA 2.46); and, without his formal causality, Augustine argues not only that there would be no order in the world, but even that there would be no world. (As we have seen, the two propositions are barely separable for Augustine.)

The right ordering of volitions, I said, reflects the right ordering of the world; and we have just established that everything that is right in the ordering of the world is for Augustine a direct consequence of God's formal causality. It follows that all right volition is equally under the influence of God's formal causality. Whatever is a formal cause of the order of the world, is also a formal cause of the rightly ordered will. To put the same point a different way: the Good Life is the formal cause of the Good Will. The natural aspiration of human volition, and the right direction for human volition, converge: on the Good Life in Augustine's most adequate characterisation of it, as lived out in the beatific vision of God. That, for Augustine, is the ultimate meaning of the directedness or rationality or form of voluntary action: the active soul's natural and (almost) inevitable gravitation (*pondus*) is towards its source and final purpose, in God.

This is the conclusion about the directedness and the rational explicability of the will at which I have been aiming all along in this chapter. The conclusion is that Augustine, just as much as Aristotle, has a doctrine of the rationality of voluntary action – even if something rather different is meant by the Augustinian doctrine. For Augustine too, we do not have anything worthy of the name 'voluntary action' unless we have behaviour which not only has an efficient cause of the right sort (v. Ch. 6), but can also be explained by seeing it as aimed at and (so to speak) shaped by some good – and in particular, of course, at the good of all goods, God himself. It follows that Augustine takes it that the rationality of voluntary action is an essential feature of such action.

However, some doubts may remain. In particular, my conclusion equates the formal causality of the good will with that of the will as such. But to many modern minds there will seem to be an unbridgeable gap between a conclusion about what the will ought to be motivated by, and one about what it is motivated by.

The best way of dealing with such doubts is to turn to a question which may already have seemed pressing anyway: the question 'What about *bad* will?' I attribute to Augustine the claim that it is normally a condition of some action's being voluntary that it should be rational, i.e. directed towards some good objective; and that ideal voluntary actions are directed in an ordered way towards the good life as a whole, and to its ultimate manifestation in the beatific vision. Can this claim be convincingly maintained in face of the objection that there is in Augustine plenty of evidence for a doctrine of volition towards bad objectives? That is the question of the next, the final, chapter.

8

Bad Will and the Mystery of Evil

It is commonly held that Augustine's ontology, in which evil is treated as a privation, does no more than evade the problem which it is professed to solve; and that his deeply Christian sense of the reality of moral evil caused him to relapse into Manichaean-ism with his doctrine of original sin, in which the Not-Being, the Nothing out of which man was created, is transformed into a Something with fatal power. In fact the originality of Augustine appears just in his steady refusal to hypostatise evil.

John Burnaby, *Amor Dei*, p. 37

The first man is summed up in one act: he took the fruit and ate of it. About that act there is nothing to say; one can only tell it; it happens and henceforth evil has arrived.

Paul Ricoeur, *The Symbolism of Evil*, p. 244

The Apostle meets the problem by leaving it unsolved.

Robert Wallis, chapter heading in his translation (1887) of Augustine's *contra Duas Epistolas Pelagianorum*

8.1. INTRODUCTION

In Chs 5–6 I argued that Augustine, just like Aristotle, teaches that the absence of compulsion and the absence of ignorance are negative conditions of voluntary action, and that the presence of the right sort of efficient causation, and of knowledge, are positive conditions of voluntary action. The conclusion of Ch. 7 was that Augustine, somewhat like Aristotle, is also committed to the view that voluntary action is normally *rational* in an important sense (though not quite the same sense as Aristotle's). The relevant sense is that Augustine believes that voluntary action, to be understood as such, must at least be directed towards some good (and ideally, of course, to one very particular good, the supreme good of God himself). Augustine's doctrine of the rationality of action, then, is a weaker one than Aristotle's, and not precisely the same as Aristotle's; but (as I have argued) it is nonetheless a doctrine of the rationality of action.

In Ch. 4 I suggested that the three conditions of voluntary action which I had argued for from Aristotle's writings pointed us to a way of dealing with the puzzle about akrasia raised in Aristotle's system. To conclude this book and my study of Augustine, I will now suggest that the three parallel conditions of voluntary action which I have argued for in Augustine suggest an analogous treatment of an analogous problem.

The analogous problem is that posed for Augustine by the admitted existence of what he calls *mala voluntas* – bad voluntary choice or action, or (as I shall call it for the sake of brevity) 'bad will'. Bad will – he believes – exists, and like akrasia can be characterised as wilful wrongdoing (deliberate choice of the worse over the better). Because of this belief Augustine, being both a Christian and a classical philosopher, is confronted by a dilemma.

On the one hand: the Christian Scriptures (e.g. Rom.1:20–21) affirm that there is wilful wrongdoing. Admittedly, in the Bible, the origin of wilful wrongdoing is as mysterious as the origin of suffering. But that it is a reality is strongly affirmed.

On the other hand: against Scripture, classical philosophy from Socrates to the Stoics denies the possibility of wilful wrongdoing, of a knowing, deliberate choice of evil. Even the Plato of the *Republic* presents an account of akrasia, not as a matter of the rational soul's choosing to follow desires it knows to be wrong, but as a matter of its being overpowered by those desires. Now, as I have argued in Ch. 7, Augustine's philosophical psychology was not radically different from the kind of accounts which the writers of the classical era had proposed. Like theirs, his took as its most basic principle the axiom that all desire is desire of something intrinsically good. Thus the idea of a free choice to do wrong was just as problematic for him as for Socrates (or Aristotle). To offer an account of the psychology of wilful wrongdoing, in the terms of a classical theory of action like this, was simply impossible. Augustine was too good at philosophy to miss this – although (as we shall see) he was also too fond of rhetoric to keep himself from ever indulging in the inconsistency of exploring other, ultimately less fruitful, lines of thought.

So the problem which haunts Augustine's theory of the voluntary is a conflict between the givens of revelation and philosophy. If voluntary action has the inherent directedness towards the good which Augustine, in line with his philosophical tradition, says it has, how can there be even one case of genuine deliberate choice of the worse over the better – as opposed to action which looks like such a choice, but is really ignorant or compelled or irrational action?

It may now be clear why I say this problem is analogous to Aristotle's problem about akrasia. In what follows, I hope to make it clear why I also say that Augustine's treatment of this problem of 'bad will' is – up to a point – analogous to Aristotle's treatment of the problem of akrasia.

8.2.   BAD WILL

How can there be bad will? To see Augustine's response to this question, we need to look in detail at how he actually uses the vital words *mala voluntas* and associated phrases. The evidence will suggest two points:

1. If the phrase 'bad will' is to be used as an explanatory tool in Augustine's theory of action, then it cannot be used to mean 'a choice of something evil in itself'. What Augustine's use of it marks, is not a belief that his talk of bad will explains any choice of something evil in itself, but a belief that at this point in the theory of the voluntary, explanations necessarily run out. For voluntary action is, in Augustine's view, necessarily directed towards the good. Therefore we cannot explain behaviour as voluntary action by supposing it to be directed towards something evil.
2. Hence Augustine's account of the origination of bad will is not only incomplete, but necessarily incomplete.

Both points – I shall argue – play vital parts in Augustine's own philosophical strategy. But this may be far from obvious at first sight. I now present evidence against both (1) and (2).

2a.   Evidence against (1)

The 'directedness' thesis which I have been attributing to Augustine, the claim that all choice is of something intrinsically good, runs clean against the normal line of exegesis of Augustine, which, on the contrary, credits him with a 'neutrality' thesis about the will, according to which the will is not necessarily directed towards anything. Now Augustine does often talk as if his doctrine of will does mean that one can have choices between a good and a bad where it is a matter of 'indifference' (in Hume's sense) which one chooses. Consider these five passages:

(i)   'Unless the movement (*motus*) by which the will is turned hither and thither were voluntary (*voluntarius*), a human would neither be praiseworthy when he turned his will to higher things, nor blameworthy when he twisted away as it were the hinge of his will to lower things.' (dLA 3.3)

If the will is a hinge between higher or better things (*superiora*) and worse or lower things (*inferiora*), then it may be said that, as a hinge between a door and a door frame is not truly part of either, the point of the image must be that the will itself has a neutral position between good and bad options, and is not, by its nature, committed to a general policy of preferring either the good to the bad or vice versa.

(ii)   'God ordained that there should be not only great goods, but also middle goods and minimal goods... No one uses the virtues badly, but one can use the other goods – that is, the middle and minimal goods – not only well but also badly.... Now the will is a middle good...'. (dLA 2.50, 2.52)

The claim that the will is a 'middle good' does not, of course, mean that the will is *in the middle*, neutral, between good and evil. Middle goods are still *goods*; they are in the middle between 'great goods' and 'minimal goods', not between goods and bads. The claim is not that the will is in itself neither good or bad; it is rather that the will is the kind of good which can be used or misused.

(iii)   In the dDA, Augustine insists that our having both good and evil desires is no evidence for the two souls, one good and one evil, which the Manichaeans claimed to discern in the human psychology:

The Manichaeans... would have me learn that there are two souls in the human from this fact: that we sometimes give assent on the bad side, and sometimes on the right side. But why is this not rather a sign of a single soul, which can by its free will (*libera illa voluntate*) be carried off in this direction, and then back again in that? When this happens to me... very often one thing is freely available even though another is what I ought to do (*illud libet, hoc decet*), and I fluctuate in the middle between them (*quorum nos in medio positi fluctuamus*). (dDA 10; cp. Conf. 8.5)

(iv) 'What makes the difference is the quality of the human's will. If that is perverse, then his emotions (*motus*) will be perverse... because of the variety of things that are desired and avoided, just as the human's will is attracted or repelled, so likewise it will turn towards these or those affections.' (dCD 14.6)

The claim is, clearly enough, that the will can equally be either right or 'perverse'. This seems to imply that it is equally likely to be either, which again suggests its neutrality. Augustine seems also to be positing a cause for its turning either way, in the environment in which the will is to be found. Cp. dLA 3.74, where he remarks that 'nothing excites the will to do anything except what is seen' (presumably Augustine means *sensed* rather than merely seen). He seems to suggest here that the causes of sin are, in a sense, in our environment: a claim which I shall consider below.

(v) Most decisively of all, consider dSL 58, where – it might seem – the 'directedness' thesis is explicitly rejected:

Free choice (*liberum arbitrium*) was naturally given to the rational soul by the creator, as that middle power (*media vis*) which can either set itself on faith or turn to infidelity.

2b. Evidence against (2)

At first sight it seems arguable, too, that Augustine's acccount of the origination of bad will is not in any important sense incomplete. He seems to have plenty to say to back up the claim that bad will is itself the origin of evil – under at least five different heads.

(a) On at least one occasion he says that sin, and with it presumably bad will, arises from two sources, one being 'one's own thinking', the other 'the persuasion of another' (dLA 3.29). In either case, of course, it remains true that what is done is voluntary. Compare dGCPO 2.42: 'In truth the originator of sin is the cunning of the devil, the deceiver, and the consenting will of the human.'

(b) Sometimes he describes bad will as arising from pride, in particular when he is dealing with the fall of the angels:

> But because that angel loved himself more than God he was not willing to be subordinate to him; and he swelled with pride, and defected (*defecit*) from the highest being, and fell. (dVR 26)

> For we never arrive at a bad deed (*malum opus*) unless there has been a preceding bad will. And what beginning of a bad will could there have been except pride? For pride is the beginning of every sin. (dCD 14.13)

(c) Sometimes he says that bad will originates in a choice of a private good as a result of a turning away from a communal good:

> No one loses truth and wisdom unwillingly (*invitus*); for no one can be separated from them by place. What is called 'separation from truth and wisdom' is that perverse will by which the lower things are prized.... We have [in truth and wisdom] what we may all enjoy equally and communally. (dLA 2.37)

> For it is a perverse loftiness, when one has deserted that first principle (*eo principio*) to whom one's soul should cleave, to be made and to become in some way one's own first principle. (dCD 14.13)

This mode of description is readily compatible with the mode which describes bad will as being due to pride, as shown by a passage in the dCD where the two modes are run together (I put in boldtype those parts which refer to the 'privacy' mode of description, and italicise those which refer to the 'pride' mode):

> Others loved **their own powers more, as if they themselves were their own good for themselves,** and so ebbed away from that higher good which makes happy **all things alike, turning to their own goods.** *They held to the citadel of overweeningness rather than the highest eternity; the cleverness of vanity rather than the most certain*

truth; the **love of partiality rather than undivided charity**; they became *proud*, **deceived**, and *envious*.' (dCD 12.1)

(d) Sometimes, as we have seen, he argues that the origin of the bad will is in some sense to do with the environment in which the will is placed. dCD 14.6 and dLA 3.7 have been quoted already. There is also 83DQ 40:

[In answer to the question 'Since there is only one sort of soul, where do people's different wills (*diversae voluntates*) come from?':] There are different desires in the soul according to the different things that are seen (*diversis visis*); from a diversity of desires comes a diversity of subsequent pursuits; from a variety of pursuits comes a variety of dispositions; from a diversity of dispositions comes a diversity of wills.

Which brings us to (e): Augustine's very frequent descriptions of bad will as originating in, or a concomitant of, or something connected in one way or another with, disposition or habituation (*consuetudo*). This is perhaps Augustine's commonest way of characterising bad will, especially in the later works.

The idea is clearly present in the 83DQ passage just quoted, where it is given unusually precise formulation. Here what is seen leads to desire; desire to pursuit; pursuit to disposition; and disposition to will. Elsewhere, the idea is usually less sharply focused, but often seems to be essentially the same: we have the bad or good will that we have because of our habituation, our constitution, the way we are already. (Notice the apparent circularity of this account, if the will is what moves us to pursue what we desire in the first place. Cp. the discussion of the idea of a reflexive will in Ch. 6.)

So in the EEGal, the stage of unsuccessful struggle against sin, 'under the law', is that stage where the sinner 'is dragged about by the weight of this world's desires', and (hence) 'leaves aside justice' (EEGal 46). In the dLA, we read that

It is no wonder that because of ignorance someone should not have free choice of the will to pick out what action he should rightly do; nor that when that carnal habituation, which the compulsion of transient mortality somehow imbues in us naturally, resists the agent, he should see what he ought to do and will it (*velit*), and yet not be able to fulfil it. (dLA 3.52)

Even where good impulses are present, they are smothered by the weight of custom and, the suggestion is, contrary bad impulses.

In the later writings, this kind of description of the bad will as will under the influence of cupidity or concupiscence, the gravity of original sin which drags us away from the choice of the good, is the subject of whole books (such as *de Gratia Christi et Peccato Originali*, Bk 2). As a proponent of the theology of the Fall, it is natural for Augustine to want to argue that, in Adam and Eve, bad will led to bad habituation; whereas in us bad habituation leads to bad will. So we read that

> It happened by our freedom of choice (*per arbitrii libertatem*) that humanity came to be sinful; but now a penal viciousness following on that choice makes compulsion (*necessitas*) out of our freedom. (dPIH 9)

And again, that

> It is from the vices of nature (but not from the foundation of nature) that there is a compulsion to sin (*peccandi necessitas*). (dNG 79)

But one begins at times to wonder whether, with reference strictly to fallen humanity, Augustine is arguing that concupiscence causes bad will, or that bad will causes concupiscence. Or is it that concupiscence *is* bad will? Or a mishmash of all three? For example, the progression from habituation to will noted above in 83DQ 40 is actually reversed in the *Confessions*, where the subject of the description is not Adam but Augustine:

> A perverse will turns into a desire (*libido*); and so long as the desire is obeyed, it is turning into a habituation; and so long as the habituation is not resisted, it is turning into a compulsion. (Conf. 8.5)

So which comes first in fallen humans, bad habituation or bad will? In the later works, the rather vague and general upshot of teaching about will and habituation tends to be that whichever way round it is, 'we are carnal, weak, hateful through our sins and wound round with the shades of ignorance' (dCD 10.24). The two states of bad habituation and bad will seem to become welded together in Augustine's thinking to the extent that to talk of one is to talk of the other. (Compare the way in which, as noted in Ch. 5, ignorance and difficulty became for the later Augustine no longer exculpating factors, but the very hallmark of culpability.) 'Which comes first?' is treated by the later Augustine as being, at least with reference to fallen humans, a chicken-and-egg question.

One characteristic argument is that the sinner has freedom from righteousness, the righteous person freedom from sin, but both are, nonetheless, free:

> Certainly a freedom (*libertas*) perished through our sin, but it was that freedom which was in paradise, the freedom of having the fullness of justice together with immortality... free choice has not perished in the sinner to this extent, that through free choice itself they sin to the uttermost who sin with enjoyment and from love of sinning; it pleases them to do so because they are free to do so. (cDEP 1.5; cp. dLA 1.37)

Cp. my discussion of the distinction between freedom as 'not being able to sin' or as 'being able not to sin' in Section 7.4.

The existence of bad will is not inconsistent with that of free will; but the range of options for a bad will is limited, and different from that available for a good will. Bad will, one might almost say, *becomes* original sin:

> Sin is hidden until the evil which fights back against justice is made evident by justice's prohibition, when one thing is ordered and approved [by justice], but another is found pleasant and is allowed to dominate [by sin]. (cDEP 1.17)

8.3.   AN INCOMPLETE ACCOUNT?

I have amassed a good deal of evidence against my two leading claims (1) and (2) about the bad will. How then am I to defend those claims? I will begin by treating of the evidence against (2). This treatment, I hope, will show how my defence of (1) is going to go.

(2) was the claim that Augustine's account of the origination of bad will is necessarily incomplete. This has suggested the retort that, on the contrary, Augustine's account of the origination of bad will is full, detailed, and therefore perfectly adequate.

Augustine's account (or rather 'accounts'), as given above, may well be full and detailed. But nothing he says under the five heads considered above deals adequately with a central problem which confronts his doctrine of bad will. There is a serious lacuna in his teaching as so far expounded: one which can only be remedied by taking (with Augustine himself, in many places) a view of the origination of bad will radically different from all the above five. This lacuna, I will now argue, seriously compromises any attempt to extract from Augustine's writings a consistent doctrine of the will in the sense required, for example, by Dihle (1982). What is this lacuna?

It is one which has already been observed by at least one sharp-eyed Augustine scholar, in Brown (1978). Let us begin with Brown's response to the suggestion that 'Pride is the cause of the fall', a suggestion in effect equivalent to (b) above:

> What a grand solution this is: Satan turned away from God because he was proud, and thereby became a self centred rebel. But just a minute! Why was he proud? Did God create him proud? Certainly not, for then God would be responsible for his fall. Did he make himself proud by the free exercise of his will? So he must have done, if Augustine's intent to defend the initial free-dom and responsibility of the will is to remain intact. If Satan made himself proud, then this act of will is itself the fall, and not a 'cause' of his falling. Pointing to pride therefore cannot constitute an explanation for the fall (an account of why the first evil will willed as it did). It is only the substitution of a synonym for the inexplicable free act of falling itself. This substitution of 'becoming proud' for 'falling' or 'first willing evil' is attractive because, by drawing an analogy to the everyday human sin of pride, it makes Satan's act more vivid... but it explains nothing, it in no way renders Satan's fall understandable.

(Brown (1978); for further discussion of Brown v. Chappell (forthcoming))

Brown's point applies in an obvious way to what I am consider-ing, the question of what Augustine can tell us about the origination of bad will. It will not do to say (b) that pride is the source of the bad will: for unless there is already a bad will, how can there be any (culpable) pride? And this point, about what Ricoeur might call the 'already'-ness of sin, can be deployed against the other four

explanations of the origin of bad will offered in response to the
allegation that Augustine's account is necessarily incomplete.

(a) Action which counts as a case of sin, and so of bad will, may
     well originate either through 'one's own thinking' or 'the
     persuasion of another'. But either way, it will not be sin (or bad
     will) unless the thinking or the persuasion was not a sufficient
     and necessary condition of the action's occurring. For if either
     was such a condition, then the agent was not free to do
     otherwise than she did, and so was not responsible. Thus, if
     (a) is an explanation of the origination of sin, in the sense of
     wilful wrongdoing, it cannot be a *complete* explanation; but, if
     (a) is a complete explanation, it cannot be an explanation of *sin*.

(c) To say that bad will originates in the turning away from the
     shared good to a private good simply prompts the question
     whether this turning away is itself a bad action. If it is not a bad
     action, then why does bad will result from it? If it is a bad
     action, then must not bad will be present already when it is per-
     formed – in which case the origin of bad will has not been
     given? The idea that bad will can be characterised as a 'turning
     aside' from the 'communal good' (or (b) as pride) seems all
     right. The idea that it can be (efficient causally) explained in
     these ways does not.

(d) As for (a): action which counts as a case of sin, and so of bad
     will, may well originate through the influence of factors in the
     environment which are perceived. But if so, it will not be sin (or
     bad will) unless the environmental influence in question was
     not a sufficient and necessary condition of the action's occur-
     ring. For if that influence was such a condition, then the agent
     was not free to do otherwise than she did, and so was not
     responsible. Thus, if (d) is an explanation of the origination of
     sin, it cannot be a complete explanation; but, if (d) is a complete
     explanation, it cannot be an explanation of sin.

(e) is the most interesting of the five accounts; but (as noted) it is
     very unclear precisely what this account comes to. If, on the one
     hand, the point is either that concupiscence originates in bad
     will, or that the two are equivalent conditions, then it is patent
     that the origin of bad will has not been explained. If, alter-
     natively, the point is that bad will originates in concupiscence,
     then the same problem as for (b) and (c) recurs. Is this con-
     cupiscence itself bad? If it is not, then why does bad will result

from it? If it is, then must not bad will be present already when the concupiscence arises? Again, in either case, the origin of bad will has not been explained.

I take it that these arguments vindicate at least the claim that Augustine's account of the origination of bad will is incomplete – if not my stronger claim (2) that Augustine's account of the origination of bad will is necessarily incomplete. The lacuna I have indicated is simply this: that not one of these supposed accounts of the origination of bad will *is* such an account. None of them delivers the goods required by actually telling us where bad will comes from. And this does seem to suggest that there is something incomplete about Augustine's account.

8.4. A NECESSARILY INCOMPLETE ACCOUNT?

What more is needed, then, for me to move from saying that that account is incomplete to saying that it is *necessarily* incomplete? The missing steps – as I shall now argue – are provided by Augustine himself. Augustine himself gives us (the makings of) a valid argument to the conclusion that such attempts at explaining the origination of bad will as the above five cannot, in principle, succeed; and indeed, that no attempt whatever to explain its origination could succeed.

This argument which I attribute to Augustine explains, with Brown, why 'the first evil will must be inexplicable'. But the argument I propose gives us more reason for saying that than Brown's argument does. It also leads us from the establishment of the second claim made at the start of this chapter (the incompleteness thesis) to the establishment of the first claim made there (the directedness thesis).

That there is this argument in Augustine will allow us to see (a)–(e) in a rather different light. On the best interpretation of his work, Augustine is not offering us any kind of positive explanation of the origin of bad will at all. Rather, what he means to offer us is an explanation of why there can be no such explanation. Hence it will emerge that neither (a)–(e), nor anything else in Augustine's writings, count as possible ingredients for a 'theory of will' which is to explain the origin of evil by reference to the neutrality, relative to good and evil, of the will's power to choose. One might, indeed, take the failure of (a)–(e) to explain the origin of bad will as a kind of *reductio ad absurdum*: a demonstration of the hopeless task which any similar attempt at explanation of bad will is, necessarily, setting itself.

For, sometimes almost in the same breath as he offers us one of (a)–(e) – or some other attempt at explaining bad will – Augustine also makes remarks like these:

> A wicked will (*improba voluntas*) is the cause of all evils... but if you seek [and find] the cause of this root [of evils], then how can that evil will be the root of *all* evils? The root of *all* evils is then rather the cause of the evil will. And when you find *that*, you will be asking for *its* cause too, and there will be no limit to your search. But, in the end, what can there have been before the will itself as the cause of the will? (dLA 3.49)

Augustine says quite clearly here that it is impossible to explain the origination of bad will. But why should that be? Because 'what is not anything, cannot be known' (dLA 2.54). Is Augustine, then, saying that the origin of bad will is *nothing*, or nothingness?

It seems clear that Augustine is indeed saying something like that. This is a recurring idea in his thought. The claim that there is some sort of connection between wickedness and nothingness is first hinted at in a piece of folk etymology in the dBV:

> Wickedness (*nequitia*) is the mother of all the vices because it is not-anything (*nequidnam*), that is, because it is *nothingness* (*nihil*).' (dBV 8; cp. Cicero, *Tusculanae Disputationes*, 3.18)

In the dDA, likewise, the origins of evil in general are said to be, at best, highly mysterious. The Manichaeans' urge to look into the questions of pain and sin is an urge 'to look into secret matters' (dDA 9). The Manichaeans' attempts to make problems for Catholics by raising unanswerable questions about sin and pain are disingenuous, says Augustine, for these are questions without answers:

> 'If evil comes from humans, where do humans come from? If from angels, where do they come from?' – as if evil were connected by some sort of chain to God. They think that they triumph by asking these questions – as if to ask was to understand.

If only it were! For then no one would be found wiser than me. (dDA 9)

In the *Confessions*, Augustine's long meditation on the stealing of the pears (Conf. 2.4–10) gives us another question which remains unanswered: *Why* did Augustine steal the pears? He says he got a 'kick' out of stealing the pears – because it was forbidden (2.4). Was this his reason for stealing them? But such a motive seems to him hardly an adequate reason for doing anything! Yet why else should Augustine have done it? For the taste of the pears (2.4), for their fairness (2.6), for the company of the young rogues with whom he did the deed (2.8), for the joke of the thing (2.9)? None of these answers seems to satisfy Augustine. The action remains puzzling to him precisely because it was so random, so aimless, so lacking in motivation. Once again, this suggests to him the link between wickedness and nothingness, the idea that wickedness is mysterious because of its essential nothingness:

Now let my heart tell you, O God, what it was looking for there – that I should be so *gratuitously* wicked (*gratis malus*), that there should be no cause of my malice except malice! (Conf. 2.4)

Who will unwind that most tortuous and involved knottiness? It is unclean: I do not wish to attend to it – I do not wish to see it. (Conf. 2.10)

But what does it mean to talk like this? What is gained by saying that the origin of bad will is nothing, or nothingness? I believe that the answer to this can be given by reminding ourselves of what was established in Ch. 7 as a fundamental principle of Augustine's philosophy of action: the 'directedness' thesis.

The 'directedness' thesis, we saw, is the claim that all voluntary action is rational in the sense of being necessarily directed towards some good or other. To put it another way: to explain an agent A's piece of behaviour B as a voluntary action is (1) to posit a good G at which B could have been directed by A, and (2) to surmise that B was directed at G by A.

Now, how might such an account apply to the kind of action which is typical of bad will: a deliberately wicked action, a piece of wilful wrongdoing? The suggestion being canvassed here (in the form of claim (1)) is that it is precisely in its application to wilful wrongdoing that such an account must necessarily break down. We may make a sharp distinction between the case in which someone does what is, let us say, 'objectively' wrong, but where that action is nonetheless the best action available to him (simple wrongdoing); and the case where someone does what is 'objectively' wrong even though he knew it was wrong and could have avoided it (wilful wrongdoing).

Simple wrongdoing, so defined, will be perfectly easily explicable: the agent had no choice, or the agent at least did the best he could. But wilful wrongdoing, so defined, will not only be inexplicable: it will be necessarily inexplicable. The agent was not compelled; the agent was not ignorant of what he was doing; and the agent did not hold that what he did was really the right thing to do. And yet he did it. Such an action is, by its very nature, inexplicable, simply because the explicability of an action can only mean the possibility of relating it to some good at which it is supposed to aim. But if no good whatever is aimed at by an action as correctly described, then of course we cannot specify any good to which it is related; and hence it is necessarily true that we cannot explain it. Our ambitions to explain human actions, and to see them as cases of wilful wrongdoing, are ambitions which necessarily, in the nature of the case, pull against each other.

This, I believe, is an argument which Augustine does actually make out. Formally, its premises are (A) that explanation of an action can only mean stating what good it aims at, and (B) that action on bad will, 'wilful wrongdoing' in the strictest sense, means action which aims at no good whatever. From these it validly derives the conclusion (C) that wilful wrongdoing in this sense is inexplicable.

Direct exegetical evidence can be found for all three steps of the argument. Plenty of evidence has already been given for (A) in Ch. 7. I here present the evidence for (C) and (B); in that order, since (B) is the more complicated of the two.

(C) 'Let no one seek to know from me what I know I do not know: except perhaps so that he may learn not to know what (let it be known) cannot be known.' (dCD 12.7)

So where can this impetus to sin (*motus peccandi*) come from? If I answer this question of yours by saying that I do not know, perhaps you will be the sadder; but at least that would be the true answer. For that which is nothing cannot be known.... Since the impetus to turn away from God is defective (*defectivus motus est aversionis*), and since every defect arises from nothing – see what follows. (dLA 2.54; and cp. dLA 3.2, 'What point is there in asking whence this impetus comes into existence?')

(B) What does Augustine mean by his claim just quoted, that 'the impetus to turn away from God is *defective*'? One way of clarifying it is to compare dLA 2.54 with dCD 12.7:

Thus let no one ask me for the efficient cause of bad will (*efficientem causam malae voluntatis*). For it has no efficient cause, but a *de*ficient cause (*deficiens*), since a bad will is itself not an effect but a defection (*non effectio sed defectio*). For to defect from God, this is to begin to have a bad will. But the causes of such defections... to want to find these is like wanting to see darkness or hear silence. (Both of these are of course known to us; yet not through their appearances, but through their lack of appearances (*non in specie, sed in speciei privatione*).) (dCD 12.7)

The analogies which Augustine offers here are worth considering. There is no sight at all without light rays; no hearing at all without sound waves. The absence of either is something which can only be understood relative to the presence of either. The Manichaeans' mistake – their dualism of equal and opposite good and evil – is like thinking that, since whiteness and other varieties of colour are caused by light-waves, so blackness and other varieties of obscurity must be caused by dark-waves: it is to think that evil is one of the things which can be explained, when in fact its very presence is the negation of explanation. But what is it which is absent, in the case of an act of wilful wrongdoing, which is present in some other case and there makes explanation possible?

Note that Augustine speaks here of the 'deficient cause' of wilful wrongdoing, in sharp contrast with the 'efficient cause' which some other things have. What other things? I suggest, in line with (A), that the contrast is between actions which are cases of wilful wrong-doing and actions which are not. Then actions other than wilful wrongdoing will have 'efficient causes'. An action which has an 'efficient cause' will be a normal, non-skew, explicable case of action: either a good action, or a piece of non-wilful wrongdoing. The case of wilful wrongdoing, the case where (as Augustine's punning has it) the agent defects (*defecit*) and there is not so much an 'efficient cause' as a 'deficient cause', will be the queer and inexplicable case.

This will sound somewhat odd if we take Augustine's phrase *causa efficiens* in the obvious way, simply to mean 'efficient cause' in (something like) the Aristotelian sense. Does Augustine really mean to talk about efficient causation in any very strict sense in this context? Or is his choice of this term dictated not so much by philosophical considerations as by a rhetorical (and pun-making) impulse, by his playing-off of *deficere, deficiens, defectio* and (if I am right to bring in dLA 2.54) *defectivus*? The way this passage (at any rate) continues suggests that, if he were to have made this distinction, he would have said that here he was talking about a presence (or absence) of *final* causality, not of efficient. The defection from God is not here seen as underdetermined by efficient causality, so that it would be random. Here it is underdetermined by final causality, so that it is inexplicable. (Hence my scare-quotes around 'efficient cause' as here used by Augustine.)

In other places, however, there is clear evidence that Augustine thought that talk about the causes of bad will did not exclude talk about efficient causes. For example dLA 3.48–49, as already quoted, where Augustine is searching for the 'root of bad will', for the first term in an explanatory series that certainly seems to be of an efficient-causal sort. The point here is that, while a bad will exercises efficient causality over other states of affairs in the world, nothing else can exercise efficient causality over it. For if it were so, it would (as Augustine holds) not be able to do otherwise, and so not responsible (cp. my arguments v. (a), (d) and (e) above). Likewise, we read that

> The cause of the misery of the bad angels is this, that they turned aside to themselves from him who supremely is and became absorbed with themselves (*ad seipsos conversi sunt*), who are not supremely real.... But if a cause is sought for this bad will, none is to be found. For what is it that makes the will bad, when it is the will that makes the deed (*opus*) bad? Thus the bad will is the efficient cause (*efficiens*) of the bad deed, but there is no cause of the bad will. For if there is some such thing, then it either has a will or has not. If it has a will, then clearly it either has a good will or a bad. But if it has a good will, who would be so stupid as to say that a good will is what makes a bad will? (dCD 12.6)

The angels' misery has its (efficient) cause in their bad will; but their bad will is not similarly caused by anything, for if it were it would not be culpable – which (Augustine has already decided) it is.

If this evidence adds up, then it shows that Augustine does indeed teach that actions which are wilful wrongdoings are necessarily inexplicable, because to explain a voluntary action is to indicate the good at which it aims, and a wilful wrongdoing aims at *no* good. And this in turn shows what I meant by the claim that his account of the origin of bad will is not only incomplete, but necessarily incomplete. For (as I have also claimed) necessarily, there can be no explanation of what is inexplicable. And this is (or ought to be) Augustine's final line of defence against all comers on the question 'Where does evil come from?'

Thus there is a fundamental distinction in Augustine's thought, not always as carefully drawn by the saint himself as one might have liked, between what I have called 'simple wrongdoing' and 'wilful wrongdoing'. There is no mystery about simple wrongdoing; it is explained by reference to the good at which the agent is (mistakenly) aiming. But there is a mystery about wilful wrongdoing: because the action in question is not aimed at any good, mistakenly or otherwise.

8.5.   MANICHAEAN DUALISM AND *PRIVATIO BONI*

To illustrate this remark: consider Augustine's response to the Manichaean doctrine of the 'two souls', in his important anti-Manichaean pamphlet *de Duabus Animabus*. In line with their dualist metaphysics, the Manichaeans argued for a morally dualist psychology. On their view, just as evil was simply the mirror-image of good, so evil desire was simply the mirror-image of good desire. The existence of such radically opposed desires in each person was taken to be evidence for the existence of two souls in each person. The Manichaeans' good soul is perfectly good, and their bad soul is perfectly bad: the good soul, which is part of the 'very substance of God' (dDA 16), pursues the greatest available good by the shortest available route. The bad soul, which is absolutely nothing to do with the good God (dDA 16), pursues the greatest available evil with equal assiduity. It is as if a mediocre chess player's mediocrity were due to the evenly balanced influence on her of the ghosts of two Grand Masters haunting her soul. Both urge moves on her; but one is playing straight chess, the other suicide chess.

Thus in metaphysics, the Manichaeans were centrally committed to this claim:

(M) Just as there are substances whose very nature is to be good, so equally there are substances whose very nature is to be evil.

And in moral psychology, they were centrally committed to this claim:

(P) Explanations of action can just as well have the form: 'A does B because A thinks it will bring about C, and A thinks C is a good result' as the form: 'A does B because A thinks it will bring about C, and A thinks C is a bad result.'

Now Augustine believes that both these claims are incoherent, and for related reasons. To begin with the Manichaeans' (M): Augustine believes that the idea of an evil substance is a contradiction in terms. Existence as such is, in his view, a good (dNB 17, dVR 44); goodness pertains to substances naturally, since they were all made by God (dNB 12): 'Every kind of thing (*natura*) is a good kind of thing' (dNB 3; dLA 3.22).

Therefore there is no symmetry between the good and the bad; the mirror-image idea is exactly wrong. For a substance to be bad is not for it to partake of an equal and opposite quality to goodness: it is for it to be, somehow, a privation of good (*privatio boni*), less than it naturally should be (dNB 17, Ench 11, dVR 44). As Augustine remarks at dNB 6, any nature which can be corrupted must have some good in it.

The existence of evil is *parasitic* upon the existence of good. Evil is not so much like a bad quality or thing, as like the absence of a good quality or thing (dNB 17). Different evils have no independent natures of their own, as good things have (dDA 1). They take their natures entirely from the good things of which they are 'privations' (dDA 6), just as the sense of any negative proposition depends not so much on the negation itself as on the affirmative proposition which it negates (dDA 6). To assert that '*x* exists', where *x* is evil, is itself to assert something which (if true) detracts from *x*'s evil. Hence there can exist no perfect evil except non-existence; which

(Augustine thinks) means the same as 'Perfect evil does not exist' (dNB 9, 17).

Here is the relevance of the *privatio boni* argument to the 'two souls' hypothesis. All substances, as such, are good (dNB 17); the soul is a substance (dDA 7); so all souls, as such, are good (dDA 1); so there is no evil of souls symmetrical in kind to the goodness of souls.

> The first vice of the rational soul is the will to do what the highest and inmost truth forbids. Thus humanity was expelled from paradise into this age – from eternal to temporal things, from plenty to want, from strength to weakness. Not, however, from substantial good to substantial evil; for no substance is evil.... There is a form of good which, if the rational soul loves, it sins, because it is of a lower order than that soul. But it is the sin itself which is bad, not that substance which is loved in the sinning. (dVR 38)

Likewise with the Manichaeans' (P); as has already been pointed out, the idea of explaining an action with reference to the bad aim which it pursues is also, for Augustine, a contradiction in terms. Wilful wrongdoing, bad will, cannot be explained symmetrically to good will, deliberate choice of the good. For Augustine's doctrine of the directedness or rationality of voluntary action commits him to the view that explanation of any voluntary action means relating it to a desired good. To perceive something as a bad is, necessarily, to be disposed to avoid or avert it, not to pursue it. Someone who (like the Manichees) does not believe this has simply misunderstood, or misused, the word 'bad'.

So Augustine's response to the Manichaeans' metaphysical and psychological doctrines (M) and (P) is to reject these two symmetries. If there were such symmetries, then Augustine would indeed be forced to admit that something like the Manichaean 'two souls' hypothesis is true. But, Augustine argues, there is no such symmetry between good and evil, either in moral psychology, or in metaphysics. The moral psychologist should say, rather, that there are two kinds of bad action: wilful wrongdoing, where no good is chosen, which (as we have seen) is not explicable at all; and simple wrongdoing, where the wrong good is chosen through ignorance or compulsion (culpable or otherwise), which is explicable as a degenerate case of good action.

Why then am I not bound to admit the existence of two souls? Because we can better and much more economically (*expeditius*) take it that there are two sorts of good things. Neither of these is foreign from God's making; but they affect the human soul in different ways. (dDA 19)

Augustine's argument is that wrongdoing, at least of the simple variety, does not display desire of any evil, but desire of some inappropriate kind of good. His examples of goods which are often inappropriate tend to be physical goods, *sensibilia* as opposed (usually) to *intelligibilia*, spiritual or intellectual goods. While both sorts are repeatedly affirmed to be good, still intelligible goods are far better than sensible goods:

Everything that is perceived by touch or sight, or in whatever other ways corporeal sensation can occur, is as much inferior to those things which we grasp hold of by the understanding, as those senses are inferior to the intelligence itself. (dDA 2)

The pursuit of intelligible goods must take precedence in any well-ordered life over that of sensible goods. As I suggested in the last chapter, the right ordering of one's desires reflects the real ordering of the cosmos: good desire has as its formal cause Reality with a capital r, which is ultimately identifiable with God Himself (dLA 1.16–20; cp. dNB 1,3, dDA 2–4).

As justice, for Plato, is 'giving each his due', so the just life, for Augustine, is giving to each kind of good the attention which its place in the order of goods makes proper. And the unjust life, correspondingly, is failing to do so (dLA 2.48–52). No object of choice is bad, and no act of choice is bad, except in the sense in which it could have been better (dVR 78). 'Sin is not the desire for *bad* natures; it is the abandonment of *better* natures' (dNB 34). In the dDA, the image Augustine uses for this 'abandonment' is that of imitation; the image also appears in the *Soliloquies* (2.11, on falsity and resemblance), and in the dVR (66). The point stressed is that imitation is not bad because of the intrinsic badness of the models which it takes, but because of the unfittingness of the imitation to the nature of the creature guilty thereof: 'Natures are made bad by sinning not because they imitate bad things, but because they imitate things badly' (dDA 20).

8.6.   INCOMPLETENESS AGAIN

It may seem that this account works well enough to describe 'simple' wrongdoing, but does not apply to wilful wrongdoing. The above account, emphasising against the Manichaeans the derivative nature of sin, applies nicely to those who are already in the bondage of sin, and cannot help but follow their wicked propensities. What it completely fails to explain is how anyone not already in that state could get there in the first place.

> For it can happen that by a soul's own will, in its desiring what is not permissible for it to desire – that is, in its sinning – good souls can become bad ones. (dDA 20)

Augustine's words are 'it can happen'; but what he does not give us, here or anywhere else, is any indication of *how* this can happen. The notion of simple wrongdoing is a clear and comprehensible one. But the existence of simple wrongdoing, it turns out, must always be causally dependent on the prior existence of wilful wrongdoing. And this concept is radically incomprehensible. Which shows, again, the necessary incompleteness of Augustine's account.

The account, in fact, yields a regress, as hinted by dCD 12.6 (quoted in 8.4). If simple wrongdoing is failure to act on the right or appropriate good desire, this failure to act on the right good desire must itself have been either a voluntary choice to fail, or an involuntary failure. If it was an involuntary failure, then the agent could not help acting on the wrong good desire, and so was not culpable for her failure. If it was a voluntary choice to fail, then the agent could help it; and so was culpable for her choice to fail to act on the right good desire. But if the agent was culpable for this choice, then this choice must have been a (simple?) wrongdoing. And the definition of simple wrongdoing is 'an agent's failure to act on the right good desire'. So the agent's choice to fail to act on the right good desire was itself due to another failure to act on the right good desire. And again: this failure was either a voluntary choice to fail, or an involuntary failure…

To put it another way. Augustine says explicitly that we should explain wrongdoing by pointing out the good at which its agent aimed:

But when we ask about the misdeed 'For what reason was it done?', it is not normal to believe any explanation unless it is evident that it could have been done either through desire for some one of those goods which we call the lower goods (*quae infima diximus*), or through fear of losing such a good. (Conf. 2.5)

But if I do so explain someone's wrongdoing, then (on Augustine's theory) I have not yet completely explained his motivation. For in doing the wrong act, he (*ex hypothesi*) voluntarily aimed at a good, but an impermissible good: that was why it was wrongdoing. But *why* did he so aim? To explain this is to specify the good at which he aimed in so lowering his sights below the threshold of what is permitted. But if he thought there was a good to be achieved by lowering his sights in this way, nonetheless, if his action was wrongdoing, he must have been able to choose a better good: so why didn't he? And so on.

This regress appears because of Augustine's refusal to allow the Manichaeans their symmetry between pursuit of good and bad objectives. Wherever it is possible to explain wrongdoing, we must necessarily explain it as simple wrongdoing. Now such explanation seems to depend upon a prior notion of wilful wrongdoing. But, unlike simple wrongdoing, wilful wrongdoing is not explicable in terms of a pursued good. But that does not mean it is explicable in terms of a pursued evil; for there is no such type of explanation. What it means is that wilful wrongdoing is not explicable at all. And here, once again, the necessary incompleteness of Augustine's account of bad will is obvious. My suggestion is that this kind of necessarily incomplete account is no mishap; it is what Augustine is aiming at.

8.7.   AUGUSTINE AND VOLUNTARISM

I conclude that, for Augustine, wilful wrongdoing simply cannot be explained: it is a mystery. In the case of a piece of wilful wrongdoing, the agent sees and acknowledges what it is right to do, but, somehow, inexplicably, acts contrary to this knowledge. That Augustine considers this kind of renegation *inexplicable* is his concession to the claims of classical philosophy; that he admits that it is *possible* is his concession to the doctrine of Scripture.

That, of course, was the dilemma I mentioned at the outset. Revelation says that there is wilful wrongdoing; philosophy says that there cannot be. Augustine's most adequate view of the origin of wilful wrongdoing rather cleverly combines elements of both sides. First, analogously to Aristotle's treatment of the problem of akrasia, Augustine argues that wilful wrongdoing is rationally inexplicable in the sense explored above. Second, however, he insists that wilful wrongdoing does occur – the evidence being in the revelation of Scripture. The fact of wilful wrongdoing is a revelation to faith; to intelligence, it is a mystery.

So, besides the analogies which I have suggested, there is also an important contrast between Aristotle's and Augustine's theories about wilful wrongdoing. Aristotle's theory (as I argued in Ch. 4) suggests the conclusion that the existence of full akrasia would be a logical impossibility. Augustine's theory, on the other hand, suggests the conclusion that the existence of bad will is logically inexplicable. Aristotle's position is that 'There can't be wilful wrongdoing; therefore there isn't.' Augustine's (best) position is that 'Wilful wrongdoing makes no kind of sense; yet there it is.' In this contrast is the biggest difference between Aristotle's and Augustine's theories of action. It is the point at which they most decisively part company; and it is the point at which one should acknowledge that, if what I called Aristotle's rationality condition of voluntary action does usually have an analogue in the conditions of voluntary action which Augustine assumes, there is a crucial exception to this rule. For Augustine thinks that wilful wrongdoing is, in the sense I have explored, 'irrational'; but this does not lead him to deny that it is voluntary.

It is also the point at which the commentators start talking about Augustine's alleged belief in 'voluntarism', or 'irrationalism', or in a 'theory of the will'. So Brown, in the article already quoted, undertakes to focus on 'that primal act in which Adam freely turned his (wholly undetermined) 'voluntas' away from God' (Brown (1978), p. 318).

So also Dihle writes:

The key role attributed to will in Saint Augustine's corresponding systems of psychology and theology resulted mainly from self-examination. It is not derived from earlier doctrines in the field of philosophical psychology or anthropology, and seems to mark a turning point in the history of theological reasoning. From Saint

Augustine's reflections emerged the concept of a human will, prior to and independent of the act of intellectual cognition, yet fundamentally different from sensual and irrational emotion.... It is mainly through this entirely new concept of his own self that Saint Augustine superseded the conceptual system of Graeco-Roman culture.'

Dihle (1982), p. 127

If the argument in Part II of this book has found favour, it should now be evident why, as I take it, this standard view gets Augustine wrong. He is not offering us a 'theory of the will' of the kind supposed by Brown (1978), Dihle (1982), MacIntyre (1985), Thonnard (1941) *et alii*. If he has a 'theory of the will' at all, it is about 'the will' in a much thinner and less general sense than these commentators suppose. The key role, in his understanding of wilful wrongdoing, is not played by a concept of will, but by a concept of bad will.

Contrast these two claims, a specific one and a general one:

X. For Augustine, the human agent is – somehow – mysteriously capable of wilful wrongdoing which is irrational action. In such action, *and nowhere else*, a voluntary choice is made which has no rational justification even from the agent's own viewpoint.

Y. For Augustine, voluntary action *in general* has not, and does not need, any kind of rational justification.

I believe that (X) is perfectly correct. But (X) is not consistent with (Y), which I take it is the claim central to the 'voluntarist' view of Augustine's theory of action. Nor can (Y) itself be sustained as an interpretation of Augustine.

My reasons for saying this should already be clear. In the first place, I have already argued at length – the claim was central to Ch. 7 – that Augustine is committed to the theses (i) that voluntary action is, or is usually, rational in a particular sense, and (ii) that voluntary action is rational in this sense only insofar as it is directed towards something good. Therefore (in the second place), it is simply untrue that either good action, or simple wrongdoing, is lacking in rational justification. And hence (thirdly), it is emphatically not the case that Augustine believes that voluntary action in general either has not, or does not need, any kind of rational justification.

True, he certainly argues that wilful wrongdoing has no kind of rational justification. But the whole point of this as a hypothesis about wilful wrongdoing is that wilful wrongdoing is the *exceptional* case. What makes it so mysterious is exactly that it breaks an otherwise unexceptioned rule: the rule that all voluntary action, by nature, necessarily has some kind of rational justification.

It may now be evident how I can answer one important remaining question. In 8.2, I amassed a fair amount of evidence for the contradiction of the 'directedness' thesis: the thesis of the neutrality of the will. How can I account for this evidence? Do I simply have to dismiss it as an inconvenient inconsistency? I think not. I take it that these passages are affirmations, not of (Y), but of (X).

That is: Augustine is affirming, in these words, the brute fact of our ability to renege on what we recognise as the right course of action. Even at his most emphatic in these passages, Augustine says no more than that the will 'is that middle power which can either persist in faith or turn aside to infidelity' (dSL 58). Need even this affirmation imply any more than Augustine's acceptance of the paradox I have already attributed to him – that bad will is inexplicable, and yet it happens? I suggest not: I suggest that there is, in fact, nothing in these passages that shows Augustine supporting any stronger thesis than (X). Hence they are no evidence for the claim that he holds (Y).

The traditional interpretation of Augustine sees him not as a 'rationalist' (i.e., one who insists that, as such, voluntary action should normally be in some sense rational) but as a 'voluntarist' (i.e., a subscriber to (Y)). But I believe that those who follow the traditional interpretation are standing Augustine on his head. The tradition has it, apparently, that Augustine is a thoroughgoing 'voluntarist' who occasionally makes remarks which can be misinterpreted as 'rationalist'. I am arguing that, on the contrary, Augustine is a thoroughgoing 'rationalist' who occasionally makes remarks which can be misinterpreted as 'voluntarist'.

Of course, anyone who dissents, as I am doing, from such a long and honourable tradition of interpretation as the 'voluntarist' reading of Augustine has work to do. The onus is on him, first, to justify his dissent by exegesis, and second, to explain how the traditional explanation arose.

I hope I have by now fulfilled the first part of this onus in this chapter and the last. In closing, I add some remarks in fulfilment of the second part of the onus.

8.8. FROM AUGUSTINE'S RATIONALISM TO AUGUSTINIAN VOLUNTARISM

Tracing the sources of what I take to be the mistake of classing Augustine, with (e.g.) Ockham, Scotus and Hume, as a thorough-going 'voluntarist', is no easy matter. To do it properly would call for a huge historical study which I have no intention of attempting here. But I think one may, at least, legitimately point to three errors of exegesis, and one of inference.

The error of inference is the mistake of supposing that, if (on Augustine's theory) renegation from any good action to wilful wrongdoing by bad will is possible, then, when any good action is not reneged on but actually performed, a prior affirmation of that good action by *good* will must be necessary.

The underlying image here (the 'intuition pump', as Dennett (1984) would say) is a common one in the philosophy of action (thanks to Plato's *Republic*). It is of the execution of an action as a legislative process. It is (we have seen) demonstrable that, in a case of wilful wrongdoing, any process of means–ends reasoning which could lead to that action is neither necessary nor sufficient for its performance. What is both necessary and sufficient, for this bad intention to be promulgated as a wilfully chosen bad action, is a kind of 'royal assent', a 'numen' or mon-arch's nod. And this, of course, is the contribution of the 'will' – which in the case of a wilful wrongdoing is, so to speak, 'ruling by decree'.

The inference is that if this 'royal assent' is necessary and sufficient in the case of wilful wrongdoing, then it must be at least necessary in the case of any voluntary action at all. But why suppose this? Why cannot wilful wrongdoing simply be an anomalous case of action – as I have argued Augustine took it to be? But if wilful wrongdoing is anomalous, then there will be no sense in arguing that what is typical of such consciously-chosen bad action must be typical of action in general. Hence admitting that in a bad action the 'will' 'rules by decree' will not constrain us to admit that all action is causally rooted in such government by decree.

This idea, that the will is involved as an extra component in every good or bad action, is suggested by the first error of exegesis, a misunderstanding of dCD 14.6:

Will is indeed to be found in all these movements (sc. the emotions); indeed all of them are nothing other than acts of the will (*voluntates*). For what are desire and happiness but a will assenting to those things which we want? And what are fear and sadness but a will dissenting from those things which we do not want?

Note, in the first place, that Augustine is not here analysing actions, but emotions. More precisely, he is building a conceptual bridge between emotions and attitudes. Desire (*cupiditas*), as an emotion, is a general wanting; as an attitude, it is a policy to obtain what is desired by the emotion. The difference between the emotion and the attitude is that attitudes are chosen, deliberately adopted, and voluntary, whereas emotions are not. So I am not (directly) morally responsible for my emotions; but I am directly responsible for my attitudes.

It is, in fact, a piece of over-enthusiasm which leads Augustine to say that 'Indeed all of them are *nothing* other than acts of the will'. For in the passage in question he has just distinguished *motus* (here = 'emotion') rather carefully from *voluntas* ('will'; or 'emotion + will' (= 'attitude')). ('It makes a difference what is the quality of the human's will; for if that is perverse, then these emotions will be perverse too.')

The point is that one can, to a degree, be detached enough from one's emotions to choose whether or not to adopt their content into one's attitudes. That is why we are responsible for our attitudes, in a way in which we are not for our emotions. This point has nothing to do with the mistaken idea that there is a need for some separately identifiable assent of a faculty called the will in any action – as opposed to the idea that any action must be voluntary to be recognised as an action at all. (Cp. my remark in Ch. 5, that the best way overall to understand Augustine's talk about *voluntas* is to treat it as all being, fundamentally, no more than a way of talking about voluntary action.)

The second error of exegesis concerns a passage in dCD 12.9 which has been misread:

Since then there is no natural cause of the evil will, ...if we are to say that there is no efficient cause even of the good will...'

The voluntarist interpretation of Augustine seems to me to require that this 'if' should be introducing the kind of rhetorical 'if' clause which is equivalent to an affirmative statement. The passage would then have Augustine saying that good will is, just as much as bad will, uncreated and without causal antecedents of any kind. But this is certainly not the meaning of the passage, as simply reading on quickly shows:

> If we are to say that there is no efficient cause even of the good will, we must beware lest we should think that the good will of the angels was not created but is coeternal with God. *But since the angels were created, how could it be said that their good will was not created?* (dCD 12.9)

The passage, in fact, says the exact opposite of what it is often thought to say. The good will of the good angels, unlike the bad will of the bad angels, *is* created, and has a causal antecedent, in the creative activity of God.

This enables us to deal with the third error of exegesis, which is the building of doctrines on a famous phrase which has already been quoted:

> But what, in the end, could be before the will as the cause of the will?' (dLA 3.49)

Taken on its own, this might well seem to be the claim that will in general has no antecedents of any sort, and would not be will if it had. But (as I have shown in Ch. 5) to take it this way is to ignore the context of the remark, which makes it plain that it is only *bad* will which is under discussion here. Hence no general theory of what the antecedents of any act of will must be is here being established. Augustine's question should properly be read as 'What could be before the *bad* will as its cause?' For, as we have already seen, Augustine explicitly says that good will does have causal antecedents: in the creative activity of God. Compare dCD 12.9, above, with dCD 5.9:

> From this it appears that there is no efficient cause of anything that is made unless it is a voluntary cause [viz. God's will].... In God's will is the highest power, which aids the good wills of created spirits, judges the bad wills, and directs

all wills.... But a bad will is not from him, for it is contrary to the nature (*contra naturam*) [in which it is found], which is from him.

The implication is plainly that a good will, which is not contrary to the nature in which it is found, is from God just as much as that nature is.

That good will has causal antecedents in the creative activity of God is also exactly what we should expect if it was right to say (Ch. 7) that the Truth is for Augustine the formal cause of the good will. And another reason for taking this view is given by the clear asymmetry, in Augustine's works on grace, between attributions of praise (which are always to God) and attributions of blame (which are always to creatures). Again and again the refrain is: 'What have you that you did not receive?' (v., e.g. dSL 58). This, again, is just what we should expect if good will, so far from being uncaused, comes directly from God.

My conclusion, then, is that Augustine is right to argue against the Manichaeans that, in his terms at least, good will is radically asymmetrical to bad will. For good will is explicable; it conforms to the form of the good life delineated in Ch. 7; its aim is always some good or other; and it is even subject to the efficient causality of the Creator. Bad will, on the other hand, is a surd in the equation, 'an incomprehensible given which steadfastly and in principle resists causal explanation' (Brown (1978), p. 315); and it is deliberately left as such by Augustine. It partakes not of formal, nor of final, nor even of efficient causation; it is something which we simply cannot account for.

Moreover, it is to be noted that there is – in spite of the literature – no valid inference from the phenomenon of bad will as the tyranny of bad desire to a general voluntaristic hypothesis. It is a mistake to claim that there is or could be, in the anatomy of a 'normal' Augustinian voluntary action, some extra job of assenting which always needs to be done by the will, over and above the simple choice and pursuit of a good. It is not the rational act which is the exception to the rule (however rarely that rule may be observed in a fallen world). The exceptional case is the irrational, inexplicable act of renegation which Augustine calls bad will, and which gets the fallen world going in the first place.

8.9.   CONCLUSION

It only remains to ask: What has been established by my examination of Augustine's theory of freedom and the voluntary, and by
comparison of that theory with Aristotle's?

In the first place, I may hope to have justified my adoption, in my
study of Augustine's theory, of the methodological axiom followed
in my study of Aristotle: the axiom, namely, that giving an account
of the nature of voluntary action is sufficient and necessary for
giving an account of the nature of free action. If I am right about
what is involved in voluntary action, on Augustine's best account
(and in particular if voluntary action involves the ability to do otherwise than one does), this axiom has indeed been a useful and clar-
ificatory one to follow, not only in the case of Aristotle but also in
the case of Augustine. Augustine's theory of freedom is widely (and
rightly) seen as a mishmash of difficult and conflicting ideas. If the
methodological axiom which I have used is put to work, we can, in
fact, extract a good deal of coherent and interesting theory from the
(not always consistent) plethora of Augustine's writings on the topic
of freedom.

And secondly: it has emerged that there is a parallel problem in
Augustine's theory to the problem posed by the apparent existence
of akrasia for Aristotle's theory; a parallel problem, with a not-quite
parallel solution. Aristotle (I suggested in Ch. 4) could have argued
for the logical impossibility of full akrasia, meaning voluntary
action which does not admit of rational explanation in the very strict
terms of Aristotle's theory of practical rationality. Augustine has a
looser theory of practical wisdom (rather than Aristotle's practical
rationality), and a commitment to the teaching of Scripture that his
analogue of full akrasia, wilful wrongdoing, actually exists and is
nothing less than fully voluntary action. Hence it is that Augustine
is bound to say that wilful wrongdoing – however mysterious, however inexplicable and however contrary in its direction to the directedness of practical wisdom towards the good – does, nonetheless,
occur, and is voluntary action and therefore culpable, even if it is not
explicable. And so it turns out that, while voluntary action always
and necessarily has three conditions for Aristotle – concerning ignorance, compulsion, and irrationality – for Augustine there is a
counter example to these three postulated conditions. In the case of
wilful wrongdoing we have voluntary action which is nonetheless
irrational.

This is the great difference between Augustine and his Classical predecessors. It is a difference which (I have argued) has been widely misinterpreted by the alignment of Aristotle and other classical writers with 'rationalist' understandings of the origination of action, and the alignment of Augustine with 'voluntarist' understandings thereof; as if Aristotle had been a proto-Kantian and Augustine a proto-Humean. But this difference between Aristotle and Augustine is, for all that it has been misrepresented, a profound and important one; and if the schematism under which I have attempted to analyse their theories of freedom and the voluntary has brought out that difference in a new and interesting light, that at least is a success of a kind.

List of Works Cited

NB that this is not a bibliography. Many works which would deserve mention in a bibliography are not mentioned here; only books actually cited or referred to are included.

(I) WORKS OF ARISTOTLE, WITH ABBREVIATIONS

APo	*Analytica Posteriora*
APr	*Analytica Priora*
dA	*de Anima*
dAR	*de Arte Rhetorica*
dC	*de Caelo*
dGA	*de Generatione Animalium*
dI	*de Interpretatione*
dMA	*de Motu Animalium*
dPA	*de Partibus Animalium*
EE	*Ethica Eudemia*
MM	*Magna Moralia*
Mph	*Metaphysics*
NE	*Ethica Nicomachea*
Phys	*Physics*
Pol	*Politics*
Top	*Topics*
VV	*Virtues and Vices*

(II) WORKS OF AUGUSTINE, WITH ABBREVIATIONS

(The dates AD as given are not polemically asserted, and may well be only approximately right.)

cAcad	*contra Academicos* (386)
cDEP	*contra Duas Epistolas Pelagianorum* (422–3)
cIOP	*contra Iulianum Opus Imperfectum* (423)
Conf	*Confessiones* (399–401)
dBV	*de Beata Vita* (386)
dCD	*de Civitate Dei* (413–26)

dCE	*de Consensu Evangelistarum* (402)
dGCPO	*de Gratia Christi et de Peccato Originali* (418)
dDA	*de Duabus Animabus* (392-3)
dFRV	*de Fide Rerum quae non Videntur* (400)
dGLA	*de Gratia et Libero Arbitrio* (426)
dLA	*de Libero Arbitrio* (387-8)
dMag	*de Magistro* (389)
dME	*de Moribus Ecclesiae* (388)
dNB	*de Natura Boni* (404)
dPMR	*de Peccatorum Meritis et Remissione* (411)
dPIH	*de Perfectione Iustitiae Hominis* (415–16)
83DQ	*de Diversis Quaestionibus LXXXIII* (388–95)
dQA	*de Quantitate Animae* (387–8)
dSL	*de Spiritu et Littera* (412)
dVR	*de Vera Religione* (391)
dTrin	*de Trinitate* (399–419)
EEGal	*Expositio Epistolae ad Galatos* (394–5)
Ench	*Enchiridion* (423)
EPRoms	*Expositio LXXXIV Propositionum Epistolae ad Romanos* (394–5)
Retr	*Retractationes* (426–7)
RomsIE	*Epistolae Pauli ad Romanos Incohata Expositio* (394–5)
Sermon	*Sermons* (390–430)
Simp	*ad Simplicianum de Diversis Quaestionibus* (395)
Sol	*Soliloquia* (386–7)

(III) OTHER WORKS

Allan (1955): D. J. Allan, 'The Practical Syllogism', in *Autour d'Aristote* (Louvain, 1955).

Anscombe (1957): G. E. M. Anscombe, *Intention* (Oxford: Clarendon Press, 1957).

Anscombe (1965): G. E. M. Anscombe, 'Thought and Action in Aristotle: What is "Practical Truth"?'. In Bambrough (1965).

Austin (1956/7): J. L. Austin, 'A Plea for Excuses', *Proceedings of the Aristotelian Society*, 57 (1956/7), pp. 1–30.

Austin (1961): J. L. Austin, 'Ifs and Cans', in J. O. Urmson and G. Warnock, (eds), *The Philosophical Papers of J. L. Austin* (Oxford: Clarendon Press, 1961), pp. 153–80.

Bambrough (1965): Renford Bambrough (ed.), *New Essays on Plato and Aristotle* (London: Routledge & Kegan Paul, 1965).

Bible, Authorised Version of, 1611.

Boethius, Anicius Manlius Severinus, *Consolatio Philosophiae*. Text, and translation (1609) by 'I.T.', in Loeb Classical Library (London: Harvard University Press, 1936).

Brown (1978): Robert Brown, 'The First Evil Will Must be Incomprehensible: A Critique of Augustine', *Journal of the American Academy of Religion*, 46 (1978), pp. 315–29.

Burnaby (1938): John Burnaby, *Amor Dei: a Study of the Religion of St. Augustine* (London: Hodder and Stoughton, 1938).

Burnet (1900): John Burnet, *The Ethics of Aristotle, Edited with an Introduction and Notes by John Burnet* (London: Methuen, 1900).

Chappell (forthcoming): T. D. J. Chappell, 'Explaining the Inexplicable: Augustine on the Fall', forthcoming in *Journal of the American Academy of Religion*.

Charles (1984): David Charles, *Aristotle's Theory of Action* (Ithaca: Cornell University Press, 1984).

Charlton (1988): William Charlton, *Weakness of the Will: a Philosophical Introduction* (Oxford: Clarendon Press, 1988).

Cicero, *Tusculanae Disputationes*. Text and translation by J. E. King in Loeb Classical Library (London: Harvard University Press, 1927).

Cooper (1975): John Cooper, *Reason and Human Good in Aristotle* (Cambridge, Massachussetts, 1975).

Clark (1978): S. R. L. Clark, *Aristotle's Man* (Oxford: Clarendon, 1978).

Davidson (1980): Donald Davidson, *Essays on Actions and Events* (Oxford: Clarendon, 1980).

Dennett (1984): Daniel Dennett, *Elbow Room: the Varieties of Free Will Worth Wanting* (Oxford: Clarendon, 1984).

Dihle (1982): Albrecht Dihle, *The Theory of Will in Classical Antiquity* (Berkeley: University of California Press, 1982).

Finnis (1991): John Finnis, *Moral Absolutes* (Catholic University of America Press, Washington, DC).

Foot (1978): Philippa Foot, *Virtues and Vices and Other Essays in Moral Philosophy* (Oxford: Clarendon Press, 1978).

Gardiner (1969/70): Patrick Gardiner, 'Error, Faith and Self-Deception', *Proceedings of the Aristotelian Society*, NS 70 (1969/70), pp. 221–44.

Gauthier-Jolif (1970): Gauthier and Jolif, *L'Ethique à Nicomaque* (Louvain: Publications Universitaires, 1970).

Gilson (1960): Etienne Gilson, *The Christian Philosophy of Saint Augustine* (London: Victor Gollancz, 1960).

Gosling (1990): J. C. B. Gosling, *Weakness of the Will* (London: Routledge, 1990).

Gosselin (1949): Gosselin, annotated French edition and translation of dNB (in Oeuvres de Saint Augustin series, Vol.1) (Paris: Desclée, de Brouwer et Cie, 1949).

Hardie (1980): W. F. R. Hardie, *Aristotle's Ethical Theory*, Second Edition (Oxford: Clarendon Press, 1980).

Hare (1952): Richard Hare, *The Language of Morals* (Oxford: Clarendon Press, 1952).

Hare (1963): Richard Hare, *Freedom and Reason* (Oxford: Clarendon Press, 1963).

Hare (1971): Richard Hare, 'Practical Inferences', in Richard Hare, *Practical Inferences* (London: Macmillan, 1971).

Hume (1739): David Hume, *A Treatise of Human Nature* (1739), ed. L. A. Selby-Bigge (Oxford: Clarendon, 1964).

Hume (1775): David Hume, *An Enquiry Concerning Human Understanding* (1775), ed. L. A. Selby-Bigge (Oxford: Clarendon, 1975).

Irwin (1987): Terence Irwin, *Aristotle's First Principles* (Oxford: Clarendon Press, 1987).

Joachim (1955): H. H. Joachim, *Commentary on the Nicomachean Ethics*, ed. D. A. Rees (Oxford: Clarendon Press, 1955).

Keillor (1989): Garrison Keillor, 'The Current Crisis in Remorse', in *We Are Still Married* (London: Faber, 1989).

Kenny (1975): Anthony Kenny, *Will, Freedom and Power* (London: Duckworth, 1975).

Kenny (1979): Anthony Kenny, *Aristotle's Theory of the Will* (London: Duckworth, 1979).

Kirwan (1989): Christopher Kirwan, *Augustine* (London: Routledge, The Arguments of the Philosophers Series, 1989).

Lear (1980): Lear, J., *Aristotle and Logical Theory* (Cambridge: Cambridge University Press, 1975).

Lemmon (1962): E. J. Lemmon, 'Moral Dilemmas', *Philosophical Review*, 71 (1962), pp. 139–58.

Lucas (1994): Lucas, J. R., 'The Lay-out of Arguments' in Krawietz, McCormick and von Wright (eds), *Prescriptive Formality and Normative Rationality in Modern Legal Systems: Festschrift for Robert Summers* (Berlin: Duncker & Humblot, 1994).

MacIntyre (1985): Alasdair MacIntyre, *Whose Justice? Which Rationality?* (London: Duckworth, 1985).

MacIntyre (1990): Alasdair MacIntyre, *Three Rival Versions of Moral Inquiry* (London: Duckworth, 1990).

Mackie (1982): J. L. Mackie, *The Miracle of Theism* (Clarendon: Oxford, 1982).

McDowell (1978): 'Are Moral Requirements Hypothetical Imperatives?', *Proceedings of the Aristotelian Society (Supplementary Volume)*, 1978.

Melden (1961): *Basic Actions* (London: Routledge & Kegan Paul, 1961).

Murdoch (1970): Iris Murdoch, *The Sovereignty of Good* (London: Routledge & Kegan Paul, 1970).

Nietzsche (1968): Friedrich Nietzsche, *Götzerdämmerung*. Translated by R. J. Hollingdale as *The Twilight of the Idols* (Harmondsworth: Penguin Books, 1968).

Plato, *Laches, Protagoras, Meno, Euthydemus*. Text and translation by W. R. M. Lamb in Loeb Classical Library (London: Harvard University Press, 1924).

Plato, *Republic*. Text and translation (2 vols) by Paul Shorey in Loeb Classical Library (London: Harvard University Press, 1935).

Plotinus, *Enneads*. Text and translation by A. H. Armstrong in Loeb Classical Library. 8 vols (London: Harvard University Press, 1978).

Rackham (1926): *Aristotle's Nicomachean Ethics*. Text and translation by H. Rackham in Loeb Classical Library (London: Harvard University Press, 1926).

Raz (1978): Joseph Raz (ed.), *Practical Reasoning* (Oxford: Clarendon, Oxford Readings in Philosophy, 1978).

Ricoeur (1967): Paul Ricoeur, *The Symbolism of Evil* (New York: Harper and Row, 1967).

Rorty (1980): Amelie Oksenberg Rorty (ed.), *Essays on Aristotle's Ethics* (London: University of California Press, 1980).

Ross (1925): W. D. Ross, *Oxford Translation of Aristotle* (Oxford: Oxford University Press, 1925).

Ryle (1949): Gilbert Ryle, *The Concept of Mind* (London: Hutchinson University Library, 1949).

Sartre (1949): J.-P. Sartre, *L'Etre et le Néant: Essai d'Ontologie Phénoménologique* (Paris, 1949). (Translated by Hazel Barnes as *Being and Nothingness*.)

Sorabji (1993): Richard Sorabji, *Animal Minds and Human Morals* (London: Duckworth, 1993).

Stoutland (1970): 'The Logical Connection Argument', *American Philosophical Quarterly*, 1970.

Stoutland (1976): 'The Causation of Behaviour', in *Essays in Honour of G. H. von Wright*, Amsterdam 1976.

Strawson (1962): 'Freedom and Resentment', *Proceedings of the British Academy*, 1962.

Thonnard (1941): F. J. Thonnard, annotated French edition and translation of dLA (in Oeuvres de Saint Augustin series, vol. 6). (Paris: Desclée, de Brouwer et Cie, 1941).

Tolstoy, *War and Peace* (1867). Translated Rosemary Edmonds (Harmondsworth: Penguin Books, 1961).

von Wright (1978): Georg Henrik von Wright, 'On So Called Practical Inference'. In Raz (1978), pp. 46–62.

Wallis (1887): Robert Wallis, translation of cDEP, in *Augustine's Anti-Pelagian Writings*; vol. 5 of Schaff (ed.), The Select Library of the Nicene and Post-Nicene Fathers (Grand Rapids, Michigan: Eerdman's, 1887/1971), pp. 374–435.

Wiggins (1980): David Wiggins, 'Deliberation and Practical Reason', in Rorty (1980), pp. 221–40.

Williams (1993): Bernard Williams, *Shame and Necessity* (Oxford: University of California Press).

Wittgenstein (1967): Ludwig Wittgenstein, *Philosophical Investigations*, ed. G. E. M. Anscombe and Rush Rhees, with an English translation by G. E. M. Anscombe, Third Edition (Oxford: Basil Blackwell, 1967).

Index of Names

213